PRIVATE
MEANS
PUBLIC
ENDS

PRIVATE
MEANS
PUBLIC
ENDS

PRIVATE BUSINESS IN
SOCIAL SERVICE DELIVERY

Edited by
Barry J. Carroll
Ralph W. Conant
Thomas A. Easton

New York
Westport, Connecticut
London

Library of Congress Cataloging-in-Publication Data

Private means – public ends.

Includes index.
1. United States – Social policy. 2. Social
service – United States. 3. Privatization –
United States. 4. Industry and education –
United States. 5. Public welfare – United States.
I. Carroll, Barry J. II. Conant, Ralph Wendell,
1926–   III. Easton, Thomas A.
HN65.P69   1987   361.6′1′0973   86-25251
ISBN 0-275-92429-7 (alk. paper)

Library of Congress Catalog Card Number: 86-25251
ISBN: 0-275-92429-7

First published in 1987

Praeger Publishers, 521 Fifth Avenue, New York, NY 10175
A division of Greenwood Press, Inc.

Printed in the United States of America

∞

The paper used in this book complies with the Permanent
Paper Standard issued by the National Information Standards
Organization (Z39.48-1984).

10 9 8 7 6 5 4 3 2 1

Contents

Preface   *vii*

Introduction   *ix*

1   Business Goals and Social Goals   1
    Barry J. Carroll

2   Communicating National Priorities to Business   8
    Barry J. Carroll

3   Motivating the Private Sector: What Role for Public
    Policy?   20
    Barry J. Carroll and Thomas A. Easton

4   The Entrepreneurial Approach to Privatization   37
    Ralph W. Conant and Thomas A. Easton

5   Privatizing the Acute Care General Hospital   50
    Harold W. Demone, Jr. and Margaret Gibelman

6   The Privatization of Prisons: Panacea or Placebo?   76
    Gilbert Geis

7   The Realities of ''Profitization'' and Privatization in the
    Nonprofit Sector   98
    Robert P. Corman

8   Strategic Marketing of Social Services   119
    Diane J. Garsombke and Thomas W. Garsombke

9   Privatization: A Game-Theoretic Analysis   135
    Justin F. Leiber

10 Privatization: Carnage, Chaos, and Corruption   146
    Frederick C. Thayer

v

11   Privatization in Perspective   171
        Norman Elkin

Index   *179*

About the Contributors   *189*

Preface

This book is a timely response to the U.S. crisis in public funding for public needs. Budgetary cutbacks and growth restrictions are endangering the American dream and the only answer may be to recruit U.S. business as the godfather of the future.

Education is our highest domestic priority, and so it is the central focus of this book. Public education has been falling behind the demands of our technically oriented society, and the problem is national. Business, like other sectors of society, has a major stake in the quality of our nation's schools. The size of the stake, and the existing involvement of business in the search for solutions, show in the size of the financial burden imposed on the private sector by the costs of remedial training.

The task of improving the educational system seems too big and too expensive to be left entirely to the public sector. Yet our educational institutions need help, not condemnation, in solving their problems and gearing up to play a strategic role in shaping the nation's future. Fortunately, U.S. business has traditionally shown a capacity for leadership in times of crisis. The question is, will business recognize the present crisis in public education and respond with its best leadership and talent? The answer is that if the problem is convincingly defined and appropriate public policies are implemented to focus the attention of business leaders on this long-term national priority, the chances are good that the private sector will respond.

We believe other areas of national concern also merit the serious attention and leadership of the business community. These include equal opportunity, health care, corrections, security, employment, day care, research and development, and more. *Private Means—Public Ends* is designed to encourage and inspire a business-led effort to mesh America's public service systems with today's needs and tomorrow's vision. It is an action-oriented book that presents a challenge to business to lead by example. It is also a future-oriented book that urges a sound program of public–partnership for the 1990s. In part, it sets forth and analyzes a philosophy of public service and cooperation toward common purposes that eschews the old paradigms of right and left, conservative and liberal, master and servant, hierarchy and anarchy.

This book says the problem-solving and communications skills of business, and the profit-making discipline that expands the total wealth of society, can be productive alternatives to the statism, paternalism, and welfarism that do no more than redistribute wealth and foster dependency.

Introduction

The delivery of "public" services through private organizations is not a new idea in the United States. Public services themselves, at least in the broad variety we see in the modern world, are a much newer idea. Unfortunately, public services may not be as lasting an idea as many people commonly assume.

That the state should provide for the welfare and education of all its citizens is a concept that comes mainly from modern socialism. In earlier times, communities and local organizations, not governments, took care of the elderly, the destitute, and the disabled. Even so, many unfortunates were left to beg in the streets or starve. Socialism tries to plug these holes in the safety net by substituting compulsory taxes and professional bureaucracies for voluntary charity and largely voluntary administration.

When welfare was largely left to individual charity, and education was an industry of the churches, governments did occasionally get into the welfare business, as in the provision of foster homes for orphans and abandoned children. However, even then they often contracted out the provision of services to individuals who were glad to have the extra income. What institutions governments did operate were usually those no private individual could or would handle, such as prisons and insane asylums. Until this century, there were far more private schools in this country than public ones. Many private students had their way paid by communities that lacked a public school system. This system remains in use in many Vermont communities today, although it has vanished elsewhere as education has evolved into a true public service, provided by government for the public good. Many other services, however, such as waste disposal, waste treatment, and power generation, have never evolved beyond a hybrid, mixed system of more or less regulated private and public delivery systems.

Our historical memory is short. Today's generation takes for granted a vast array of federal, state, and local programs that support every conceivable form of social service across the spectrum of health, education, welfare, and even legal and political services. So accustomed have we become to the availability of these services that we find it difficult to imagine a time when most of them did not exist. Yet that time was only a little more than 50 years ago, before the Great Depression and the response of the Roosevelt New Deal. Prior to 1932, the federal government had very few social programs, and state and local governments had even fewer. In the 1950s we were still debating the advisability of federal aid to education, and in the early 1960s we were barely into federally sponsored housing and hospital programs. Medicare and Medicaid did not come until 1966. Legal aid was a creation of Lyndon Johnson's War on Poverty, as were comprehensive approaches to urban blight, a mere two decades ago.

The 1980s brought the Reagan presidency and a strong reaction against the new array of government programs for social services. This reaction seems to be due less to the cost of these programs, or to their contribution to the national deficit, than to growing doubts about their effectiveness in improving education, mitigating poverty, reducing crime, and providing efficient public transportation, affordable health care, and trouble-free prisons. If government is failing in its efforts to provide essential services, should we not reconsider the role we have given government in these areas? That is what this book is about. It is an exploration of the whole question of the division of responsibility for public services between the public and private sectors.

The editors, Barry Carroll, Ralph Conant, and Thomas Easton, wish to disclaim at the outset any label on the enterprise of conservative or liberal, right or left wing, socialistic or capitalistic. Any such labels, in our view, place needless constraints on an inquiry that asks: "What works best?" The political landscape of world history is strewn with the victims of ideologies whose only purpose was political power. If a reader is impelled to discover the philosophical leaning of this inquiry, let that reader be saved the trouble. We are pragmatists. We are realists. We do not believe any particular system will work forever or that any division of responsibility worked out in the 1980s will necessarily continue to serve even into the next century. We believe that a workable system needs continuous attention and adjustment, that no system should be locked into any set of arbitrary rules and principles.

The idea for this book came out of a project Barry Carroll undertook in 1983–84, when he was serving as special assistant to the Secretary of Education in Washington, D.C. The aim of the project was to discover, by interviewing corporate chief executive officers, ways in which the nation's businesses could contribute to improving public education and what incentives they required to make the effort. The project and its results are described in Chapters 1–3. Discussions between Barry Carroll and Ralph Conant of the implications of that study lead to the idea of examining other areas of private-sector participation in public services.

In planning the book, we decided to explore only two additional public service areas—prisons and hospitals—as plausible examples of privatization with which there is recent experience. By limiting our in-depth examples to just three areas of public service, we were able to examine in greater depth several key aspects of privatization.

In Chapter 3, Carroll and Easton build on Carroll's survey of chief executive officers to explore the factors that seem likely to motivate private enterprise to contribute to public services such as education, even when the gains to private business are neither great nor immediate. Carroll's survey found that when direct profit is removed as the primary motivator, tax incentives can be an effective substitute under some conditions. A sense of "corporate responsibility," a peer ethic of involvement in the broader affairs of the community, can be established over time under the right circumstances. Business can also be induced to help in public service areas if convinced of the urgency of an unmet social need and if presented with a concrete plan of action that spells out the role of the private sector. Recognition of the contribution of private business helps spur cooperation as well, as does assured protection from liability.

In Chapter 4, Conant and Easton discuss the crucial role that entrepreneurs can play in the provision of public services. They point out the increasing part entrepreneurs are playing in fueling an unprecedented expansion of the national economy and the opportunities for profit that a growing number of entrepreneurs are seeing in the public sector. In education, many private corporations are developing in-house educational facilities for training executives and new workers or are hiring contractors to operate such facilities. Other companies are building and operating hospitals and prisons, among other once-public institutions. All are drawn into public service by various factors, chief among which is the prospect of profit.

In Chapter 5, Harold Demone, Jr., and Margaret Gibelman focus on the privatization of health care and the way this lucrative field has become a major industry in the years since private enterprise first discovered it. In Chapter 6, Gilbert Geis discusses how corrections has become a vexing problem for many parts of the public sector. Solutions to the problems have involved the private sector in various ways, despite such disincentives as close monitoring by public regulators, pressures from public interest groups, and the uncertainty associated with ever-shifting public policies.

In Chapter 7, Robert Corman turns our attention to the third sector of society, not quite private, not quite public, but nonprofit. This sector is a traditional alternative to government-sponsored public services. At times in the past, services that are now potential targets for privatization were in the province of the nonprofit sector. Corman points out that, as privatization occurs, some of the nonprofits will be observing, criticizing, participating in, and challenging (and sometimes ignoring) the activities that mark the trend. This is because many of the nation's nonprofit organizations see themselves as speaking for and protecting those who often have trouble speaking for and protecting themselves—low- and moderate-income populations, the mentally and physically handicapped, ex-offenders, the elderly, and children, precisely those to whom many public services are addressed.

In Chapter 8, Diane Garsombke and Thomas Garsombke consider the special problems of marketing public services, especially the problems created for entrepreneurs by conflicts among "external constituencies." Political interest groups can severely constrain the marketing strategies of private entrepreneurs in public service businesses. If such constraints affect profits, the entrepreneurs need to learn to compromise and seek effective alternatives.

They also discuss the pitfalls that await private businesses working with public bureaucrats, whose values can be very different from those of private-sector workers. Of course, the closer the entrepreneur is to the public bureaucracy, the more acutely all of these problems affect his or her operation. Conversely, the more distance the entrepreneur can place between her operation and the controlling bureaucracy, the less it may affect her normal private-sector style of functioning.

In Chapter 9, Justin Leiber asks, who stands to gain and who stands to lose in the shift to privatization? What works for the public? Where are the trade-offs, and how are they accomplished? How do we find the balance point where the public benefits are optimized and the private return is maximized? Leiber suggests that the allocation of responsibilities in public services between the public and private sectors must be continuously reevaluated to achieve a dynamic equilibrium and avoid the stasis of too rigidly structured societies. The aim is to make the economic system adaptive to changing conditions and to an improved understanding of what works and what does not.

Leiber's approach to discovering the balance begins with the "prisoner's dilemma" of game theory, in which the partners in a social or other transaction must decide whether or not to cooperate in their search for gain. The best strategy in order to maximize gains—instead of minimizing losses—is to cooperate at first, but then always to return tit for tat, betrayal for betrayal, cooperation for cooperation. That is, the player who takes quick revenge for lack of cooperation but is also forgiving, does better in the long run than one who takes no revenge or is not forgiving. Leiber concludes, with us, that a pragmatic approach to negotiation is a far more fruitful social strategy than ideology.

In Chapter 10, Frederick Thayer makes a strong case *against* privatization for most public services. He begins by challenging the privatizers' assumption that most public services will benefit from the profit incentive that supposedly leads to efficiency and reduced costs. The commonness of bribes, kickbacks, deliberate cost overruns, and other corrupt practices, which he sees as inevitable consequences of competition, moves him to deep skepticism of the ability of the private sector to deal honestly with the public. Cost cutting, he notes, leads to lower pay scales, union busting, increased unemployment and underemployment, poorer equipment maintenance and employee training, and unreliable quality. He also points out that some services, notably education, have a defined market in which competition must result in inefficient duplication of capacity. He then argues that to ensure quality and public safety, privatization demands costly government oversight or regulation of suppliers hard pressed by competition.

The chapters on privatization of hospitals and corrections provide examples of public services where experience offers clues and guidelines to both the advantages and the pitfalls of privatization. A searching examination of these particular experiences and others like them will surely yield lessons that could serve as the basis for private decisions about entering into public service areas for profit and, more importantly, for the formulation of public policy in the rapidly developing privatization movement.

Geis indicates that specialized facilities are more effectively privatized than others. Demone and Gibelman suggest that matters such as accountability and the availability and quality of health care may be more important than efficiency and hence better justifications for public-sector health care. They find, in fact, that the failure of the efficiency and profit promised by the privatizers to materialize may be contributing to the current decline of the hospital privatization trend and the movement of the private-sector health-care companies into preventive health care (HMOs) and medical insurance.

Yet even such amenable public services as prisons and health care warrant close public scrutiny before and after their privatization. Monitoring and regulation are essential to making privatization redound to the public benefit, as both Leiber and Thayer stress. These oversight activities must be carried out by government agencies, with or without the aid of nonprofit "watchdogs."

On the other hand, advancing technology and the growing capital costs of maintaining and improving our health-care system (and other public services) underscore the importance of optimizing the relationship between the resources available and the measurable results. It is hard to imagine a national health-care system that both excludes the for-profit providers and gives us as good an information base for the necessary public policy debate. As in education and other social service delivery systems, the private, for-profit competitors are an invaluable mirror in which we can examine, judge, and improve the entire system.

PRIVATE
MEANS
PUBLIC
ENDS

1

Business Goals and Social Goals

Barry J. Carroll

On the surface, business and society seem to have very different goals. One depends on profit to survive. The other seeks stability and improved human welfare. Yet at a deeper level, these goals are not inconsistent. Business profit benefits from social stability and yields a prosperous society, and a prosperous society can afford to foster the welfare of its people, reducing poverty and improving freedom, nutrition, health care, and education. And a prosperous, free, healthy, educated society is a stable society, with little impetus for economic disruption, revolution, or war.

The joint interest of the U.S. government and society in an effective, efficient educational system is axiomatic. Good government in a true democracy requires a well-educated electorate. However, as we review our educational system in the mid-1980s (for example, U.S. Dept. of Education 1983; Committee for Economic Development 1985), we find that it is not fulfilling our present needs, or the needs we can foresee for the future. We are failing in our responsibilities to ourselves, our children, and our future. As a society we are *not* achieving our full educational potential.

No segment of society is innocent. All segments, including the business community, have a role to play in bettering our educational system. If they do not play their respective roles, that is because they have not been convinced that they have a responsibility, or that it is to their benefit, to do so.

In this chapter and the next, and again in Chapter 3, we focus on the role that business may play in education. We do not simply describe the ways business has helped education in the past, call for specific future programs, or address the growing role of businesses as educators, as imparters of specific job-related skills to employees at all levels. Nor are we dealing with those companies whose business *is* education, or those that sell to the education market, although both are important and growing business segments. We are more concerned here with the motivations that can impel business to find its own future programs to advance the level of educational attainment of the general populace. That is, we are concerned with marketing the idea of an increased role for business in social service delivery, particularly in education, through more contact and coordination with existing public-sector institutions.

THE PUBLIC SECTOR VERSUS THE PRIVATE SECTOR

Federal and state governments have long played an influential role in the development of the voluntary private sector, the not-for-profit corporations such as colleges, foundations, churches, and charities, which provide numerous social and cultural services to our citizens. These organizations are usually chartered by the states and are exempt from local, state, and federal taxes. Thus their importance and utility in serving the public good are sanctioned by public policy. Particularly since the time of Franklin D. Roosevelt's New Deal, however, government has taken to itself the responsibility for funding a growing proportion of the social services that were once the exclusive province of the nonprofit sector. Under the Reagan administration, debate has been renewed over what blend of government and voluntary private support will best serve the national interest.

Reagan has taken a stand in favor of a reduced role for the federal government in social service delivery and a greater role for individuals, families, local and state government units, and not-for-profit organizations. The Task Force on Private Sector Initiatives, appointed early in the Reagan administration, recommended a goal of doubling corporate philanthropy by 1987 as part of this effort (President's Task Force 1982). The Commission on Private Philanthropy for Public Needs (the Filer Commission) in 1975 urged fulfillment of a similar goal by 1980 (Filer Commission 1975). Although change has been slow, some progress toward these goals has been recorded since the 1981–83 period.

In October 1983, President Reagan urged that all 110,000 schools in the nation should become involved in partnerships with other organizations. Since then, the Department of Education (1984) has documented in some detail more than 46,000 such relationships that have already been established. Because these relationships generally appear to be useful and constructive, it seems clear that more benefits could be realized if the number and scope of these partnership activities could be expanded.

If public policy is to move in the direction of encouraging increased involvement of the private sector in partnerships with the public sector, it is important that policymakers be well informed regarding the priorities and pitfalls of this approach. To avoid wasting effort and tax dollars, policymakers should also have information on the efficacy and cost effectiveness of the various tools that might be employed. Some approaches to motivating corporate behavior, such as tax and other financial incentives, are well tested and documented. The influence of these various tools on the specific task of promoting formation of public–private partnerships such as those advocated by the Reagan administration, however, has not been studied, and more research is needed.

In an attempt to provide some of the information needed to support this task, I undertook an interview project for the Department of Education. At the time, I was a Presidential Exchange executive, on loan for a year from International Metals and Machines Corp., serving as special assistant to Secretary Terrell Bell. To meet the study's goal of discovering the incentives and disincentives for business to "buy" the idea of supporting private-sector initiatives, particularly partnerships in education, I enlisted the aid of the Secretary's ten regional representatives (SRRs) and the department's liaison staff. We then focused on the behavior and attitudes of leaders of small and medium-sized corporations operating in communities across the nation.

A STUDY OF BUSINESS AND EDUCATION

Effective marketing of any product or idea depends on careful analysis of the product from the perspectives of both seller and buyer. Considerable work has been done to ascertain the nature and scope of various types of private-sector initiatives to address social problems. However, the project that we undertook at the U.S. Department of Education (Carroll 1986) was to our knowledge the first and only "market research" attempted by any agency into the psychographics of business leaders regarding private-sector initiatives.

We pursued this research by conducting face-to-face interviews with top executive officers of 101 companies throughout the United States between March and August of 1984. The SRRs chose and interviewed ten subjects in each of the DOEd's geographic regions. When one subject declined to be interviewed, another was chosen. The criteria for choosing interviewees were that their companies be roughly evenly divided among manufacturing, service, and financial and retail operations, and that they employ more than 50 people. We deliberately avoided Fortune 500 companies, preferring instead smaller, more local companies, similar in size to most not-for-profit organizations, such as educational institutions.

The interviews were, for the most part, conducted by the SRRs in the subjects' company offices. In New York, the ten subjects were interviewed at a luncheon. In Chicago, three of the ten were seen in the same way. Most of the interviewees (71 of 101) were top policymakers with titles of chief executive officer (CEO), chairman, president, executive vice-president, or general manager. The rest were other company officers or directors, with few exceptions. Substitutes for top managers were more common in the larger companies.

The 101 interviewees represented 35 manufacturing, 37 service, and 29 financial and retail companies. Nineteen had sales of less than $10 million, 20 had sales of $10–25 million, 16 had sales of $26–100 million, and 46, including several financial companies, had sales of over $100 million. Several were insurance and utility companies, which differed in their tax environments and legal constraints from the rest.

The interviews focused on three general topics: incentives and disincentives to business philanthropy, factors that have recently influenced business philanthropy, and the specific effects of tax incentives on philanthropy and voluntarism. After the interviews had been conducted, I classified and ranked the responses, including direct quotes as appropriate. In the process, I was struck by the wide variety of responses in all topic areas. The result was a valuable measure of qualitative attitudes and their pervasiveness in the business community and, I believe, an accurate indication of how the business community might respond to certain changes in public policy.

This chapter summarizes the overall report (Carroll 1986). In Chapter 2, I address the implications of the study for how government could best communicate social priorities to business. In Chapter 3, with the aid of Dr. Easton, I turn to how public policy may be used to motivate business to increase its philanthropic activities and its participation in social service delivery in a broader sense.

SUMMARY OF THE STUDY

The analysis of our interviews with business leaders points up that, although the goals of business are focused and specific, the means by which these ends are pursued include many strategies that serve the greater public interest. Furthermore, it is plainly within the capability of many institutions serving the public, such as the various governmental bodies and agencies, to create a business environment more conducive to involvement by businesses in social service delivery. A brief summary of the findings of our study illustrates these points.

In order of importance, we found the principle factors that *discourage* corporate involvement in public educational programs to be:

- Adverse economic conditions
- The drawing of resources from the firm's main business activities

- Disinterest in or skepticism about corporate involvement on the part of not-for-profit organizations, particularly when they depend heavily on government support (such as the public schools)
- The difficulty that not-for-profit managers, particularly educators, often have in defining their missions in terms of results that can be measured and monitored
- The absence of a standard "peer ethic" reflecting a broad acceptance in the business community that such involvement is expected and normative
- Potential liability exposure for some types of activities (such as internships)

Our analysis indicated the principal factors that *encourage* corporate involvement to be:

- Tax incentives
- Public recognition for corporate efforts
- Clear statements of need and setting of priorities by responsible community representatives
- Leadership by various levels of government
- Protection from liability in connection with good-faith efforts

In recent years, the business community has endorsed a broad concept of social responsibility. This attitude, coupled with the Reagan administration's reassessment of the federal responsibility for some areas of social service delivery and encouragement of greater private-sector involvement, apparently stimulated the higher level of business philanthropy witnessed in the 1981–83 recessionary period (Council for Financial Aid to Education 1983). Also, according to many of our interviewees, the business community is becoming increasingly concerned about some social issues that directly affect them, such as the inadequate development of basic skills among new entrants into the work force (Committee for Economic Development 1985).

Beyond educational issues, many in business and government and the public at large have begun to question the basic premise of whether many forms of nominally "public" services are, or can be, furnished as efficiently by units of government as they could be by private business. Transportation, health-care delivery, corrections, mail and parcel delivery, even garbage collection, are all being scrutinized, and there are many examples of private enterprise serving these public needs with exemplary efficiency and economy. Leaving aside for the moment the subject of how and whether businesses should actually tackle the jobs, which the other contributors to this book will treat at length, let us look at our study that focused on education to see how business CEOs felt about helping the schools to do their jobs better.

We found that the businesses represented in our survey supported local causes proportionately more often than larger companies do. However, this emphasis apparently did not carry over to support for elementary and secondary education. Despite a more local focus for their work force, and often for their markets as well, many of these businesses apparently have not yet fully realized the direct relationship between healthy schools and a healthy business environment, especially as expressed in the competence of entry-level employees. They are generally content to let local and state governments retain full responsibility for ongoing program funding and standards. Positive incentives will probably be necessary to induce them to expand significantly their awareness and involvement.

In conducting this project, we devoted special attention to evaluating the opinions of CEOs of businesses concerning current incentives. We also explored the potential for expanding or restructuring such incentives. For a majority of CEOs, tax treatment (or, more precisely, the marginal cost of giving in after-tax dollars) has a major effect on the inclination to make contributions. Another large segment of the group, however, said they would not be affected by an improvement in tax incentives. Their reasons, they said, were that they responded only to specific needs, were not earning enough income to make gifts, or were constrained by specific provisions of the tax codes that applied to their type of business.

The executives we surveyed tended to agree that a carefully drawn tax incentive would help to stimulate voluntarism. However, they also clearly indicated that smaller companies are not well suited to "lending" employees during business hours. Many such companies already encourage off-hours volunteering by employees. Enough executives warned of the potential they saw for cumbersome (and expensive to process) reports and abuse, that we question whether such a tax incentive for voluntarism would produce enough additional social services to be cost effective for smaller businesses or for the federal government in terms of the reduction in tax revenues involved.

In our DOEd study, a proposal for a marginal tax incentive for gifts in cash, conversely, was widely accepted. This reflects the previous and continuing success of similar incentives in stimulating capital investment, energy conservation, research and development, and construction. The suggested incentive was in the form of a tax credit for gifts supporting elementary or secondary school improvement when and to the extent that total giving exceeded a set percentage of pretax earnings. Seventy-four percent of the executives who responded supported this proposal, which would reward only well-above-average involvement. We therefore suggested that this concept warranted more study as a realistic way of motivating a significant portion of the business community to increase its support of business–education partnerships. It would simultaneously help to achieve the doubling of corporate support of all not-for-profit organizations to 2 percent of pretax earnings, as recommended by the Commission on Private Philanthropy for Public Needs, known as the Filer Commission (1975), and the President's Task Force on Private Sector Initiatives (1982).

Our report also pointed to the need for expanded programs at all levels of government to recognize business executives who take the lead in encouraging their companies to participate in not-for-profit activities such as school partnerships, as well as in helping communities organize, identify, and set priorities for corporate support. Such increased recognition would also help to motivate corporate support.

If the various levels of government truly wish the private sector to increase its help in meeting public needs, they must strive to make the goals of business more congruent with those of government. In order to do this, public policymakers must be very sensitive, not just to the profit motive of business, but also to the finite constraints of skills and time, and of money, all of which successful businesses manage with great care.

REFERENCES

Business-Higher Education Forum. 1983. *America's Competitive Challenge: The Need for a National Response* (Washington, D.C.).

Carroll, B. J. 1986. *Talking with Business* (Washington, DC: U.S. Government Printing Office).

Committee for Economic Development (CED). Policy Committee. 1985. *Investing in Our Children, 1984: Business and the Public Schools*. (New York: Committee for Economic Development).

Council for Financial Aid to Education (CFAE). 1983. *A Profile of Corporate Contributions* (New York).

———. 1984. *Corporate Support of Education 1983* (New York).

Department of Education (DOEd). Office of Planning, Budget, and Evaluation. 1984. *Partnerships in Education: Education Trends of the Future.* (Washington, D.C.: U.S. Government Printing Office).

Education Commission of the States. 1983. *A Summary of Major Reports of Education*, report no. EG-83-4 (Denver, CO).

Filer Commission. 1975. *Report of the Commission on Private Philanthropy and Public Needs* (Washington, D.C.: U.S. Government Printing Office).

Northeast Regional Exchange. 1983. *Education under Study: An Analysis of Recent Major Reports on Education*, 2d ed. (Chelmsford, MA: Northeast Regional Exchange).

President's Task Force on Private Sector Initiatives. 1982. Incentives Committee Report, *Building Partnerships* (Washington, D.C.: U.S. Government Printing Office).

U.S. Department of Education. 1983. *A Nation at Risk* (Washington, D.C.: U.S. Government Printing Office).

2

Communicating National Priorities to Business

Barry J. Carroll

The central purpose of our Department of Education study (Carroll 1986) was to take the pulse of corporate decision-makers. We wanted to see, by asking them directly, what incentives or policies best stimulate or deter their involvement in the delivery of social services. We expected that we would then gain additional understanding and corroboration by probing what factors in the business environment have recently affected the actions of these business leaders.

The project was conceived and conducted in 1984 to help policymakers develop and maintain a balance of policies that would encourage achievement of the goal of doubling business involvement in social service delivery (particularly in the form of business and school partnerships). As is done in most of the literature on the topic, we measured the involvement of business in terms of the percentage of pretax earnings taken as tax-deductible contributions. Our findings therefore have cogent implications for more effective national policies to stimulate greater individual philanthropy or local and state government policies to mobilize family and neighborhood resources for self-help efforts. Historically, tax policy, in the form of tax credits, deductions, and other reductions in taxes, has often been used to encourage individuals and businesses to "invest" in social goals deemed desirable by government. Tax policy is thus an important avenue for government to communicate its priorities to taxpayers.

An alternative means of communicating priorities is moral suasion, jawboning, or propaganda. It amounts to urging businesspeople to take steps the government wishes taken with no incentive other than appeals to patriotism or morality. However, business has become jaded about appeals by politicians to address this or that national priority. It tends to respond with little more than lip service.

Another alternative is regulation. Regulation adds negative incentives (such as permit requirements and fines) to the statement of priorities, and it can work very well, as it did when government chose to use it to clean up the nation's air and water. However, regulation is best suited to preventing undesirable business activities (such as pollution) and guiding others. Almost never can it create initiative for positive actions.

Like regulations, taxes can be and often are used to force cooperation. The difference is that with taxes, the business role is limited to providing money. Government spends it, as when, over 80 years ago, property taxes were enacted to build the nation's public school system. The goal was and remains desirable, almost everyone agrees, but government has long monopolized the roles of designer of and stimulus to educational programs. The role of business has been restricted to whatever role individual businesspeople can play as parents and citizens.

It is ironic that today business and the public have come to see relief from coercive taxes as the most important and effective means of inducing willing cooperation with social goals defined by government. Regulation, in contrast, is widely despised as overweening meddling that strangles business initiative with paper. The prevalence of this view received significant recognition under the Carter administration, with the passage of the Paperwork Reduction Act, directed largely at burdensome regulatory compliance.

The main trouble with both regulators and taxers is that they rarely see the point of view of the businesses they regulate and tax. A useful by-product of our final report for public officials, and for educators in particular, was to sharpen their appreciation of the special perspectives and concerns of the business community. Relief from taxes on profits is not the only lever available to influence business. But it cannot be ignored if the willing cooperation of business is the goal. This understanding should help foster greater and more fruitful communication and cooperation between the public and private sectors.

A MODEST PROPOSAL

Businesses welcome tax incentives, and they understand that such incentives are how government signals to the business community that serious national priorities have been identified, that the community's positive participation is needed, and that the issues are not minor, transitory, or out of public favor. Not surprisingly, businesses prefer certain kinds of tax incentives, and the most revealing and fruitful topic in our discussions with CEOs dealt with a specific conceptual proposal: *Businesses should receive a tax credit for giving to schools beyond a certain minimum percentage (the "hurdle point")* of pretax earnings. This proposal, directed at the elementary and secondary schools, attempts to reconcile three things:

- The desire for budget austerity and smaller government
- The goals identified for expanded private-sector involvement by the Filer Commission (1975) and by the President's Task Force on Private Sector Initiatives (1982)
- The urgent call for reform of American education voiced in *A Nation at Risk* (U.S. Dept. of Education 1983), the report of the National Commission on Excellence in Education, and other recent studies of our educational system (Education Commission 1983; Northeast Regional Exchange 1983)

This proposal is now being studied by the Department of Education as a possible approach to mobilizing and institutionalizing the long-term involvement of business in the schools. The Reagan administration believes that this involvement is worth encouraging. It also believes that the management skills, habits of accountability, and knowledge of the world of work, as well as the financial resources of the business community can contribute to reform in our schools. However, for a government initiative to achieve an effect that lasts beyond the term of one particular administration, the conditions favoring its implementation must be woven into the national social environment.

A large proportion of our respondents identified the tax code as a part of the environment that can and does influence their decisions. We therefore solicited their comments on the tax credit proposal described above. Of 93 executives who took a clear position for or against a tax credit, only six commented entirely negatively. They said that the system would be "totally unworkable" and would "discourage" corporations that were not contributing a high enough percentage of pretax earnings to be eligible for the credit. In essence, they objected that "the tax credit should not be tied to this minimal percentage thing."

Five CEOs responded negatively but without clearly articulating a reason. Four others said the policy was not necessary or would not be effective. Six indicated that other factors were more important, that they had other priorities, or that they felt they should support private schools and colleges over public ones. Two expressed the view that elementary and secondary schools should be supported through taxes, not through private contributions. Another voiced strong opposition, saying that he "favored tax breaks for private college tuition but not for elementary and secondary school support. " Others said that larger companies would be favored, that the proposal was too complex, that it would reduce company earnings, or that there was no advantage, given their tax situation. A few of these concerns were shared by executives who nevertheless favored the tax credit proposal.

On the positive side, we were struck by the broad and enthusiastic support for this idea. Sixty-nine executives (74 percent) out of 93 who commented favored the proposal. Based on the total of 101 interviewees, the favorable response rate was 68 percent. We classified the respondents' degrees of support as follows: moderate support, 12; generally unqualified support, 39; very positive support, 18. The last group used terms ranging from "a good idea," "sounds good," or "like the idea," to stronger affirmatives such as "very much support," "a grand idea," "excellent," and "strongly favor."

The 39 executives who expressed general support made comments such as, "It is a shame companies have to pay again for what schools should have done. Some companies in our industry would be particularly interested in this concept since they are doing some literacy training and use lower skilled people." Eight others, one a former school board member, expressed concern that any such program might have too many government strings attached: "Do not create more bureaucracy." "Keep it simple and easily understood and administered. Complexity will discourage companies from taking advantage of it and make it hard to sell smaller companies." One of these CEOs greeted the proposal in very positive terms: "It is a good sign that businesses who do more than the minimum get recognition for their effort. I like the idea of giving to the community directly instead of through government because some money is spent in administration to receive and distribute."

Six executives couched their support in statements of concern about the conditions of the schools: "Public schools are in such bad shape that any incentive for business to get involved would be a plus. Education is more important than contributions to charities. If we don't have education, everything else will fail. Corporations will buy in for the good of the community. Tax incentives are more important for creating awareness than anything else." "This proposal is fine and should cover public *and* private schools. But we will not give just to be giving, but only if the quality of the educational program merits it." "We would do *more* for a tax credit. The educational program in our city is a big need. This proposal would help increase awareness and attract more exceptional leadership by having more companies involved."

Eleven other executives favored extending this concept to a broader range of not-for-profit activities (to "all charities" or "all community and cultural activities") or, conversely, favored using the concept to emphasize narrower activities such as vocational schools, public schools only, economic education programs, or new equipment only. Four said that although they would support this tax credit, they preferred to see tuition credits or efforts to improve leadership, accountability, and recognition first.

Interestingly, seven CEOs endorsed the tax credit proposal even though, they said, their current giving or level of earnings would not allow them to realize any near-term benefit. The consensus among seven others who proposed specific terms for the proposal was that the hurdle point (the percentage of pretax earnings after which the credit would be available for additional gifts) should be from 2 to 3 percent of pretax earnings, and the credit should be from 50 to 75 percent of the amount in excess of the hurdle point. One executive proposed a credit that would increase on a sliding scale, and two proposed substituting a flat credit of 46 percent for the current deduction.

TAILORING THE MESSAGE

The business community generally acknowledges that the successful marketing of a product or idea depends on defining its value to the customer in terms of the customer's needs and interests. One of the goals of the Reagan administration is to reverse the trend toward mediocre performance in our educational system, which has been documented by so many commissions and study groups in recent years. Moreover, the President's Task Force on Private Sector Initiatives (1982) set a goal of doubling the historical level of corporate contributions to all not-for-profit activities to 2 percent of pretax earnings by 1986.

The nation operates under severe budgetary pressures on social programs, today and for the foreseeable future. Thus it should be no surprise that there is a public consensus that we as a nation need to spend our resources more wisely, with more local control and accountability, and that we need to encourage individuals and corporations to take more responsibility for, and a more active part in, assessing needs and setting priorities. These means and ends need to be reconciled in public policy.

Individual citizens have responded to the themes of this administration: self-help, patriotism, responsibility, excellence, opportunity, and so on. Although the CEOs in our research have also responded personally to these themes, they function for the most part as CEOs, in specific and very circumscribed roles. They are not usually free to indulge their personal inclinations, certainly not without first considering the economic effects on their stockholders, workers, and customers. In other words, their decision-making is defined primarily in financial terms—"the bottom line," to put it simply. Personal likes, dislikes, or impulses to altruism are typically subordinated to one basic economic concept: What return will come from this investment and how does this compare with alternative uses of the company's limited resources?

The Reagan administration stimulated a considerably higher level of corporate involvement (Council for Financial Aid to Education 1984). A substantial portion of the corporate community has shown initiative and creativity in tackling local problems without government assistance. The majority of businesses today have demonstrated "enlightened self-interest" and will continue to sustain their current involvement in the future. But there is little or no evidence that doubling of corporate involvement is imminent, or that the current level of activity will continue when another administration shifts the attention of its "bully pulpit" to other issues.

Given the diversity of opinion reflected by our executives, it seems unlikely that any single approach to encouraging business philanthropy will be broadly effective. More likely, we will need to resort to a combination of means. The fact that one approach may not be effective in motivating all businesses or in serving all not-for-profit organizations should not be a sufficient cause for its rejection. We should, instead, expect a synergistic effect from a combination of parallel efforts that would render them more effective than the sum of their individual impacts.

From our examination of the executives' views of disincentives, we can conclude that smaller businesses typically:

- Are more single-minded and direct in their pursuit of economic gain (profit)
- Will seldom seek opportunities to serve the community, but will be generally responsive if approached with clearly defined needs and plans
- Will never be as reliable a source of support as government, but are well suited to involvement in special efforts with an economic, skill-training, or public relations component
- Are far more interested in measurable results than in process and will demand that their involvement "make a difference"
- Are averse to working with government because of the expected paperwork burden and hence tend to stay clear of contacts and entanglements with government units if possible

From our analysis of incentives and recent giving behavior, we conclude that these small and medium-sized businesses generally:

- Respond to leadership from several levels of government and would welcome help in assessing community needs and priorities
- Appreciate recognition by others but try to keep a low profile
- Tend to be sensitive to economic incentives, especially tax policy
- Have accepted the idea that companies have a legitimate economic interest in some areas of social services
- Sense that government is withdrawing somewhat in these areas
- Are concerned about the declining quality of basic skills, attainment, and attitudes of young people entering the work force

WHERE DO BUSINESSES GIVE?

Our investigation of the marginal costs of giving showed a definite and substantial, elastic relationship between the marginal costs and the philanthropy that the CEOs in our research could justify. Looking at current giving habits, we note that our survey respondents appeared to favor community-based organizations more than do larger companies, but that elementary and secondary education does not receive any particular benefit from this emphasis. Moreover, local schools would probably receive little additional benefit from any expanded support that might be stimulated by a broadly based incentive.

We explicitly asked our CEOs where their present contributions to social needs are directed. We asked them which activities and organizations are the major recipients of their largesse and which ones might be favored by a tax policy that provided more encouragement for giving. Table 2.1 lists their responses by frequency.

The three categories (0–12%, 13–32%, and 33% or more) we could call low-, moderate-, and high-interest brackets. Compared with the study group of the Conference Board and the Council for Financial Aid to Education (1983), a group that included a large proportion of very large companies, our group seemed less supportive of education and more supportive of community organizations. The CFAE has determined that approximately 37 percent of total corporate philanthropy goes to education. Although our research format was not directly comparable, and the scope of our sample was much smaller, it seems unlikely that our group could be giving

TABLE 2.1
Business Contributions to Social Needs

	Number of businesses indicating present (and expanded future) contributions, by percentage of each company's contributions		
	0–12%	13–32%	33% or more
Primary/secondary education	28 (15)	7 (10)	12 (8)
Community organizations	6 (12)	19 (15)	50 (21)
Total local	34 (27)	26 (25)	62 (29)
National charities	31 (21)	9 (4)	10 (2)
Higher education	23 (12)	21 (14)	18 (7)

Note: Nineteen CEOs gave no reply to any questions on this topic. Of those who did reply, many said they would distribute increased philanthropy in the same proportion as current giving. Not all respondents gave replies that totaled 100 percent; some left out one or more classes of recipient completely; and many apparently varied in their interpretations of the recipient classifications.

anywhere near this proportion. Only 28 percent of our respondents gave more than a third of their contributions to education.

The local focus of our group was very clear. Two-thirds gave more than 33 percent of their contributions to local organizations. Of those giving to national causes, nearly two-thirds gave less than 12 percent to these causes. This local focus, however, does not seem to include much more support for local elementary and secondary schools. Only a quarter of the respondents indicated that one-third or more of their gifts went to schools, whereas 60 percent said that less than 12 percent of their gifts went to schools. We surmise that this group is not much more supportive overall of elementary and secondary schools than the group in the CFAE study. That group gave 4 percent of all its contributions (approximately $100 million in 1983) to elementary and secondary schools.

The sparse data concerning expanded contributions supports few conclusions. We find some evidence that our sample of smaller businesses would continue to favor community organizations with a high proportion of expanded support, and that they might be somewhat more supportive of schools. The executives' comments reflected a great sense of pride in their companies' participation in a wide spectrum of local activities. Three comments captured frequently repeated themes: "We give to higher education, then to elementary/secondary and vocational education for programs fostering economic development." "We don't believe corporations have a role at the elementary/secondary level except in vocational education." "Too much in the way of taxes is going to the local school boards now."

Of the 34 executives who commented about their allocation of expanded philanthropy, 11 said they would make no change. The other 23 indicated a wide variety of organizations and activities they would prefer to emphasize. Twelve mentioned education, including eight who specifically cited elementary and secondary education. Four specifically mentioned that they would favor whatever class of charity was subject to the tax incentive.

EMPLOYEE VOLUNTARISM

Our discussions indicate that an incentive targeted at voluntarism might stimulate some activity, but that small businesses would resist losing much time from the workday of employees, particularly that of blue-collar workers. They generally support "after hours" voluntarism already. Therefore, tax-credit incentives would probably be a costly way of motivating them to organize and administer additional voluntarism among employees. Furthermore, a significant minority of the executives expressed skepticism about this approach, citing the potential for abuse and the likelihood of burdensome administrative requirements.

When we explored with CEOs the use of tax incentives to encourage company-sponsored voluntarism, we presented a scenario in which a carefully controlled and defined tax credit was made available to businesses to stimulate this kind of contribution. Of the 94 executives who responded, 38 favored a tax-based incentive, but expressions of lukewarm or qualified support were common. Often a tax-based incentive was relegated to third or fourth priority, compared with other factors.

Representative comments went as follows: "We are very interested. This would be an incentive, a catalyst." "Employees' increased sense of self-worth helps the company." "A tax credit would be great for Adopt-a-School and would be a terrific incentive." "A calculated tax credit for contribution of staff would stimulate company-sponsored voluntarism. We do some now." "It would have to be significant in order to encourage paid employees to volunteer. We might have to hire one-third to one-half a person to do the work of the volunteer." "An additional 25 percent should be plenty of incentive." "Must be simple—no paperwork or inspectors—a voucher from a volunteer agency and a limit of 4 hours per day." "If criteria were clearly defined and government involvement were minimal, this would be beneficial and would encourage local communities to allow the private sector to have more 'hands on' involvement." "Might work if it didn't cost a dollar to fill out the form, and 50 cents to read it."

Five executives thought the credit should go only to the employee, or to both the company and the employee who volunteered: "Tax credits should be only as great as out-of-pocket expenses—[I] like the idea." "It would take a big credit to compensate a company for lost work time, but a credit to employees who put in extra time would be good." "The biggest problem is finding and funding volunteers in the evening hours required."

Of the executives who considered tax incentives of less importance, most favored recognition or expanded expense allowances for voluntarism first. "Recognition, peer pressure, then tax incentives." "Recognition is most important, then a deduction for a 'loaded' wage rate, then persuasion by peers." Loaded wage rate in this context means the inclusion of expenses beyond direct wages (workers' compensation and unemployment insurance, Social Security taxes, fringe benefits, and overhead charges that vary with direct wages). Although these costs are tax-deductible, these CEOs think that additional financial incentives tied directly to such expenses would stimulate voluntarism more effectively than a tax deduction alone would do. "We would donate services and supplies, but we need a break beyond simply writing off the wages and materials. It could be an exemption on payroll taxes or a tax credit." One suggested, "Take costs as a credit rather than a deduction."

Several executives said that their considerable involvement in volunteer activities was motivated purely by the satisfaction of achieving the intended results, either in developing skills needed by the company or in improving the community. Two CEOs indicated priorities for corporate involvement that probably would not be covered by a credit approach: "Our company's [affiliated] foundation is not interested in supporting public education financially. We are interested in addressing the underlying problems in public education."

Among our interviewees, 54 described the activities in which they were already involved without any short-term financial incentives or made negative comments about the use of a tax-based incentive: "[It] could be an administrative nightmare; it would have to be an awfully good credit to work." "This is not the best way. Leadership is better; use current networks, share expertise in special projects." Some CEOs referred to the need for "clearer expression/definition of agency needs and publicity for past success" as the important motivators. "It would take a $10-an-hour credit to influence me."

Several CEOs clearly regarded welfare and voluntarism as antagonistic approaches to social service delivery: "Cut food stamps and plow the money back into elementary/secondary education." "Business can/should get involved to strengthen local schools. The local economy will grow with well-educated people but will stagnate and decline with noneducated people, who become a drain on it through welfare." "Voluntarism could be stimulated by reducing government social service programs. It would force people to accept individual responsibilities."

The executives' comments indicated that some larger companies prefer to donate staff time for volunteer work rather than provide direct cash support. In smaller businesses, however, individual employees typically have broader responsibility, and so their absence during business hours is more keenly felt. "Small business without special staffs can't do much volunteering." "If a school came to us for volunteer help, we might be amenable, but involvement of employees would be on their own time."

Other reasons executives mentioned in arguing against a voluntarism incentive were: "Our internship program with a community college was vetoed by our union, which objected to [our paying] the school instead of the students." "If you work for this company, you work for it 100 percent. We contribute money, but not people on company time at any level."

Four executives related voluntarism to company size: "Our small company, which employs unskilled labor, doesn't have the time or flexibility to involve company personnel in outside activities even with a realistic incentive." A related comment was: "Volunteer work is not so bad for white-collar personnel during business hours. Blue-collar workers must be replaced, however, or work slows, causing reduced profits and lost orders. A credit would have to be awfully big to compensate for this." "Because our company is small, we lack flexibility in scheduling, which is always tight."

Three of these four executives indicated current personal involvement and active encouragement of employee voluntarism.

CONCLUSION

Tax policy is an acknowledged alternative to other methods of communicating social priorities to the business community and enlisting their aid in achieving social goals. Among the most popular tax mechanisms for aiding communication are measures such as income tax deductions and credits that relieve taxpayers of some portion of their tax burden in exchange for some desired behavior, such as charitable donations. These measures permit precise targeting of the message: If government wishes business to invest in the public schools, it need only phrase the credit offer so that no other charitable donation qualifies.

Our conceptual proposal for a tax credit that rewards only above-average contributions and is targeted toward a specific and acknowledged need (that is, the reform and improvement of elementary and secondary education) enjoyed widespread support. The approval of these business leaders is particularly important, because the information assembled by the Department of Education (1984) on partnerships indicates that support in kind, in shared resources of people and facilities, and in the "leadership effect" that such involvement can have in communities, is often more significant than financial support. As a result, the benefits a school receives are often far greater than would be expected from the dollars involved.

This "leverage" or "multiplier" effect is, of course, above and beyond the leverage on federal dollars (taxes foregone), which would be matched in effect by corporate contributions under such a policy. The cumulative effect should be to generate additional funding, gifts in kind, and voluntarism for specific purposes that support excellence in our schools far more efficiently (in terms of the federal investment needed) than would a direct federal grant with no matching corporate commitment.

In the context of our overall findings, our public policy prescription is that the appropriate federal, state, and local government units should take the following actions:

- Continue and expand existing programs to recognize the contributions of business to the community
- Identify and call to the attention of the business community the problems and needs of the community and the schools
- Conduct further research to discover the optimal structure for a marginal-tax-credit incentive to encourage business to increase its investment and involvement in education

We encourage educators and other social service managers to take the following actions:

- Meet with leaders of the local business community and describe the specific problems and needs of the local schools or agencies
- Inquire about the needs of the businesses in the area for basic skills, work habits, pre-employment training, and personnel recruiting
- Develop modest programs that serve mutual needs and can attain measurable results in a few years' time, and solicit business support to get such programs started

We further recommend that business and professional leaders take these actions:

- Give private-sector initiatives a high priority on the agendas of the trade associations, chambers of commerce, and professional societies to which leaders belong
- Initiate contacts with government officials and school administrators, individually or through intermediary organizations such as local education foundations, business–education partnerships, or other community service organizations

REFERENCES

Carroll, B. J. 1986. *Talking with Business* (Washington, D.C.: U.S. Government Printing Office).

Council for Financial Aid to Education (CFAE). 1983. *A Profile of Corporate Contributions* (New York).

_____ . 1984. *Corporate Support of Education 1983* (New York).

Department of Education (DOEd). Office of Planning, Budget, and Evaluation. 1984. *Partnerships in Education: Education Trends of the Future* (Washington, D.C.: U.S. Government Printing Office).

Education Commission of the States. 1983. *A Summary of Major Reports on Education* (Denver, CO).

Filer Commission. 1975. *Report of the Commission on Private Philanthropy and Public Needs* (Washington, D.C.: U.S. Government Printing Office).

Northeast Regional Exchange. 1983. *Education under Study: An Analysis of Recent Reports on Education*, 2d ed. (Chelmsford, MA).

President's Task Force on Private Sector Initiatives, 1982. Incentives Committee Report, *Building Partnerships* (Washington, D.C.: U.S. Government Printing Office, p. 43ff).

U.S. Department of Education. 1983. *A Nation at Risk* (Washington, D.C.: U.S. Government Printing Office).

3

Motivating the Private Sector: What Role for Public Policy?

Barry J. Carroll and Thomas A. Easton

One thing that the governments of all industrialized nations—communist, socialist, or capitalist—have in common is that they all provide their citizens with many services, from transportation to health. The differences are ones of degree. Capitalist nations leave many more services to the private sector.

Why does a capitalist nation provide any services at all? Perhaps the public becomes impatient with the workings of a free market in responding to its needs. Or perhaps society prefers to rest its broad, continuing needs in the hands of an entity it can trust to remain in existence longer than is possible for most businesses. Or perhaps it prefers the stability of funding possible only to an organization with the authority to levy taxes. Or perhaps, despite government notoriety for inefficiency and high costs (covered, of course, by personal and corporate taxes), the public trusts its government more than it does its capitalists to meet its needs for certain services that could become pernicious monopolies in private hands.

More to the point may be the nature of the profit motive. Businesses decide whether to undertake any activity based on the market. Are there enough people who will buy the service or product to justify the investment? How will it be financed and who will provide the needed capital? Who will bear the risks involved? Any broad societal need has to be secondary.

In short, an ultimate profit is the bottom line. There are no exceptions, for business does nothing unless it can see some benefit for itself or its investors. Nevertheless, the private sector will provide some public services that are not profitable in readily measurable monetary terms. The key is the existence of other gains, such as tax incentives, improved community image and public relations, better employee skills, or community amenities, that enhance the personal or family lives of needed employees.

The benefit need be neither large nor certain, but it must be perceived as real and significant. Public officials are not immune to this frame of mind, since the pressure from innumerable interest groups for services invariably exceeds the general public's willingness to bear the cost collectively. Some policymakers may thus be eyeing with great interest recent proposals in Congress to add to the list of state lotteries a federal lottery. One obvious benefit of such a nationwide numbers game would be income to offset the national deficit without increasing taxes.

The lottery strategy would also provide less obvious benefits. One might be to provide a way to encourage businesses to invest money and other resources in helping to provide unprofitable public services. To a straightforward tax deduction or tax credit might be added free lottery tickets, perhaps one ticket for each $100 in corporate resources devoted to specified services. The list of qualifying services would provide an effective way of communicating social needs to business. The jackpot, which would be considerably larger than any present state lottery's prize, would serve as a major incentive for business participation in meeting social needs. Consider that a company that donates $10,000 to the public schools, the Red Cross, and so on would gain a tax deduction or credit, as now, plus 100 chances for a $20 million payoff.

Corporate profit is the bottom line. Companies help provide social services when they see a profit in those services. Companies that turn a social service into actual businesses (*vide* private prisons, hospitals, mail delivery, transportation, and garbage collection) realize that profit in a very direct way. If we could show where such direct profits lie for other services, we might expect the private sector to take over those services quite eagerly.

Unfortunately, many social services are in the public sector precisely because their immediate costs are much higher than their immediate yields. The eventual payoff for investment in these services might prove high enough in the long run, but not in the short run, and perhaps in other forms than cash profits. For example, what if a company were to spend money to encourage preventative health care for its young workers? The benefits to the employer in lower absenteeism, longer productive lives of workers, and lower medical bills will be two or three decades away. Encouraging the education of future workers also costs *now*. And here too the reward is delayed. The company that helps a local school system improve its services to the community contributes to the quality of those who may be its own future employees, but it will not be hiring those higher-quality workers for many years, if at all. Some of them will pursue careers elsewhere. The imperative of the bottom line almost always dictates that such long-term investments cannot (and will not) be made without some strong external incentive such as a generous government tax credit or deduction, or some new plan like the lottery we suggest above.

How well do such incentives work? Carroll's Department of Education study (1986) addressed the efficacy of tax policy. It also examined such other motivating forces as recognition, communication of needs, leadership, help with liability problems, and others.

TAX POLICY

Many of the chief executive officers interviewed for the Carroll study indicated that they were motivated to help provide public services by the desire to make a difference with measurable results, to accomplish some significant achievement besides success in the marketplace. However, the study's major finding was that a favorable *tax policy* is the most effective incentive for CEOs to undertake initiatives in the nonprofit public sector. Fifty executives identified this incentive, compared with 44 who selected the next most commonly cited incentive, "recognition." Specific measures to which the executives said they would respond relating to education were tax incentives to support employees' continuing education (30), to support company-funded scholarships for tuition and fees of employees' children (25), and to promote sponsorship of educational programs targeted at marginally employable persons in the community (27). Only 13 respondents went beyond mere agreement, calling tax incentives "very helpful," "very important," "number one," and "essential." One stated that there is "no other meaningful incentive." Another said that "a credit like the ITC [investment tax credit] would result in the greatest increase in [either] corporate or individual giving." Yet another remarked, "There are no nonprofits; we're all here to feed ourselves."

Several comments shed further light on the executives' reasoning. "Use local, state, and federal incentives as a *handle*. We must be able to justify to stockholders. [We] like the continuing education credit for tuition support." "The targeted-jobs tax credit program is good. We are heavily involved and have gotten back over $1 million. [It] helps the target population and our company. Business all over should look into this program." "Tax incentives are needed to accomplish many things such as moving into inner-city locations and hiring untrained and disadvantaged [workers]." "Economic incentives override all others; over the long term, we see this having multiple benefits and a big payback." "Yes to tax incentives and better preparation of students for work." "[Incentives] should be to foster company matching-gift programs with employees." "[They] can be a mutual benefit."

Two respondents thought the incentive should be for individuals as well as for corporations, and four others emphasized the value of such a credit in expanding existing continuing education and tuition rebate programs and in stimulating other companies to offer such benefits to employees. Two executives emphasized the importance of using a tax credit rather than simply an expanded deduction (the latter was recommended by the Filer Commission) (1975).

Several of the above comments support the thesis that because income for small businesses tends to be taxed in lower brackets, small companies would have proportionately less incentive than larger companies to participate under an expanded-deduction approach. One executive cited as very effective the Pennsylvania Neighborhood Assistance Act, which provides a credit that reduces the marginal after-tax cost to the company for neighborhood improvement philanthropy from 50 cents to 22 cents on each dollar contributed.

Opinions about the appropriate amount of a credit varied from 100 percent ("Why not a plan by which if business provides a service which saves the government one dollar, we credit the company with a one-dollar write-off?") to more moderate proposals, such as, "[You] don't have to make support to schools by business free; just provide some incentive" and "A 10 percent flat tax incentive, I am in favor of it."

The CEOs of several companies that were in a loss position still approved of tax incentives. They would derive no long-term benefit, but they said, "No gain for us, but try to do it anyway; helpful unless [the] economy changes."

Although, as one executive stated, "tax incentives are a cornerstone for most corporations," support for such a policy was neither universal among the respondents nor without reservations. Several executives reflected their concern that such a tool be used prudently in comments such as: "Tax incentives are an easy answer, but nonetheless generally true. Be sure to control the levels." "Although more liberal IRS [Internal Revenue Service] policies are called for, perhaps education vouchers would be a better approach." "It is very important that incentives be adopted which are simple and understandable."

RECOGNITION

Another incentive with widespread support is *corporate recognition*. Forty-four executives commented in favor of expanded programs of recognition, 11 using superlatives to describe its importance as a motivator of business. However, some small businesses may be reluctant to publicize their philanthropy. One CEO put it this way: "We do a lot of public service now, but we don't toot our own horn. If someone else reported [what we do] we would be delighted." Another said, "There is often a lack of sufficient recognition for smaller companies. The corporate giants always seem to be the only ones to get stroked. Yet often the smaller company has a much higher proportionate level of giving. The smaller firm senses the importance but has limited absolute resources." A joint study of philanthropy relative to the size of companies conducted by the Conference Board and the Council for Financial Aid to Education (1983) supports the thesis that smaller companies on average *do* contribute a higher percentage of assets than larger companies.

According to these studies, altruism was mentioned as a reason for philanthropy by only 8 percent of their (mainly large) corporate survey respondents. Similarly, only a small proportion of Carroll's 101 respondents indicated that altruism was their motive for philanthropy or *pro bono publico* involvement in public education. Comments reflected the goodwill obtainable from community involvement, but those comments mainly related such activity to a more purposefully profit-oriented motive: "In good times, we do many things for which we receive no credit [but] in what is a local company, local PR recognition—appreciation for charitable activity—is a real incentive." "Employees appreciate working for public-spirited firms." One respondent observed that expanded programs of recognition are needed "so that your own employees know you are involved" and "so that we recognize the positive side of business's and education's relationship in the media."

Underlying the feeling toward public service of most large businesses and many smaller ones is the attitude that "some companies' donations are really image building, linked with the company agenda, actually a PR way of advertising their products." Because smaller companies tend to provide fewer "household word" products, however, they think of recognition more in terms of employee and community goodwill.

Even among the nearly 50 percent of the survey respondents who favored expanded recognition, however, opinions on the value of various types of recognition differed. They ranged from the highly commended service business leader's view that he sought only "pride in being recognized for what you are doing" to another CEO's comment that "Recognition is good, but a cash benefit is more important."

Several executives volunteered suggestions for specific forms of recognition: "I strongly support an 'E' flag and pin approach like in World War II. It needs to be done with class and stature." "This is extremely important, a letter or certificate from the President or Secretary [of Education] would be a tremendous incentive." Instituting such a program for business was mentioned as "an excellent way to recognize leadership."

COMMUNICATION OF NEEDS

Carroll's respondents gave first and second place to tax policy and recognition as ways to stimulate business participation in meeting social needs. Third place went to *improved communication of needs by the community*. Carroll's research format distinguished between community needs for volunteer help and the needs of local not-for-profit organizations for funding and equipment, but his executive respondents made little distinction in their responses: "We need an inventory of what the community requires, to better determine how the private sector can respond." "There are only vague parameters for giving, a lack of guidelines." "The public and private sectors together should identify economic and social needs of the community, then make a joint commitment." "State and federal agencies should help schools specify needs for volunteers and other help for good work habits and motivation among students." "Corporations need to see the overall picture." "Business needs clear objectives, better planning, and the belief that [our support] will make a difference."

Several CEOs pointed out that business is particularly interested in a two-way street: "Mutual benefits are the key to selling business." "There is a strong need between industry and education to explore each other's resources." "Adopt-a-School sounds too one-way and paternalistic; use Partnership." "It is wrong to assume the private sector knows nothing about education. We think the best kind of education prepares young people to be productive workers." "We believe in supporting schools if they stress the right curriculum—the three R's." But one executive commented, "Government is better at communication with industry on job-training needs than on the subject of developing the work habits needed to hold a job."

Speaking about tackling needs once they are identified, one executive suggested an incremental approach: "Start with a project that is relatively easy and see it through. You can build on positive results and take action to correct the negatives."

GOVERNMENT LEADERSHIP

Government leadership is another important incentive, or facilitator, for private-sector initiatives. Twenty-two executives affirmed that the government can, at various levels, take an active part in stimulating business involvement in cooperative arrangements: "It just has not been made important. If government or industry or civic leaders were to make it important, our business would do a lot more. Political pressure is needed."

The type of government involvement was addressed in the following comments: "We like talk sessions with the government like this. We like the President's involvement." "The credibility of the Department [of Education] with the private sector rose considerably as a result of your asking

[our] opinions, and I believe you are now in a position to forge lasting links." "Government leadership is needed to promote programs for improving motivation and higher achievement in the early grades before negative attitudes take hold." "The Department of Education should foster cooperative arrangements. The opportunities in electronics alone are unlimited." "The Department's interest and involvement with private sector initiatives is timely. Business is favorably disposed."

Three executives mentioned the importance of "educating corporate executives so they can see the mutual benefits." One noted that younger managers do not seem to have this perspective. Several CEOs specifically asked for "feedback from the Secretary [of Education] on this survey to learn what other companies are doing." One wanted "a list of positive projects."

Some CEOs, however, disagreed with these views. One commented: "Incentives are feasible for tackling a temporary problem—a business task force can help straighten it out; but in the long term, elementary and secondary schools should be supported by taxes." Four other executives said that government involvement was neither helpful nor effective: "There is too much of this. Corporations can set their own goals." "Let the needs come from people, not political types."

LIABILITY RELIEF

In these days of massive awards to litigants who claim damage by corporations, either in the normal course of business or during some side-line activity such as a school tour, many people think that the cost of helping public organizations (in the form of increased insurance premiums or of liability judgments) is simply too great to justify the risk. As a remedy, some people have proposed a "Good Samaritan" law to grant substantial immunity from liability to individuals and companies that act in good faith to further a public purpose.

Asked about this method of alleviating liability concerns, 16 executives expressed some support for the idea, while four dismissed the issue as "not important": "No one cares about this but a few lawyers." However, specific comments indicate that a significant part of the business community has some concern about this issue, even though "most insurance policies cover this." One CEO said, "We no longer sponsor a handicapped picnic event at the company or field trips to our plant because of liability exposure." Another said that the issue "comes into play with our summer jobs program. The workers' compensation exposure is a drawback." Still another remarked that the "Good Samaritan law in Massachusetts resulted in large food contributions." The most cogent comment on the value of such a law was this: "Such legislation could provide confidence to industry that they have strong protection against liability." We must conclude, however, that liability is not a widespread concern.

OTHER INCENTIVES

Other possible incentives mentioned by the executives were "seed money" to help get broad-based community partnerships off the ground and "increased parental involvement in the schools." Many CEOs favored programs that contained an economic education component and were oriented toward needed specialties, such as "apprenticeships," "engineering and utility regulation," and "technical skill development." Several CEOs said that such school reforms as career ladders, merit pay, and elimination of tenure would attract their support. One executive noted that not only was "the credibility of the company within the community strengthened by involvement in giving and voluntarism," but that such activity "helps develop leadership within management; broadens their image, abilities, and knowledge within the community."

WHY VOLUNTEER?

Carroll concluded from his interviews of CEOs that the basic motive for any corporation to help meet community needs is not altruism but the company's own benefit. That benefit can take the form of public relations or of management broadening. It can also, of course, take a more directly economic form, as one respondent explained: "We spend a great deal on retraining. We are not happy with the products of the public schools. Improved schools would reduce training costs." By contrast, several executives voiced a broader perspective: "It is crucial for all businesses to understand that their success depends on the well-being of school districts in their city and insist that commitment lead to improvement in the quality of life for the community, and that a more literate society emerge."

Corporate philanthropy is not a new phenomenon. In the years since World War I, businesses have maintained a level of giving of about 1 percent of pretax earnings (Conference Board 1983). Businesses today claim over $3.4 billion in tax deductions for gifts to tax-exempt organizations. To test the statements of executives on what they indicate motivates them to serve the public weal, Carroll followed up the initial discussions of incentives and disincentives by asking the respondents their opinions on what factors they thought had *recently* influenced business philanthropy. He sought an explanation for the fact that despite a severe recession, corporate philanthropy rose as a percentage of pretax earnings between 1981 and 1983 (Council for Financial Aid to Education 1985). Even after eliminating some aberrations caused by one large bequest and another extraordinary transaction, and after taking into account the fact that part of the percentage increase was due to a drop in earnings rather than to an increase in contributions, the absolute dollar amount contributed by the corporate community increased during this period. Through the survey, Carroll hoped to gain some insight into the factors that contributed to the increase and to check on the validity of the respondents' assessments of incentives.

Corporate Responsibility

Carroll's initial finding from the first round of discussions with CEOs was that corporate giving is usually subordinated to the profit motive in one way or another. In the second phase of the interviews, the same respondents most frequently cited *corporate responsibility* as the reason for their voluntary contributions. Forty-seven executives cited this reason. Since this was nearly as many respondents as had said they favored tax incentives to encourage business philanthropy, Carroll checked to see how much overlap there was between the two groups. Exactly half of those who favored tax incentives identified a sense of corporate responsibility as the reason for the current higher level of giving. However, only four CEOs used superlatives such as "key," "definitely," and "extremely" in asserting the importance of corporate responsibility, which may indicate that this phrase is more of a cliché among some executives than a strongly held belief. Cliché or not, the phrase "corporate responsibility" is an accepted concept among business leaders, as is evidenced by such comments as: "[Social responsibility] has become a truism of American business." "I feel there is a more basic realization of need." "There is a growing awareness that government is not the best way to address the problems of the poor, uneducated, etc." "There is a moral obligation to help others."

One executive cited "a sense of community responsibility" on the part of business. Business "senses a greater vacuum [in the area of social services] and perceives limits to public financing." Seventeen CEOs referred to somewhat lower tax burdens as one factor motivating them. As one said, "After the tax decreases, it seemed only fair to contribute more." Not only is there "recognition of these cuts," but as another executive put it, "I feel there are more skills in taking advantage of tax incentives around today."

Fourteen executives referred to the effect of inflation: "It took more dollars than before to hold the line." "There has been a recognition of the effect of inflation on social services." "The poor economy made need more obvious. Community leaders, especially corporate executives, were far more aggressive [in fund raising]." Responses ranged from a tit-for-tat altruism ("Our company believes that if the community supports you, you should return that support to the community") to more pragmatic reasons ("There is a general feeling the private sector is more cost-efficient than a government-run agency"). Others commented: "There is more corporate conscience in tough times," and "We should contribute more to society, especially in difficult economic times." "If all stopped relying on government, we would volunteer more."

And one CEO pointed out, "There is a realization by more stockholders that contributions are a legitimate use of corporate dollars, and there is a desire of management to improve the quality of [community] life."

The Role of Leadership

Carroll's interviews thus detected a clear impulse in the business community to try to do more when times are tough. This impulse seems to work against the more predictable tendency to put profits first. It was thus no surprise to find several comments that reflected less enthusiasm for this new role: "This [corporate] responsibility could be overstated," noted one executive.

Several CEOs preferred to stress other motives, such as President Reagan's leadership, as primary contributions to businesses' expanded philanthropy. Of the 34 executives who mentioned this factor as an influence, several referred to the timeliness of the president's emphasis. First evident in the establishment of a new White House Office for Private Sector Initiatives in 1981, this emphasis became a continuing theme in speeches throughout the president's first term. "We feel the nation was ready for the president's approach to home rule—the importance of state and local control." Many CEOs felt the president's goals were "important and attainable." The president's emphasis, referred to by several executives as "jawboning," was effective in "highlighting government withdrawal and creating a feeling of obligation."

Eight CEOs used superlatives to describe the president's leadership. One called it "the biggest single factor" in bringing about his city's 2 Percent Club (composed of companies that pledge contributions of 2 percent or more of pretax earnings). Another said, "There was a reaction from business to support the Reagan administration in a positive sense via contributions."

Several CEOs, however, expressed different views. One said, "We are too small (100 to 300 employees, $10 million to $25 million in sales) to be affected by speeches and programs from Washington." A second supported the president's effort but said, "It won't happen by jawboning alone. The government must put its money where its mouth is—tax credits, for example."

Although many CEOs did not refer specifically to the president, 43 referred to a vacuum created by the shrinking role of the federal government. Other causes for this vacuum were identified: "Proposition XIII [California] caused a great increase in requests." "When government money is reduced, other sources had to be sought. Fund seekers get more creative in their quest for funds." "OPEC changed things. We see a trend of government withdrawing and the private sector stepping in, especially small and medium size business." "There is a growing awareness that bureaucracy can't do the job." This changing role is reflected in some business organizations. "CEOs have placed this function at a higher management level where they can monitor the efficiency [of recipients] and have higher accountability."

The Need for Competence

A widespread concern of the executives Carroll studied was the quality of the workers coming into the work force. Twenty-nine respondents cited the low level of basic skills and the need for retraining of workers as stimulating increased business philanthropy. "Poor writing is endemic. Employees can use calculators but don't understand mathematical concepts." "There is a need for better educated employees, but the schools are graduating students who are less well prepared." "If [high school students] learn only to have a good attitude toward basic skills and improving themselves, the company can train them for a specific job." "Business involvement seems to be the only answer."

Line business executives tend to define the basic skills needed in the work force much more broadly than literacy and computation skills: "There has to be more emphasis on motivation, personal characteristics, and job entry skills—to succeed at work and to ultimately improve profits and customer satisfaction." Several executives mentioned their in-house training programs and the critical need to retrain workers from obsolescent industries.

Other Motives

Among other reasons for increasing corporate philanthropy were: "There is a need to maintain a positive corporate image." "Good corporate citizenship makes firms look solvent, secure, and successful. Anything that reflects on the community, such as the school system, reflects also on business." "There has been an unproductive and adversarial relationship between management and labor. There was resentment over some extravagant bonuses. Channeling more of pretax earnings into charity brings rewards in the long run."

The reasons executives give for the recent philanthropic performance of the business community are thus generally consistent with their appraisal of the incentives and disincentives they said would affect their actions. The withdrawal of government support and the substitution of the Reagan administration's program, combined with a growing sense that business has an interest in the health of the community rather than simply in short-term profits, have more than offset the adverse impact of the recession on giving.

THE COST OF GIFTS

Because CEOs cited tax policy so often as a powerful influence on their thinking, Carroll also explored what effect tax incentives have on philanthropy and voluntarism. The aim was to elaborate on the previous remarks of some executives alluding to the relationship between the cost of a gift to a corporation *before taxes* and its cost *after taxes*.

For example, if the marginal tax rate (the rate levied on the last dollar earned) is 46 percent, a one-dollar gift to a charity by a company costs the company only 54 cents after taxes. The gift reduces the taxes paid by 46 cents. If the company regards the gift as an investment that will pay some return in the future, even if the return cannot be precisely determined (as in the case of a gift to a school), one conclusion is inescapable: If the after-tax cost of the gift is reduced, the return on investment must increase.

Ignoring theoretically sounder techniques, most businesses analyze investments by the "quick and dirty" payback method. That is, they calculate the time needed for the return on the investment to equal the original investment. Usually, they take into account the effects of tax incentives for investment such as ACRS (Accelerated Cost Recovery System), the investment tax credit, and an energy tax credit, if appropriate. Most businesses insist on rapid payback, usually in three years or less, without much regard to the true economic life of the investment. The reason is simple, and it owes something to the "bird in the hand" philosophy: The longer the time required to recover the investment, the more risk is involved. The investment could be made obsolete by better technology; the end product might be made obsolete in the marketplace; or the economy could turn sour, leaving the company with the cost of financing the investment and little or no income. The use of the payback concept helps in controlling risk as well as in estimating how long capital recovery will take.

In recent years, U.S. business has been compared unfavorably with the Japanese because of the American emphasis on short-term return of capital rather than on long-term planning and investment. Asked why the Japanese have been able to develop a longer-term approach, some scholars have noted that the Japanese have had several advantages over their U.S. competitors. Although the Japanese economy has cycles, they reflect varying speeds of expansion, rather than alternating expansion and contraction. The Japanese government is involved in setting industrial policy, organizing international marketing, and managing competition in key targeted markets. The Japanese sustain growth in many industries by using international trade to counterbalance the cycle of domestic demand, thereby smoothing overall demand. This practice permits financing growth with far higher levels of debt than U.S. banks would ever permit domestic companies. Reduced risk also supports lower interest rates, and these reduced financing costs in turn permit development and marketing efforts to be planned for the longer term without the necessity of a quick capital recovery. In short, Japanese companies are able to invest on a longer-term basis in large part because they have developed ways of reducing the risk of such investment.

We do not make this observation to advocate any specific methods the Japanese use in their overall strategy. Rather, we wish to illustrate how, through several complementary policies, they have created a business environment that reconciles a relatively free market with the long-term needs of a nation highly dependent on trade in a rapidly changing high-technology age. Although the U.S. government structures the business environment in many ways, its effort seems less consistent in identifying and addressing national priorities. One priority on which there is a widespread consensus is that we must improve our educational system to support our nation's international competitive position. We should be implementing long-term policies to that end.

The responses of Carroll's executives indicate that large segments of the U.S. business community regard philanthropy as a type of investment. They want to see results from these expenditures. Specifically, they want to see results that relate to the business purpose of their companies. If giving is in fact a business decision for those companies, it is certainly a long-term investment. A gift to an elementary school might help a program that serves the child of a valuable employee whom the company wants to attract or to retain for many years to come.

Looking even further ahead, the company is thinking of the investment in that child's education as having a long-term payback, coming primarily when the child emerges from high school or college with a good foundation in basic skills of value to the community and the company. The business is fostering a healthier school because this will ultimately produce a healthier business environment. It follows that if government policy can increase the short-term payback (which is the same as reducing the investment) for the same long-term return, businesses will be more inclined to undertake such investments.

Carroll and his team asked executives to estimate the effects they thought various marginal costs of their contributions would have on their level of giving. This was a difficult question for many of them. It was hypothetical and called for rapid analysis of many factors and a conclusion that many respondents would have preferred to consider over a much longer period with fewer undefined variables. Nevertheless, 58 executives gave opinions that permit some useful generalizations about how businesses might respond to policy alternatives. Table 3.1 summarizes their responses.

We will not attempt a detailed analysis of these data because of the small sample size. It seems significant, nevertheless, that a large proportion of the CEOs surveyed indicated a substantive response to the marginal costs of giving. When Carroll and the SRRs asked the CEOs about personal giving, they found that the CEOs would handle their own money in almost exactly the same manner if there were an individual tax incentive. This fact tends to confirm Martin Feldstein's judgment that corporations as well as individuals would very likely show price elasticity in their giving.[1] His research has shown that private giving has an element of elasticity that ranges from 1.15 to 1.30—that is, a reduction in the cost of giving yields an increase in giving larger than the cost reduction.

TABLE 3.1
Effects of Changes in Marginal Costs on Giving

Corporation's after-tax cost for $1 gift	Number of companies that would increase giving by percentage shown[b]					
	None	5–10%	11–15%	16–20%	21–25%	More than 25%
$0.54[a] (current cost)	NA	NA	NA	NA	NA	NA
0.50	3	7	1	—	—	—
0.35	5	18	22	1	1	—
0.25	4	6	14	6	14	3

NA, not applicable
[a]Excluding state and local income taxes.
[b]Not all companies responded to all marginal cost alternatives.
Source: Compiled by the author.

The additional qualitative comments that the executives volunteered shed additional light on the basis for their projections. Twenty-five respondents favored tax credits. Twenty of these specifically commented that tax credits would increase giving: "With a 25 percent credit, contributions could be doubled at the same net cost." "Giving would be relatively proportionate to reduced tax liability." "I don't like to think we would give just because of tax considerations, but it is realistic." "We would give at least one to one, but would need time to adjust our planning. We are very civic-minded. We would have to ask ourselves, what is our after-tax cost?" "There is an inverse relationship—the lower the after-tax cost, the higher the giving." "[We] would give at least the [newly] available tax dollars." "Industry would be more generous if the increased benefits didn't go to Washington but to the education and community groups it was meant to help. The more hands it goes through, the more is siphoned off in unproductive ways." "We would give $2 for every $1 tax incentive." Two CEOs suggested a graduated tax credit: "The greater the contribution, the greater the tax break. Great incentive!"

Thirty executives said, in effect, that their companies and perhaps others would not be motivated by a tax credit. Their reasons varied widely. One type of response could be called *needs based*: "Taxes are not too heavy; need is a more important criterion than a tax break." "Commitment is more important than tax credits for either corporations or individuals." "Our company would not be motivated by unique incentives, only by perceived need."

Another frequent response could be called *income based*: "The percentage [of giving] would grow as a factor of income." "Can't increase for a while, too much in debt." "Only if we can spare it, and only to selected private groups such as blind, diabetes, etc., not to a United Crusade." "We don't think our giving would represent much money at our current level of business." "If the tax incentive were increased, it would encourage us [to give] if we were making money."

A third response could be characterized as *government policy limited*: "I am personally nearing retirement and giving at the maximum amount deductible each year and am therefore not likely to increase giving." "We are extremely generous now, and I am unsure how a reduced marginal cost would affect our plans." "We currently give the maximum amount of pretax income to a related foundation." "We already give 10 percent of gross income to our church." "We are projecting gifts of 5 percent of pretax earnings this year." (Several executives appeared to be unaware that the ceiling for the annual amount of gifts deductible, which they considered a constraint, had been raised from 5 to 10 percent of pretax earnings.)

Some industries, such as banking, utilities, and insurance, have special factors and methods of operations that give them a unique perspective on tax policy. Bankers, for example, usually invest assets in tax-exempt bonds to the point at which their bank's taxable earnings drop into lower brackets, for the after-tax returns on such bonds are usually greater than those on taxable loans or bonds. "Our bank is not paying taxes; if the shelters were abolished, my individual giving and my bank's giving would go down." "A reduced marginal cost of giving probably would not affect our bank, but might affect others."

As to the amount of a credit needed to motivate business philanthropy, one executive said, "It would not take a significant reduction [in marginal cost] to increase giving." Four others indicated that a reduction in marginal cost from 54 cents to 50 cents would have no measurable effect. One said that a reduction from 54 cents to 40 cents would be a "meaningful incentive to give." Another said that "new tax incentives would really have a significant impact, but I feel very strongly that credits are a better approach than [expanded] deductions." Five said they favored comparable individual and corporate tax incentives. Only three executives denied unequivocally that there is a cause-and-effect relationship between the level of philanthropy and the marginal cost of giving for business in general.

CONCLUSION

The prevailing opinion among the business executives Carroll interviewed is that an increase in tax incentives would increase corporate philanthropy directed at education and other public needs. Yet this opinion is far from universal. Some executives oppose tax incentives, most of them saying that since they are already active in the community, increased tax incentives would not affect them. "Most companies do not have the capacity to adopt a school. Some coordinating mechanism is needed to make modest contributions from many sources more effective." "Most companies can absorb such costs as providing a visiting lecturer, student internships, or informal career days. The range of activities is unlimited." "Legislation should be considered to allow states and schools to create foundations to accept volunteer work and money—for education only—not for athletic support, where it goes now." These comments reaffirm the perceived need for mediating structures to help match the needs and resources of companies and not-for-profit organizations.

Many CEOs expressed concern about the possible strings attached to, and the paperwork burden of, a tax incentive. Three executives worried about the potential for abuse of any tax incentive: "Be careful, some [companies] might overwhelm the schools in their fourth quarter in a rush to get full allowable credit." Four executives were quite adamant that the government should stay completely away from the subject of voluntarism: "Forget the credit for voluntarism. It is nonsense."

Yet ignoring incentives is practical only if business contributes on its own, without encouragement of some form. And while some businesses do have enough of a sense of corporate responsibility to need no incentives, many do not. Incentives clearly have a role to play. The question we must ask is whether tax incentives are adequate to society's needs. If they are not—and the extent of society's unmet or poorly met needs suggests that this is so—we need to devise other means of encouraging business to help.

These other means could include programs to expand recognition, communicate needs, provide leadership, and limit liability. They might even include that national lottery we mentioned. The ways of encouraging business to help meet social needs that seem likely to be most effective have in common their effect on the bottom line. They reduce the costs of helping, or they enhance the rewards. The most effective encouragement of all may involve permitting business to turn social needs such as prisons, health care, and so on into profit-making activities.

We do not believe we have examined all conceivable ways of encouraging business to help meet social needs. We do believe that if government is to reduce the burdens of taxation and regulation, it must find new ways to ensure that the tasks it now takes as its own are accomplished. It must devise imaginative solutions to social problems that allow it to leverage its available funds. It must not follow the path of the past, for that leads to more regulation, more taxation, and an unbearable pressure to increase the deficit that already threatens to strangle the U.S. economy.

NOTES

1. Dr. Feldstein, who had conducted a major study ("Tax Incentives and Charitable Contributions in the United States: A Microeconomic Analysis") for the Filer Commission in 1975–76 on tax policy effects on individual taxpayers' charitable deductions (Filer Commission 1975) expressed this opinion in a personal conversation with Carroll on December 20, 1983.

REFERENCES

Carroll, B. J. 1986. *Talking with Business* (Washington, D.C.: U.S. Government Printing Office).

Conference Board. 1983. *Annual Survey of Corporate Contributions*, report no. 833 (New York), p. 16.

Council for Financial Aid to Education (CFAE). 1984. *Corporate Support of Education 1983* (New York).

_____ . 1985. *Corporate Support of Education 1984* (New York).

Filer Commission. 1975. *Report of the Commission on Private Philanthropy and Public Needs* (Washington, D.C.: U.S. Government Printing Office).

4

The Entrepreneurial Approach to Privatization

Ralph W. Conant and Thomas A. Easton

If private enterprise is to assume responsibility for providing some of the social services we now assign to government, it must be convinced of opportunities for profit in those services. The private sector will surely avoid involvement in public services where the profit is marginal or at risk. Thus, large corporations whose wealth and reliability qualify them to assume responsibility for public services may shun these services as unprofitable or too unlike their present activities to be worthy of consideration. Thanks to the near bankruptcies of cities such as New York, and to the political winds, which blow with unpredictable fury, they may even see public service activities as severe threats to their financial health.

However, we need not look to big business as a replacement for government in the realm of public services. Social service providers need not be large organizations at all. It may be just as reasonable to meet social needs of many kinds through *small* organizations, such as the small businesses that are springing up all over the country in this age of entrepreneurship (Easton and Conant 1985b).

Entrepreneurs, singly and in small groups of partners, are responsible for just about every business that exists in the United States. Corporate spinoffs are a distinct minority. Many people thus look to entrepreneurs to solve the problems that face the country today. Some of these problems involve impending shortages of everything from industrial raw materials to public funds. In essence, these problems are those of the "limits to growth" prophecies that emerge from computer simulations based on the dubious assumption that present trends will continue unchanged into the future.

One major objection to the "limits to growth" pessimism comes from Julian Simon (1981), who reminds us that history shows a constant trend of improving standards of living, largely because people have always been able to find substitutions for resources in short supply. In Simon's view, "there is no physical or economic reason why human resourcefulness and enterprise cannot forever continue to respond to impending shortages and existing problems with new expedients that . . . leave us better off than before the problem arose." He might have had in mind the way automakers responded to demands for more fuel-efficient cars once the price of fuel soared in the early 1970s, although that response falls short of solving the problem of diminishing petroleum supplies. *That* problem will be solved only when need finally prompts the conversion to synthetic fuels and electrically powered cars.

Kirzner (1983) agrees with Simon, observing that resourcefulness and enterprise are the prime traits of entrepreneurs, to whom every "problem" is an opportunity. When in need, they seek and find new raw materials, new sources of energy, and new technologies. In addition, they are already seeking and finding new ways to deliver social services, and they will continue to do so. The problems exist, and so do the opportunities. The potential is limited only by the entrepreneurial imagination, for there is demand for almost every service that government now provides (would government provide these services otherwise?). The entrepreneur's task is to find a way to provide those services at a profit, direct or indirect.

ENTREPRENEURS AND CAPITALISM

The literature on entrepreneurs credits the economic dominance of capitalism to the power of entrepreneurship. Kirzner (1979, 1983), for example, says that the entrepreneur is why capitalism works. Kirzner's point is that the ideal economic systems of most free-market economists assume that buyers and sellers have perfect knowledge of the marketplace. Yet no economic system approaches that ideal. Knowledge of the market is always imperfect. There is always room for intelligent, perceptive people to correct inefficiencies, improve marketing, and devise new products that satisfy unmet needs, adding knowledge and initiative to create value. These are the people we call entrepreneurs. Their "secret" is their ability to spot the opportunity to make a profit, and the end result of their opportunistic activities is increased supply and variety of products and services, more jobs, more profit, more investment capital, and an expanding national economy.

Gilder (1984) considers the entrepreneur the main hero of our time, disagreeing strongly with those modern economists and politicians who see this individual only as someone to be exploited through punitive taxes and beaten down with laws intended to "protect" society from his or her "depredations." It is true that entrepreneurs are motivated by the prospect of personal gain, but that in itself is neither sin nor crime, at least in a capitalist society.

ENTREPRENEURS AND EMPLOYMENT

The Internal Revenue Service reports that there are about ten million self-employed Americans. The Small Business Administration tells us that about four million businesses employ fewer than 20 people. Dun & Bradstreet reports that in 1984 635,000 new businesses incorporated. These figures show that roughly a tenth of the U.S. work force are entrepreneurs, and researchers have found that many more are potential entrepreneurs (Easton and Conant 1985b).

Vesper (1983) notes various studies that credit small businesses of less than 50 employees with providing three out of four new jobs. Drucker (1984) tells us that between 1970 and 1980, small and new businesses provided most of the U.S. economy's 20 million new jobs. Before 1970, three-quarters of all new jobs came from big business and governments. By contrast, in the 1980s, Fortune 500 firms (the nation's largest) lost about three million jobs, while businesses under ten years old created over 750,000 jobs and hired more than a million employees. Drucker adds that less than a third of all these jobs were in high-technology areas and that entrepreneurship is booming not only in the United States, but in Europe as well. China, the world's largest nation and socialist in its form of government, is encouraging entrepreneurialism as a major policy of economic development.

Kennedy (1984) predicts that the pattern of job creation will continue to emphasize small business and entrepreneurs. He cites the enormous growth in new business formations as evidence that Americans are more willing than ever to accept risks, and notes that many companies are encouraging the entrepreneurial spirit among their employees. One result, he says, will be a fragmentation of large companies into profit centers, subsidiaries, and spinoffs. The trend is not new, however. It has its roots as far back as the 1950s (Shapiro 1983).

ENTREPRENEURS AND UNEMPLOYMENT

With entrepreneurs providing so many of the country's new jobs, it seems reasonable that encouraging entrepreneurialism could hold some promise for relieving unemployment, both by providing new employers and by helping the unemployed create their own jobs. Unemployment is a major social problem, and its reduction is a principal objective of government social services, ranging from unemployment insurance to retraining and welfare. Unfortunately, unemployment programs are not designed to stimulate self-employment. It is actually illegal for the unemployed to use their benefits to set up new businesses and to create their own jobs. In Britain and France, recent changes in the law not only allow such attempts at boot-strapping but encourage them by continuing benefits through the start-up stage of a new business. These changes have proven very successful, leading directly to the creation of some 63,000 new small businesses (Friedman 1984).

We might expect such attempts to turn the unemployed into entrepreneurs to work best where people are out of jobs because of technological changes in the industries for which they were trained. Such people are likely to have some education, experience, and motivation to retain or improve their standard of living. It may be harder to turn the never-employed into entrepreneurs. Getting the latter off welfare may hinge on turning the technologically unemployed into new employers.

Vesper (1983) has analyzed the ways in which new businesses appear and the factors that impede or facilitate the attempts of individuals to become entrepreneurs. He concludes that:

- Government should provide more venture capital for new businesses. (Generally, government sources of venture capital are available only after a business has shown clear signs of success.)
- Government should supplement present loan and loan-guarantee modes of supplying venture capital by purchasing equity in new businesses.
- Government should remove the capital gains tax on money invested in start-ups and left there for five years or more, thus increasing the incentive for private suppliers of seed capital.
- Government should deliberately favor new businesses in its purchasing policies and give established businesses incentives to patronize start-ups as suppliers, customers, and capital sources.
- Government should revise patent policies to protect patent rights more effectively and cheaply and to encourage holders of unused patents to make them available to start-ups.
- Government should expand its support of scientific and technological research and of entrepreneurial education; it should encourage entrepreneurial spin-offs from educational institutions.
- Federal agencies that deal with small business should be directed to assist entrepreneurs and their new small businesses. One agency should be named to coordinate this effort.
- Government should enhance its capability to collect and provide data on entrepreneurship to track and evaluate the results of entrepreneurial activities.

Vesper (1983) emphasizes the role of government in encouraging entrepreneurial ventures. However, there are difficulties with his suggestions. Venture capital seems to work better when it comes from the private sector, where the decision-makers are more directly and powerfully motivated than bureaucrats. Purchasing set-asides and favoritism for start-ups run head-on into problems of quality, service, and warranties. Getting more patents into private use would require changing fundamental policy, since businesses are reluctant to pay even small fees for nonexclusive licenses that permit competitors to copy their successes easily. And finally, government already pays for 90 percent of basic research in this country; business funds the bulk of applied research and product development, areas which, except in defense-related projects, government is less likely to see as appropriate fields for its efforts.

Nevertheless, these areas seem to deserve attention. Perhaps we can avoid some of Vesper's difficulties if we condense his suggestions into three main categories and suggest other steps government might take. The goal in either case is the same: to reduce the role—and the expense—of government. Our three categories are:

Money. Start-up capital from government is needed in many cases, but the greater potential may lie in removing the restrictions on money now paid to the unemployed, and perhaps in encouraging private venture capital, as by improving the tax treatment for losses.

Education. The Small Business Administration supplies pamphlets, books, consultants, and seminars for would-be entrepreneurs and small business owners. Government should also provide courses and pamphlets on how to create one's own job to the newly unemployed.

Opportunity. Government should list the unused patents it holds and make the list available to the unemployed, who may be less concerned with exclusive licenses, as a source of business ideas. It could also identify and list social needs such as those discussed in this book as further sources of ideas. For example, someone could create a business out of supplying to the unemployed information on how to become an entrepreneur.

The last of these items may hold the most potential, for when given a compelling idea, many people will find for themselves the knowledge and money they need to implement it. In creating jobs for themselves and others, they will twice help to reduce unemployment, will reduce the need for government expenditures in this area, and will reduce the country's overall tax burden. Judging from the contributions entrepreneurs have already made to the health of the nation's economy, they and others to come can be encouraged to solve many of our pressing problems, increase innovation and productivity, and improve the U.S. international competitive position (Vesper 1983).

THE ENTREPRENEURIAL POTENTIAL

Encouraging entrepreneurs not only promises to help reduce the problem of unemployment. Numerous social services now provided by government might be provided as efficiently (and perhaps more efficiently) by private enterprise. One example of a service being rapidly invaded by private enterprise is the delivery of letters and packages around the country. This service has traditionally been a monopoly of the government-run postal service, protected by law and by zealous prosecution of anyone who dared an incursion onto postal turf. First-class mail is still monopolized by the postal service, but over the years private companies such as United Parcel Service, Federal Express, and other national and local courier services have taken over the delivery of many packages and high-value and express items. Local delivery services are also handling a great deal of "junk mail." Their service is faster and their cost is less, largely because they are free to pay local wage scales. They also need not support too generous fringe and retirement plans (government generosity may be most visible in the reports of retired government employees with two or more pensions).

It has already proven tempting to many entrepreneurs to think of moving into other areas dominated or monopolized by government. Private police forces, serving as security guards, watchmen, and the like have long been common. So have private fire departments, either within the bounds of single large companies or as fee-for-service town organizations. Press reports have lately emphasized the efforts of some entrepreneurs to set up for-profit prisons, run under contract to state governments and finding their profit in improved management (Johnston 1985).

It is easy to imagine that before long someone will propose to run a city police force privately, finding its revenues in contract fees and perhaps increasing its employees' motivation by paying bonuses for decreases in crime rates or increases in criminal-capture or conviction rates. It is also easy to imagine a privately run court system that would gain its earnings from fines or from sentencing offenders to what would amount to indentured servitude. From there, it is but a small step to an integrated private police, court, and prison system, a transformation of small, entrepreneurial operations into big business. The potential for abuses would be enormous (as it is in publicly run services), and so in a system of privatized public services the chief business of government would have to be careful monitoring of contract performance through supervision and regulation.

Before World War II, public transportation was largely a matter for private enterprise. The public sector took over only toward the late 1950s, when buses, trains, and the like became less profitable as more people bought their own cars. One major result was the decline of the railroads, culminating in the public takeover known as Amtrak. Since then, public transportation has become more expensive because of higher public-sector salaries and excess bureaucracy, and it has become much more difficult for public agencies to satisfy the needs of the public for transportation.

But the private sector is once more stepping into this field (Armstrong 1985). It now operates some five percent of all urban mass transit in the United States, where in the late 1970s the figure was only 1 percent. In Maine, it supplies virtually all public transportation, with much of it run on a "demand-response" basis. In Orlando, Florida, private interests are funding a $375 million link between Disney World and a local business district. In New York City, private "subscription buses" carry 50,000 commuters a day. In Chicago, private buses have arisen to beat the high fares of the local transit authority. And the Urban Mass Transportation Administration is insisting that public agencies receiving federal funds for mass transit invite private bids for contracts. Supporters of such privatization efforts project increases in efficiency and cost savings of 10–50 percent.

Critics worry that private mass transportation will leave unprofitable, low-use areas without any service at all, or that inevitable business failures will leave the public in the lurch. But the trend is clear. More and more mass transit will become part of the realm of entrepreneurs who see opportunities in the high fares and inefficiencies of publicly run systems. They will find profit in more efficient management and in the use of smaller vehicles, "demand-response" systems, and flexible routes and schedules. And those who fail will be replaced promptly enough by new opportunists.

Health care is another service area into which private enterprise is already moving, often stimulated by business awareness of the high costs of health insurance (most of whose premiums are paid by employers). Health maintenance organizations (HMOs) have appeared in many areas, stressing preventative and out-patient health care in order to minimize costs to the HMO and, perhaps incidentally, to the patient. Private ambulance and emergency services are common, for-profit hospitals are proliferating, and many companies are offering home care for patients who need traction, oxygen, dialysis, physical therapy, nursing, and other services. Dawson and Feinberg (1984) report that the cost to the patient can be half what a hospital would charge, and that the home health care market may top $18 billion annually by 1990. The health-care field also requires public supervision and regulation.

Education is still another area of entrepreneurial opportunity. Private schools thrive in many regions of the country as an alternative to public school systems. Corporate schools provide vocational education for fees. And many corporations are finding profit in setting up their own in-house campuses, either like McDonald's, to train franchise managers, or like Xerox, RCA, Holiday Inn, Wang, and Rand, to provide their employees with opportunities for advancement and themselves with more qualified employees. Some of these corporate campuses grant academic degrees and professional certification. Still other companies are helping the public schools with money, materials, and teachers drawn from their own people

(Hechinger 1985). Some pay all or part of the costs of higher education for their employees, asking in repayment only that the employees work for their employer for some agreed-upon time after completing their educational program.

The profit to private enterprise lies in the nature of the educational problem: a severe lack of competence in the pool of would-be employees. By aiding the schools or by running their own educational programs, companies help to produce people with the training to step into waiting jobs. They improve their work force, and at the same time their productivity and profitability. In the process they spend over $40 billion a year on eight million students, according to a Carnegie Foundation report (Eurich 1985).

The same motivation lies behind many partnerships between corporations and universities, such as that between United Telecommunications, Inc., and the University of Missouri in Kansas City, which in 1984 launched a major research and graduate degree program using (in part) company funds and (in part) company researchers as faculty (Mouat 1985). There is also profit to be had for the providers of needed training. Seminars, tapes, books, and lesson plans are big earners for many small businesses and individuals, and there is an entire "training and development" industry, complete with its own professional journals.

It is this industry that provides room for educational entrepreneurs. Anyone with suitable expertise can offer classes, seminars, tapes, books, and so on. Those who lack such expertise can become publishers and manufacturers, marketers, and organizers, finding their profit in bringing together experts and the companies and students who need what they can provide and in supplying the necessary teaching materials. There is even, according to Banfield (1972), a place for private versions of public libraries, which might be better able to put educational materials in the hands of those who need them most. One kind of "private library" is the computerized data base, such as DIALOG or ERIC, which provides, for a fee and to anyone equipped with a personal computer and a modem, access to vast collections of government documents and magazine, newspaper, and journal back issues; their great benefit is the ability they provide to search quickly and thoroughly for key words.

THE NEED FOR IMAGINATION

Security, health care, and education are only three of the more obvious areas where entrepreneurs can relieve government of the burden of providing social services. There are others as well, and if they seem intractable to the entrepreneurial approach, that may only mean that they require more imagination and initiative to see where entrepreneurs might provide superior service. Let us look briefly at three of these areas: research and development, welfare, and defense.

Research and Development

The fiscal year 1986 federal budget for research and development (science and technology) proposed early in 1985 was for $57.6 billion, up about ten percent from the previous fiscal year. The increase was entirely for weapons programs. Other areas actually declined by about $500 million, continuing a trend of static or declining funding that has persisted for several years (Norman 1985).

The federal government foots most of the bill for research and development, and it gives much of the money to academic researchers, funding over 95 percent of academic research. As a result, in order to compensate for a 1 percent decline in federal support of these researchers, other sources of support (notably industry) must increase their contributions by 20 percent (Kennedy 1985).

It seems unlikely that private enterprise could take over public support of research and development completely. For one thing, there is a fundamental difference between government interest primarily in basic (and defense) research and private interest in applied research and product development. If government were to abandon basic research, it would likely go begging. And that would be unfortunate, for it is basic research that provides applied researchers and product developers with the new ideas and concepts they need. Even if private enterprise could be convinced that it was in its interest to support basic research, that would not help. Many research projects in physics, astronomy, and other fields are simply too vast for the private purse. Their funding requirements run into the hundreds of millions of dollars, enough to strain the budgets of even the largest companies, and their results are too unlikely to lead promptly to marketable products. Yet many research projects are more manageable and promising, and many universities, like the University of Missouri in Kansas City mentioned above, are finding ways to gain private funds, from outright grants to intimate partnership agreements (Kennedy 1985).

Is there any hope that entrepreneurs might be able to help resolve the funding dilemma of research and development? Probably not, if we consider much of basic (nonapplied) research. But many researchers are working in areas that can lead sooner or later (often sooner) to marketable products, and it may be possible to turn more of them into entrepreneurs themselves. Already, we have seen molecular biologists, computer scientists, and others develop the rudiments of new technologies and then leave their campuses to set up high-technology companies with the aid of venture capitalists. Perhaps venture capital companies should begin to search more actively for scientists on the verge of profitable breakthroughs and fund them at earlier stages in their careers. Encouraging these money sources to help will require changes in the tax laws governing speculative investments, so that those investments will seem more attractive.

Researchers can also put their research on a paying basis by hiring themselves out as consultants to business and industry. Many do this already, although often their aim is only to supplement their incomes (Easton and Conant 1985a). But some actually use the consultant fees they earn to fund their research. More might invest in their own research if universities or government agencies were to educate them about the potential benefits of consulting and act as clearing houses for them and their prospective clients. Such steps might successfully replace a small part of the funding government now provides for research.

Welfare

Another seemingly intractable problem area may be the welfare system. We have already indicated how encouraging entrepreneurialism could reduce unemployment by increasing the numbers of employers and available jobs and by helping people to develop their own jobs. It may seem unlikely that entrepreneurs could reduce the expense of other welfare programs, such as food stamps or aid to families with dependent children, but let us consider the perennial problem of welfare cheating. Every year, newspapers carry stories of new drives to find and remove from the welfare rolls people who are taking benefits from two or more jurisdictions, who lie about their resources or employment, or who falsely claim to be disabled.

Welfare cheating is the result of two problems. First, welfare staffs lack the time to search thoroughly for the cheaters. Second, welfare benefits often exceed what a poorly educated and poorly motivated person might earn on a job. The first problem might be eased by turning the operation of the welfare system over to private enterprise, which we could expect to be more zealous than bureaucrats, since the cheaters would reduce profits. We might also ease the problem by employing welfare recipients as caseworkers, on the same premise that banks follow when they hire bank robbers as security consultants. One sociologist (R. Willis, personal communication) suggests that such a step would gain additional benefits because the welfare recipients so employed would be harder for new applicants to satisfy.

Employing welfare recipients in the welfare system would also help to ease the second problem by providing some of them with jobs. It becomes a form of "workfare," where welfare benefits are contingent upon labor for the municipality dispensing the benefits. In many areas, this labor takes the form of street cleaning and park clean-up, but there is no reason why it should not be broadened into other areas. Nor does there seem to be a reason why municipalities could not revive the old New England system of moving indigents to the "town farm," where they worked to grow and process their food and other necessities. Some drug treatment halfway houses already operate in this manner.

Modern municipalities might find it awkward or impossible to establish a farm for their poor, but they could provide housing and operate a labor pool of minimum-wage workers for businesses in need of temporary help. The money earned by the indigents would go to the municipality to finance the system and support those people who are unable to work. Additional benefits would be provided in the training and experience gained by the welfare recipients on their temporary jobs. To take this concept into the entrepreneurial realm, municipalities could contract with private companies to operate housing and the labor pools. As a private venture, earnings would have to go to the workers, but suitable amounts could be charged for rent, food, and other necessities for company profit. The problem of inescapable debt to the "company store" would require laws regulating the conditions and limits of such debts.

Defense

The U.S. Department of Defense consumes something over a quarter of a trillion dollars every year. It is the single biggest federal budget item. Is there, can there, be any hope for entrepreneurs to replace a significant part of this critical social service?

The answer is no, if we insist that entrepreneurs replace the defense function as it stands today. It would probably even be unwise to try, for a private defense department would comprise a body of mercenaries, whose loyalties have traditionally been to their pay rather than to any particular country. However, technology is producing a new kind of defense, one that could be effective as a private enterprise.

The technology we have in mind is that of the U.S. Strategic Defense Initiative (SDI), popularly known as "Star Wars." This new technology (not yet developed) depends on a strong presence in space, whence defending forces can look down on the earth to observe and respond to hostile acts. As presently conceived, SDI would comprise orbiting laser and particle-beam weapons, as well as more ordinary weaponry, missiles and high-speed chunks of rock and metal, with which to intercept and destroy launching ICBMs. Similar weaponry will before long increase our ability to destroy aircraft, tanks, and ships, thus interdicting any type of attack, in space or on the ground.

It is not our purpose to explore the question of whether such a system would be stabilizing or destabilizing in international relations, or to discuss the technical details and feasibility of the proposed system. Rather, our aim is simply to point out one of its potentials. Bova (1985) has proposed that the Star Wars technology makes possible for the first time an international peacekeeping force with the capability of stopping in its tracks any attack of one nation upon another. Such a force might well be an arm of the United Nations, but it could also be privately operated. We imagine a private company developing and installing orbital interdiction weapons and then selling guarantees against attack to any nation that wishes to pay the price. The company would probably start on a modest scale, with only a few orbiting weapons and with contracts with one or two small nations. Once begun, the company would grow quickly as its competence and trustworthiness were demonstrated, until it could assume the burden of defense even for the world's great powers. One significant benefit would surely be a reduction in both world and national defense outlays, since a single organization would be able to replace many competing ones.

CONCLUSION

There are numerous ways in which private enterprise could take over government provision of social services, using private means to satisfy public ends. Some seem fairly easy to realize. Others seem more difficult. All have in common that they require a willingness on the part of society and government to consider private alternatives. They also require active encouragement and stimulation of these alternatives by government, as well as some aid, at least in the initial stages of any transition, and continuing regulation to ensure that the private sector provides its public services in the public interest.

It would be a mistake to think that if the private sector takes over the provision of a social service, the cost of providing that service will disappear from government budgets. This will surely happen in some cases. In most cases, private enterprise will act on contract for government, and we can expect that at best the cost to government will decrease and the services will be more efficiently delivered in a properly competitive market. This should be enough to make the transition to private social service delivery worth serious consideration.

REFERENCES

Armstrong, S. 1985. "Cities use Private Firms to Fill Transit Gaps," *Christian Science Monitor*, July 30, pp. 3–4.

Banfield, E. C. 1972. "Some Alternatives for the Public Library." In *The Metropolitan Library*, edited by R. W. Conant and K. Molz (Cambridge, MA: MIT Press), pp. 89–100.

Bova, B. 1985. *Assured Survival: Putting the Star Wars Defense in Perspective* (Boston, MA: Houghton Mifflin).

Dawson, K. and A. Feinberg. 1984. "Hospitals in the Home." *Venture* 6 (August).

Drucker, P. 1984. "Our Entrepreneurial Economy." *Harvard Business Review* 62 (January–February): 59–64.

Easton, T. A. and R. W. Conant. 1985a. *Cutting Loose: From Employee to Entrepreneur* (Chicago, IL: Probus).

Easton, T. A. and R. W. Conant. 1985b. *Using Consultants: A Consumer's Guide for Managers* (Chicago, IL: Probus).

Eurich, N. 1985. *Corporate Classrooms: The Learning Business* (Washington, D.C.: Carnegie Foundation for the Advancement of Teaching).

Friedman, R. 1984. "63,000 Entrepreneurs," *Inc.* 6 (May): 14–16.

Gilder, G. 1984. "Fear of Capitalism," *Inc.* 6 (September): 87–94.

Hechinger, F. M. 1985. "Turnaround for the Public Schools?" *Harvard Business Review* 63 (January–February): 136–44.

Johnston, D. A. 1985. "Prisons for Profit Seen as Growth Industry." *Los Angeles Times*, in *Maine Sunday Telegram*, April 14, p. 4C.

Kennedy, A. 1984. Interview. *Inc.* 6 (April): 108–17.

Kennedy, D. 1985. "Government Policies and the Cost of Doing Research." *Science* 227: 480–84.

Kirzner, I. M. 1979. *Perception, Opportunity, and Profit: Studies in the Theory of Entrepreneurship* (Chicago, IL: University of Chicago Press).

_____ . 1983. "Entrepreneurship and the Future of Capitalism," In *Entrepreneurship and the Outlook for America*, edited by J. Backman (New York: The Free Press), pp. 149–72.

Mouat, L. 1985. "University Chancellor Promotes Ties between Academia and City," *Christian Science Monitor*, January 4, p. 5.

Norman, C. 1985. "The Science Budget: A Touch of Austerity," *Science* 227: 726–28.

Shapiro, M. 1983. "The Entrepreneurial Individual in the Large Organization." In *Entrepreneurship and the Outlook for America*, edited by J. Backman (New York: The Free Press), pp. 55–80.

Simon, J. 1981. *The Ultimate Resource* (Princeton, NJ: Princeton University Press).

Vesper, K. H. 1983. *Entrepreneurship and National Policy* (Chicago, IL: Heller Institute for Small Business).

5

Privatizing the Acute Care General Hospital

Harold W. Demone, Jr. and Margaret Gibelman

Privatization has become a popular term for a major phenomenon in American society: the transfer of functions, and sometimes ownership, of a vast array of governmental activities. The thrust of current federal health and welfare policies reflects the dominant goal of the Reagan administration to diminish the role of government in virtually all areas other than national defense and to transfer government activities to the private sector. Two secondary reasons are also offered. One suggests that government service provision has been inadequate, the other that the private sector is capable of resolving the problems of escalating costs and inefficiencies that pervade the health, welfare, and other systems.

In this chapter we explore the privatization phenomenon in relation to the health industry, particularly acute care general hospitals. The changes taking place in our health-care system suggest that privatization may, in fact, represent more than the transfer of functions from government to private providers. Transfer of functions is also occurring from the voluntary sector to private, for-profit enterprises, representing an application of corporate models to health and human services.

Many approve the decreasing role of government in the ownership and management of hospitals and other health-care systems, believing that privatization will lead to cost containment, greater efficiency, and higher quality services. Others lament the effects of profit-making competition among private providers of health care, predicting that treatment of the indigent will be sacrificed and that even those covered by government insurance, such as Medicare and Medicaid, will be considered and treated as less desirable patients. What is clear is that the privatization of our health-care system is as yet so new that empirical data on its positive and negative impacts is still sparse. It is also clear that a number of policy issues, including those of equity and adequacy, arise with the privatization of hospitals, and that these issues warrant close investigation.

THE CASE FOR PRIVATIZATION

The health industry is generally freer to test organizational alternatives than other social welfare institutions. That nearly 85 percent of Americans are covered by some form of third-party health insurance provides a different set of environmental influences. The proportion of Americans with third-party coverage for their dentist or lawyer is still quite small. The proportion covered for day care and almost any other social service is essentially nonexistent, except when these other services fall under a rare "health" umbrella.

The development of the investor-owned general hospital provides an excellent case example of the testing of alternative organizational auspices and approaches. The relative success or failure of this new economic and organizational entity will probably have substantial influence within the health and human services arena, far beyond its own boundaries.

A neoconservative case for privatization in health care has been identified to include the following factors (Starr 1982):

- The welfare state is overloaded.
- Western democracies are ungovernable.
- The enlarged governmental role in resource allocation and income distribution has stimulated unrealistic expectations.
- By eliminating some of its functions, government can secure time and respite from the conflict inevitably stimulated by demands for unlimited entitlements.
- Government is inherently incompetent to perform certain responsibilities.
- The demands for efficiency in government are in essential conflict with political objectives; for example, government cannot close down unneeded hospitals.
- Public policy antennae are not sufficiently sensitive to the constant shifts in individual preferences and local conditions.
- A "new class" is created by government, financed by taxes, which becomes burdensome to the private sector and thus dampens private investment and innovations.

These arguments for privatization of the health-care system have prompted private investors to consider hospitals as potential, available sources of profit. Since the 1960s, investor-owned hospitals and hospital chains have become common. Most chains are for-profit, but some are not-for-profit. The privatization of the health-care industry now extends to general, psychiatric, substance abuse, and chronic disease hospitals; surgi-centers; rehabilitation centers; home health agencies; group homes for the retarded and mentally ill; nursing homes; and a variety of new, experimental, short-term emergency, and other kinds of medical care facilities.

Starr (1982: 417) summarizes the developments in the organization and structure of the health-care system as follows:

The redistributive and regulatory reforms of the 1960s and 1970s greatly expanded the boundaries of the political in health care. Once the government assumed a large share of the financial burden for medical services, conservatives cooperated on grounds of fiscal precedence in the expansion of political authority. Initially, the resistance came mainly from physicians, who feared government would restrict their economy and income. The opposition, while influential, was no longer sufficient to hold back state intervention. But by the late 1970s, the opposition assumed the more formidable proportions in American politics. A newly revised conservatism sought to throw back the boundaries of the political, to return tax money and government functions to the private sector—in short, to reprivatize much of the public household.

THE SHIFT IN HOSPITAL AUSPICES

The current shift in hospital ownership has precedents. Following the Reformation and the hospital management corruption of the fourteenth and fifteenth centuries, the principle was established that medical care of the poor was a community, not a religious, responsibility. In Protestant countries, the quality of health care declined seriously. To the civil authorities, the patients were a formidable burden. To the new staff, the motivation was pecuniary. Thus the church commitment to serving the poor and infirm was found to be difficult to replace by civil authorities.

Then a change occurred. A unique feature of the developing general hospital in the United States compared to those of other countries was that the great majority, in the major growth period of the early twentieth century, were voluntary, not-for-profit institutions. Elsewhere, most hospitals were constructed and operated by the government (Anderson and Gravitz 1983). The growth of hospitals in the United States, a function of several technological, social, and demographic influences, was extraordinary. During the 36 years between 1873 and 1909, the number of hospitals grew from 178 to 4,359, and the number of beds from 35,608 to 421,068, a growth of seven times the increase in the population.

By the end of the nineteenth century, the privatization of the American general hospital was well established. Through much of the twentieth century, voluntary and philanthropic contributions to general hospitals grew continuously and generously. The pattern was fully established: the general hospital was a voluntary, not-for-profit institution. As recently as 1970, the majority of hospital conversions were from proprietary to not-for-profit status (Steinwald and Neuhauser 1970).

Bays (1979) suggests that hospitals are differentiated from other economic organizations in several key respects. First, they are dominated by not-for-profit institutions (only 10 percent in 1979 were organized for profit, and they accounted for only 5 percent of the beds). Second, third-party insurance covering nearly 85 percent of the population affects the behavior of both users and providers. Last, although physicians are principally responsible for allocation of hospital personnel and capital, they are only indirectly responsible for the associated costs.

Initially, for-profit (investor-owned) hospitals were called "proprietary" and were owned by the physicians who practiced in them (Bays 1979). In 1928 these proprietary hospitals constituted about 36 percent of hospitals of all types. By 1968 the proportion had fallen to 11 percent. But by 1980 a clear reversal had occurred, in large part reflecting the dominance of the privatization theme in this society. The number of proprietary hospitals had, by 1980, grown to about 1,000 from 769 in 1968, with about half owned by large corporations (Relman 1986). These corporations purchased many of the physician-owned and some not-for-profit hospitals and established new ones. According to the National Consumers League, there are now 1,200 for-profit hospitals in the United States, about one out of every five facilities, a 40 percent increase since 1977 (Engel 1985).

PROFILING THE INVESTOR-OWNED HOSPITAL

The two largest owners of acute-care hospitals in the United States are Humana and the Hospital Corporation of America (HCA). Humana, founded in 1961, was the second largest investor-owned hospital chain through 1983. Its principal growth has been horizontal, achieved by acquiring or building acute-care hospitals (although in 1983 it began some experiments in the delivery of non-hospital-based services). Humana's primary emphasis has been in the South, with approximately 65 percent of its beds there, and in states with nominal regulation of health care.

Humana has shown considerable continuity in leadership; the same two key executives have managed the corporation since 1961. It is well known as a highly centralized corporate-type organization that makes strong use of contemporary management technologies. Each unit is a cost center, and standardization of operations is the norm.

The organization has been extraordinarily successful. In 1968, its stock was $8.00 a share; in 1982, the stock, adjusted for two splits in the same year, sold for $5.74 per share. Its monthly reports focus on such key indicators as: pretax margin, accounts receivable by days outstanding, occupancy rate, and paid hours per patient day. There is an elaborate incentive compensation system for hospital administrators, based on pretax profit, days of accounts receivable outstanding, bad debts, and growth in census. The focus is on the private paying patient who has insurance and is able to pay any differential or who has no insurance but can pay the full tab.

Both Humana and HCA operate at lower occupancy rates than most community hospitals. They both have higher gross revenue per patient day, and Humana has a shorter length of stay per patient day (Siegrist and Herzlinger 1981, 1983a).

HCA, founded in 1968, is now the largest profit-making hospital chain in this country. Like Humana, HCA demonstrates considerable continuity. Of course, this continuity is important as a variable only if the organization is successful (Siegrist and Herzlinger 1983b). By 1980 HCA was managing or operating 188 hospitals. By 1985 it was operating more than 415 health-care facilities in the United States and abroad, representing a 20 percent annual growth rate (Wayne 1985). The growth has been both by acquisition and by hospital construction. Over 60 percent of its stock in 1980 was owned by institutional investors. As with Humana, the HCA payer mix includes more privately insured, charge-based patients than the average for U.S. hospitals. A higher proportion of the profits (66 percent) comes from immediately related ancillary services (room, board, and nursing) than from routine medical care.

HCA also manages hospitals for government, religious, and other groups. In these instances, the profit margin is lower, but HCA does gain an inside position for later acquisition. (This "advantage" is less certain now, given the tenuous profitability of general hospitals.) Like Humana, it too has most of its facilities (84 percent) in the South, with only a few hospitals in the more regulated Northeast. About 40 percent of HCA hospitals are the dominant hospitals in their areas. Unlike Humana, HCA is highly decentralized. The hospital administrator is boss (Siegrist and Herzlinger 1983b).

SIZE OF THE INVESTOR-OWNED SYSTEM

It is possible to calculate the size of an investor-owned system in terms of the number of hospitals, hospital beds, or dollars. Urban, suburban, or rural locations add another dimension. In the business pages, quarterly earnings by share may be the important statistic.

The forecast on growth depends on one's perspective. The total number of investor-owned hospitals in the United States declined slightly from 1,051 to 1,019 between 1976 and 1981. Yet a revealing shift occurred inside the system. The number of hospitals in multi-institutional complexes (both profit and not-for-profit) went from 396 to 586 during the same period, up 48 percent. The old proprietary hospitals suffered most of the loss (Pattison and Katz 1983).

Relman (1983b) describes the new kind of health-care industry as virtually beginning from scratch in the 1960s. By 1983 investor-owned chains accounted for 15–20 percent of the personal health-care delivery system.

The gross income at that time probably exceeded $40 billion per year. The investor-owned hospital industry in 1983 comprised four chains owning almost two-thirds of the for-profit hospital market (over 1,000 general hospitals). In addition to Humana and HCA, the list of the largest chains includes American Medical International and National Medical Enterprises. According to *Time* magazine profit-making companies owned or managed more than 20 percent of all U.S. hospitals in 1984, more than doubling the 1979 figure (Castro 1984).

Several types of measurements can be used to determine the growth of investor-owned hospitals. In 1984 Humana facilities housed 17,000 beds, representing 2 percent of the national total. This translated to 89 acute-care hospitals in 22 states and four countries (Barron 1984). From 1980 to 1985, according to a Standard & Poor survey, more than 400 hospitals joined larger chains, the latter now accounting for more than 30 percent of total hospitals (Purdum 1985).

Time describes the U.S. health-care industry as generating nearly $1 billion per day in expenditures (Castro 1984). HCA reported 1984 revenues of $4.1 billion and earnings of $297 million. Had HCA's proposed merger with the American Hospital Supply Corporation, the nation's largest distributor of hospital supplies, been successfully negotiated, the combined market value would have been $6.6 billion. This merger would thus have constituted one of the largest ever outside the oil industry (Purdum 1985). On the day following the HCA–HSC merger announcement (which was later thwarted), HCA's stock was the most heavily traded on the New York Stock Exchange.

THE ISSUES

For-Profit Versus Not-for-Profit Health Care

There are both critics and supporters of investor-owned chains. Speaking at the 1981 Annual Meeting of the American Association of Medical Colleges, Donald MacNaughton, former chairman of the board and chief executive officer of the Prudential Life Insurance Co. and then chairman and CEO of HCA, strongly defended these chains. He noted their relative youth as the context in which to examine their real accomplishments. Compared to other community hospitals in Texas, Florida, and Utah, HCA hospitals have lower costs per admission and they have not been found to "cream" patients. Their commitment to medical, nursing, and allied health education was also noted.

The three-state comparison (Texas, Florida, and Utah) examines HCA only in relation to other community hospitals (presumably including other for-profits). In this comparative analysis, HCA revenue per admission is lower (6 percent in Florida and 5 percent in Texas). Operating expenses per admission in Florida were 21 percent lower for HCA.

The change of "creaming" of the more "desirable" patients was refuted with three points. Where HCA operates the only acute-care facility in the community, all patients requiring hospital service are treated. Citing the Lewin (1981) study, MacNaughton noted that investor-owned hospitals as a group had the same percentage of Medicaid patient days as the not-for-profit group. Last, in 1980, HCA provided approximately $845 million worth of uncollectable services and charity. It paid $72 million in taxes.

The progressive nature of investor-owned chains was also equated with their attitude toward professional education. It was found that 26 of HCA's hospitals had formal affiliations with medical schools, and about 75 HCA hospitals were affiliated with nursing schools. Similar arrangements were found to exist in relation to other allied health programs (MacNaughton 1981). For its employees, HCA finances continuing education and scholarships and encourages involvement in professional associations. A Center for Health Studies has been established to provide educational programs for the managers of HCA facilities. HCA also contributes directly to medical education and directs 1 percent of its earnings to charitable causes, many for educational purposes. Finally, HCA manages two teaching hospitals for Tulane and the University of Miami.

This positive view of the investor-owned chains, perhaps the epitome of for-profit involvement in the health-care industry, is not shared by all commentators. Arnold Relman, editor of the *New England Journal of Medicine*, wrote a special article in 1980 in which he coined the term "medical-industrial complex," with special acknowledgement to President Eisenhower's 1961 farewell address, which warned the public of the "military-industrial complex." Relman limits his "complex" to those for-profit corporations "supplying health care services to patients for a profit" (1980: 963). His analysis thus excludes, for example, the pharmaceutical industry.

Collectively, this "new medical-industrial complex" grossed about $35–40 billion in 1979, representing about 25 percent of the total expended on personal health care (Relman 1980). Relman dismisses the marketplace as an effective or useful mechanism for delivering patient care. Health care is a public good, a right of all people rather than a privilege. Tax-supported medical care through Medicare and Medicaid has grown steadily, and despite congressional and administration concerns about spiralling government costs, the growth pattern is likely to continue. About 40 percent of the direct costs of personal health care is now funneled through federal programs. And, for the majority of Americans, health coverage is provided by employers who gain tax deductions.

The corporate model has also been criticized from the perspective that people in need of health care are not actually consumers in the classic sense, and therefore the competitive model is really not applicable. Shopping for health-care bargains is not particularly popular and price is secondary to quality. Even assuming that consumers are able to make discriminating choices about the "best" hospital care, it is actually the physician who serves as middleman and makes the majority of decisions.

Another concern that has been voiced about for-profit hospitals is their reported tendency to focus on technology and procedures rather than personal services. "The result is likely to exacerbate present problems with excessive fragmentation of care, over-specialization and over-emphasis on expensive technology" (Relman 1980: 969).

An excellent example of the for-profit hospitals' concern with technology can be seen in the recruitment of Dr. William C. DeVries from the University of Utah for the Humana Heart Institute in Louisville. At the time of his recruitment, DeVries was the only American surgeon authorized to perform artificial heart implants. In explaining the move, DeVries cited his frustrations with Utah's Institutional Review Board. He apparently assumed that the ethical review process would be less cumbersome at Humana and that the scope of his work would thus be able to expand (Altman 1984). Humana also promised to fund 100 heart implants, assuming it would benefit from the scientific progress, if not the publicity. At the University of Utah, the limitations on DeVries's work were based on cost considerations, in part reflecting its public auspices and the review board's mandates and sources of accountability. At Humana, the private composition of the board made it less susceptible to public pressures and therefore freer to take bold actions.

There are several alternative views of this development by the investor-owned chain. One medical writer states that Humana was taking a major risk, but humanity would be the winner if the research were successful (Schwartz 1984). Caplan (1984), a medical ethicist, saw the red tape that frustrated DeVries as appropriate behavior by the Institutional Review Board. Matters of consent and risk should be taken seriously. At Humana, Professor Caplan worried, the FDA-required committee might not be able to remain independent because the institution had a heavy financial interest in the success of the artificial heart.

Altman (1984), a physician, notes the potential conflict of interest in patient care when a physician is working for, and has a financial interest in, a technology such as the artificial heart. He worries about the debate over the complexity of the approach, noting that considerable caution might have been most appropriate in this new medical experiment. In a follow-up story, Altman continued to examine the conflict of interest situation and to question whether an institution that will gain financially from the success of an experimental procedure should sponsor the procedure's evaluation.

An important point that runs through the arguments and questions regarding for-profit hospitals, including their experiments and innovative programs, is the extent to which government funds have permitted, and laid the groundwork for, the success of these institutions. It is, after all, the influx of federal research support into the health field following World War II that allowed for the accelerated study and development of new medical procedures, equipment, and even the artificial heart. Thus, it is public auspices and funding on which the for-profit hospital chain's spirit of innovation and commitment to experimentation are based.

The hospital chains are likely to benefit substantially from the publicity about their successful experimental procedures. *Time*, for example, sees Humana's interest in the heart implantations as proof that health is a sound financial investment. It quotes Humana's guidelines of consistency, quality, high volume, and affordable care as being comparable to the McDonalds's hamburger company's retail philosophy. Three months after DeVries moved to Humana, a Humana spokesperson was quoted as saying that "the rising tide lifts all boats. As the process receives attention and that tide rises, Humana rises with it" ("Hospital executives" 1984). A spokesperson for competitor American Medical International (a California-based hospital chain) sees the matter similarly: "Humana has certainly taken a high-visibility step. Humana was one of the first companies to brand-name their hospitals. The most effective way to promote that is a grandstand play" (Schrage 1984: D16).

Hospitals, in the view of many, are intended to serve a public purpose and prevent or cure illness among all citizens. The growth of a huge health-care industry with considerable influence on national health-care policy (like that of the defense industry on Congress) may make possible abuse and/or distortion of social purposes (Relman 1980). Indeed, if hospitals are intended to serve both patients and society, clarification of priorities is in order. In this "social good" perspective of the health-care industry, for-profit enterprises may be inappropriate. A consistently strong point of view is that physicians should not derive financial gain from the health-care market, except for their professional services (Relman 1980).

Excluding the Poor?

Critics of investor-owned hospital chains claim that seriously ill patients considered to be poor financial risks are "dumped" into public hospitals. A January 25, 1985, *New York Times* headline proclaimed: "As Companies Buy Hospitals, Treatment of Poor Is Debated" (Tolchin 1985: 1). Quoting Relman, the *Times* reported that "health care is being converted from a social service to an economic commodity, sold in the marketplace and distributed on the basis of who can afford to pay for it (Tolchin 1985: A1).

Numerous examples of the transfer of indigent patients from investor-owned hospitals to public hospitals have been cited in the press. In Chicago, it is reported that more than 500 patients have been transferred to Cook County Hospital each month from local private hospitals. A physician at a public hospital, observing this "patient dumping," commented: "every day, hospitals send us patients who are at risk of dying in the ambulance on the way over. It seems that physicians at the private hospitals are under such pressure from administrators to get rid of nonpaying patients that they sometimes misrepresent or hide important patient data" (Bernard 1985).

A study reported in the *New England Journal of Medicine* of 467 patients sent from emergency rooms of private Chicago-area hospitals to Cook County Hospital found that 24 percent, when transferred, were considered to be medically unstable and that most were transferred without their written, informed consent. Further, the death rate for these transferred patients was found to be significantly higher than for patients already in the hospital, with the delay in treatment cited as a probable cause for the difference. Of the patients studied in Cook County, 87 percent had been transferred there because they lacked insurance to cover the cost of private hospitalization. Eighty-nine percent of these patients were black or Hispanic, and 81 percent were unemployed, suggesting discrimination not only against the poor, but also against minorities (Okie 1986).

Similar patterns have been found in other areas, and in response to alleged and verified discrimination against the medically indigent, 22 states have, to date, enacted legislation to prohibit hospitals from denying care to emergency patients. But sometimes these laws do not go far enough. In Illinois, for example, the law does not appear to deter transfers from private to public hospitals after emergency care has been provided (Okie 1986). North Carolina and Georgia have enacted legislation to set minimum levels of care for the indigent that hospitals must provide. Some other states are considering a freeze on takeovers of public hospitals by investor-owned chains (Tolchin 1985).

Patient dumping is not, however, due solely to the profit-seeking motivations of the investor-owned hospital chains. The situation is compounded by government-established income eligibility levels for Medicaid and by changes in Medicare regulations that place increasingly higher deductibles within the responsibility of the patient. Medicaid does not cover all of the poor in need of medical care. Experts estimate that at any given time there are 38 million poor Americans not covered by Medicaid. Over the period of a year, it may exceed 50 million. In regard to the care of elderly patients, the federal government now pays flat fees on the basis of the average costs of specific illnesses rather than paying actual costs. This "diagnostic related group" (DRG) reimbursement policy places fiscal responsibility on the hospital if the patient is not discharged in accordance with the predetermined schedule. Some hospitals therefore may be reluctant to accept elderly, poor patients who may require longer periods of hospitalization than allowed under the DRGs, but who cannot afford to pay the difference themselves (Tolchin 1985).

Although some investor-owned hospitals do provide excellent care for the elderly and poor, the general perception is that, due to the business orientation of these enterprises, the poor are certainly the least favored clientele. Charles Davis, administrator of an HCA hospital in Dublin, Georgia, was asked while testifying before the Georgia Health Planning Review Board in 1981: "Why don't you put up a sign saying, 'this hospital will provide free care to people who are unable to pay'?" Mr. Davis replied: "I'll answer that question with a question: Why don't department stores put up signs inviting shoplifters to shoplift more?" (quoted in Tolchin 1985). It is clear that more empirical data will be needed to substantiate whether, and to what extent, investor-owned chains actually do discriminate against the poor and minorities and, concomitantly, the degree to which legislation protecting the rights of the poor and guaranteeing access to health care diminishes or obviates discriminatory practices. So, too, hard research data is needed to determine whether investor-owned chains have the potential to, or in fact do, benefit all members of a community by improving hospital facilities, using the most up-to-date technology, and so on.

Profit-Making in Health Care

The informed public and health-care community are by no means neutral on the subject of profit-making within the health-care system. There are both opponents and proponents of this phenomenon. Michael D. Bromberg, executive director of the Federation of American Hospitals, a for-profit group, says that all hospitals, independent of auspice, have to earn a profit over surplus to survive. Far from being antithetical to quality care, he claims, profit is a prerequisite (quoted in Gibbons 1984). Although the logic of this latter remark is tenuous, it is self-evident that balancing the books is an important consideration for both for-profit and not-for-profit hospitals.

James Roberts, executive director of the National Association of Free Standing Emergency Centers, is positive about competition in health care. He sees it as a stimulus for innovation in pricing and consumer choices and a general opportunity to initiate change. "Competition means the opportunity for profit and profiteering. Each of us must determine the differences between profit and profiteering" (quoted in Gibbons 1984:35).

A 23-member committee of the Institute of Medicine and the National Academy of Science was assigned the responsibility of examining the implications of for-profit health-care organizations in late 1983. The arguments they encountered were similar to those posed in relation to the use of public funds to purchase nonpublic human services, but included in addition concerns about values. The president of the Health and Medicine Policy Research Group of Chicago, Dr. Quentin D. Young, noted that the appropriate goal for for-profit managers is to maximize profit. He saw this as both legitimate and ethical in the appropriate setting, but not in the health-care industry, where the appropriate goal is "to enhance the health status of the American people. It seems . . . that these two objectives are only occasionally congruent and in many critical instances contradictory" (quoted in Gibbons 1984: 35).

Cecil G. Sheps, speaking for the American Public Health Association (APHA), was similarly concerned. He described an APHA resolution deploring "the record great growth in the size and scope of for-profit health care institutions and programs because of our belief that the overriding need of private investment in health services is to maximize profit, an operating principle we consider inappropriate to decision making in delivering health care" (quoted in Gibbons 1984: 35).

Judith G. Waxman, representing the National Health Law Program, also voiced concerns about values. She was "concerned that access to care is going to be a severe problem in for-profit hospitals" (quoted in Gibbons 1984: 39). She noted that some for-profit hospitals believe that since they pay taxes they bear no responsibility to provide emergency care for those unable to pay.

Relman sees a significant potential problem in profit-making in medicine, with the control over these problems in the hands of the physician. He urges that physicians be responsible, a role he acknowledges was easier to play when they were in relatively short supply. Under conditions of short supply, there was no economic motive to provide unnecessary services, given the high service demand. "How can the public be expected to have confidence in the profession, and how can the profession retain its own image of dedication to the public interest when physicians become entrepreneurs in this way?" (Relman 1983a: 16).

Some have voiced concern that the profit-seeking motive of investor-owned chains will lead to the exploitation of public funds. The Medicare reimbursement system was under attack by the General Accounting Office (GAO), the investigative arm of Congress. This agency wanted to find out whether Medicare subsidized the $600 million purchase of one hospital chain by another in 1981. The concern was that the reimbursement mechanism was manipulated (Clurman 1983). According to Richard P. Kusserow, inspector general of the Department of Health and Human Services, that department is illegally paying profits to home health-care agencies and other Medicare providers (Pear 1985). Concern has been expressed that even the "legal" profits paid to private hospitals seem excessive compared to profits in other industries (Kinkead 1980).

In general, Medicare reimburses hospitals for "reasonable costs" of patient care, with one exception. Profit-making hospitals are guaranteed a "return on equity capital," that is, profits (of 19–20 percent per year in 1981 and 1982). Not-for-profit institutions do not receive such benefits. The rate of return paid by HHS has always been the maximum on equity allowed by law. This is 1.5 times the average rate of interest paid by the Treasury when it borrows money from the Medicare Trust Fund. This reimbursement policy dates back to 1965 when Medicare was first established, and it is obviously one of the major reasons why profit-making hospitals and the nursing home industry have done so well.

Matters of capital are not insignificant. In 1984, for the 90 New Jersey hospitals, capital cost payments on loans outstanding amounted to 11.4 percent of their operating budget. By 1990, it is estimated, these costs will be 23.3 percent (Medicare wants a 7 percent cap) (Friedland 1985).

Questions also arise simply on the basis of the expanding size of the for-profit chains. For example, American Medical International, Inc. (AMI) tested the murky antitrust waters in 1979 when it purchased its fourth of five general hospitals in the San Luis Obispo, California, area. The Federal Trade Commission's (FTC) administrative law judge ruled the remaining county-owned general hospital "not a formidable competitor" and stated that AMI seemed in deliberate pursuit of a monopoly position (Wallace 1983: 28). It was thus ordered to sell one of the four hospitals and to secure FTC approval for any acquisition that would give the chain more than 20 percent of the licensed acute care hospital beds in either a standard metropolitan statistical area or a county, or within 30 miles of another AMI hospital.

The FTC similarly challenged the Hospital Corporation of America (HCA) in Tennessee in November 1983, charging that HCA illegally controlled costs in the greater Chattanooga area by managing or owning 22 of the 29 area hospitals. FTC spokesperson Arthur Lerner commented that "in the long run, the effect of this kind of acquisition has the potential to lessen competition significantly, to tend toward a monopoly, to raise costs for consumers, and to not give consumers as much for their money in terms of quality" (Clurman 1983: 3B). HCA responded that it offers quality provisions at competitive prices.

A common theme of commentators on for-profit hospitals is that of the potential risk to the public interest. The 1984 closing of the only physical rehabilitation unit in Austin, Texas, stimulated opposition to HCA's plans to convert the 34-bed unit to other uses. Having received approval from the

Texas Health Facilities Commission, HCA proceeded without further public discussion to shut down the unit. The major question was whether a for-profit chain could be both a good corporate community citizen and loyal provider to its stockholders (Simler 1984).

Marketing Health Services

The entrepreneurial nature of for-profit hospitals shows not only in the concern for profits (apparently even at the risk of violating the public good) but also in the use of marketing strategies to promote hospital selection and use. One consequence of the entry of investor-owned chains into competitive marketing is the concurrent effort on the part of not-for-profits to compete via the same strategies. John Milton, vice-president for marketing at North Memorial Medical Center, Robbinsdale, Minnesota, claims that "the survivors in the health-care business are going to have to make more of an effort to communicate to people what they have to offer" (Malan 1985).

Humana markets itself in several ways, one of which is to include within its referral network physicians who deal with younger rather than older patients, acute rather than chronic illnesses, wealthy rather than poor patients. To persuade the "right" patients to use their facilities, Humana looks to the "right" doctors. It erects office buildings next to its hospitals and offers space at a discount, sometimes as much as a year's free rent. It helps doctors secure office furniture and even associates and partners. It guarantees them an adequate first-year income, with Humana making up any difference (Kinkead 1980).

By "matching" the more attractive doctors with the more attractive patients and communicating this image to the public, Humana no doubt hopes to increase hospital occupancy rates. In exchange for the perks it offers, Humana keeps close tabs on its physicians, monitoring admissions to its hospitals and the revenue these admissions produce. One co-owner of Humana commented: "if the doctors don't produce for Humana, I'm damn sure I'm not going to renegotiate their office leases. They can practice elsewhere" (Kinkead 1980). This is big business, with the entrepreneur's emphasis on productivity and profits.

In summary, there are several outstanding issues regarding the use and impact of investor-owned hospital chains and, more generally, for-profit hospital systems. These issues range from the appropriateness of profit-making within the health-care system and the heretofore unusual but growing tendency to employ marketing strategies to increase the use of services, to the consequences for the less desirable patient who, it seems, may be quickly referred to a voluntary or public hospital. Unfortunately, there is little empirical data to validate or disprove these concerns and issues.

THE BALANCE SHEET

Comparative Research Studies

Following, we briefly summarize several major studies that endeavor to compare private for-profit and private not-for-profit hospitals. In some cases, the studies include public hospitals.

One problem in comparing for-profit and not-for-profit hospital care is that of nomenclature. The for-profits are investor-owned chains and for-profit unaffiliated hospitals, or proprietary hospitals. The not-for-profits generally fall into three classes: major teaching, minor teaching, and nonteaching (usually community hospitals); they can also be differentiated by their religious or secular orientation. Both profits and nonprofits can be readily distinguished on the basis of size: small, medium, and large. It may not be necessary to distinguish or control by all identified variables, but certainly major teaching hospitals, largely not-for-profit, must be classified separately. For-profit chains must also be viewed separately because of their distinctive attributes.

Bays (1979) compared 46 short-term, nonteaching California general hospitals, using diagnostic and treatment records for the 1971–72 period. Of the potential 92 comparisons, 64 were sufficiently complete, 30 from profits and 34 from nonprofits. Bays concluded that for-profits and nonprofits are essentially equal in operating costs, but that chain for-profits, if factored out separately, are less costly than the other two hospital types. In turn, nonchain, for-profit, physician-managed hospitals were the least efficient. Steinwald and Neuhauser (1970), in an earlier study, reached similar conclusions. They hypothesized that the reason for the lower efficiency of the physician-run hospitals is that doctors are dividing their time between medical practice and management.

Bays (1979) urges caution in extrapolating from his data. The sample is small and not randomly selected. Also, for-profits (compared to nonprofits) devote a majority of resources to the treatment of specific diseases. Creaming is thus possible. On the other hand, for-profit chain hospitals carried case loads not significantly different from those of nonprofits.

Lewin et al. (1981) found investor-owned hospitals in California, Florida, and Texas to be pricing services considerably higher in relation to operating costs, and hence more profitably, than the not-for-profit hospitals. Pricing differences between the groups were very large for several of the ancillary departments but small for routine services, including room and board.

A study by the Florida Hospital Cost Containment Board compared all proprietary and not-for-profit hospitals in the state for the years 1980 and

1981 (State of Florida 1981–1983). Consistent with the Lewin data, the board found for both years that the for-profit hospitals charged more and had higher operating costs than the nonprofits. The net profit after taxes for the for-profits was about the same as the net surplus of revenue for the nonprofits.

Pattison and Katz (1983) noted that their findings largely substantiate those of Lewin and associates. Using a different data base, they studied California hospitals and found that for all profitable ancillary services, the frequency of service-unit use or admission was higher in the investor-owned chains than in the voluntaries. For unprofitable or break-even ancillary services, there was little or no difference between the for-profits and the not-for-profits. The for-profits also had fewer emergency room visits per admission, and relatively more in-patient admissions. No difference in patient complexity could be determined.

With respect to the economies of scale argument (chains can purchase and provide more specialized functions more cheaply because they buy in bulk), Pattison and Katz found the total operating costs per patient day, including allocated home office expenses, were higher by 2 percent in the investor-owned chains. They concluded that "the data do not support the claim that investor-owned chains enjoy overall operating efficiencies or economies of scale in administrative or fiscal services" (1983: 353).

These recent studies, which found higher operating costs in the for-profit sector, have elicited the expected responses. Michael D. Bromberg of the Federation of American Hospitals (for-profit) does not think the debate is over. He suggests that the higher costs of the for-profit hospitals are likely a function of the age of the facilities. Since for-profit hospitals are generally newer, they have to set higher charges to amortize construction costs. When the not-for-profit move to replace their older facilities, he notes, their charges will be forced even higher than those of the for-profits (Gibbons 1984).

The most recent study would probably not affect Bromberg's defense. In 1986, Watt and his colleagues reported a comparison of 80 matched pairs of not-for-profit and investor-owned hospitals in eight states in 1978 and 1980 (the hospitals were in the South and Southwest, and in California). They found that total costs, controlled for case mix, were significantly higher in the investor-owned hospitals. The principal reason was higher charges for ancillary services. In regard to patient-care costs per case, there were no significant differences. Nor did the two groups differ in patient mix as measured by their Medicare case-mix indices or the proportions of their patients covered by Medicare or Medicaid. Several differences were found: the administrative overhead was higher in the for-profits, they were more profitable, and they employed fewer employees per occupied bed. They funded more of their capital through debt, and their capital costs in proportion to their operating costs were higher.

Watt et al. (1986) concluded that the higher profits of the investor-owned hospitals were the result of "more aggressive pricing rather than operating efficiencies" (p. 89). They also concluded that, given the current cost-control pressure, neither type of hospital has a clear advantage in accommodating the government-imposed restrictions of diagnostic related groups (DRGs).

The Unanswered Questions

At this stage in our experience with for-profit hospital chains, the limited research findings leave us with more unanswered questions than proven facts, but clearly the for-profits are not more efficient to date. As with all significant organizational shifts, questions of purpose and process arise, objections develop, and defense of the newly developed organizations occurs. Some of the issues, questions, or concerns that have been raised about the recent growth of the profit-making hospitals, and which remain unanswered, include:

- The extent to which the "creaming" of patients occurs, resulting in a two-class system
- The quality of services offered
- The level of training and capability of physicians and staff compared to nonprofits or nonchain for-profits
- The extent to which immediate profit-making is the overriding consideration, rather than long-range objectives and quality service
- Productivity trends over time
- The efficiency and effectiveness of quality control mechanisms
- The degree of emphasis (or lack thereof) on research and development, innovation, and experimentation
- The degree to which for-profit chains encourage monopoly and/or corruption
- The extent to which quality can be held constant while costs are reduced
- The tendency of for-profit investor-owned hospital chains to be vulnerable to strikes by employees
- The extent to which for-profit chains stimulate more competition while maintaining professionalism and professional values

The objections to not-for-profit hospitals generally follow some standard lines: (1) overall health care costs are too high; more specifically, hospital costs are too high relative to alternative care systems and potential benefits; (2) something needs to be done to contain spiralling costs; and (3) the test of the marketplace should be useful to the health industry.

The caveats often inserted after declarations of the need to contain health costs and to adapt corporate models to the health industry are particularly telling. Given the service that is delivered and its universal applicability, it is indeed questionable how relevant corporate models may be.

Writing for an unspecialized, non-health audience (*Harvard Business Review*), Egdahl (1984) asks, "Should we shrink the health care system?" In the process, he briefly and succinctly states the problems of profit-making health-care delivery organizations:

- Since much of their profit comes from higher prices and greater use of laboratory tests, it is hard to say how such practice will help reverse health cost trends.
- Rapid expansion of for-profit companies will increase the capital pool, adding to inflation.
- The focus on profit-making, rather than on the integrity of the entire health-care system, can be of major concern.
- Not-for-profit institutions are major sources for the training of medical students and residents, and for many other professionals.
- Most people who cannot afford to pay are served by the not-for-profit sector.
- Centers of excellence, typically academic health centers, are more costly, and under the present DRG funding system could find themselves in a precarious financial position.
- Constraints are inevitable, but the question is whether the costs will be passed on to the major health-care users, including the critically ill, old and terminal patients, and the poor.

Collectively, these problems present an unattractive picture of the impact of profit-making health-care systems. Egdahl's view is shared by others, several of whom have noted significant violations of the public interest by for-profit chains. One example is a National Council of Senior Citizens (1986) report concluding that for-profit hospitals are dangerous to the nation's health-care system. It accuses them of excess fees, inferior care, failure to provide care to the poor, and failure to contribute to medical research and education. Understandably, the for-profits reject such claims ("Study sees" 1986).

"Creaming" (taking the better patients) remains a popular accusation, even though many contracted hospitals are required by contract to treat indigent patients. HCA's Joseph Hutts replies to charges of creaming that in 1983 his hospitals provided uncompensated care to patients at a rate of 4.2 percent of revenues. The national average for all hospitals was 5.2 percent (Gibbons 1984) (if contracted hospitals were excluded from the analysis, the proportion of uncompensated care would be much lower). At the height of the DeVries controversy, Humana defended itself against creaming by pointing out that patients are not turned away from the Louisville facility. However, Humana spokesperson Robert Irvine defended referring patients to public hospitals by saying, "We are paying money through our taxes to support those hospitals. Those being paid to do it should be the ones to handle it" (quoted in Castro 1984: 85). The tax argument is interesting in itself, for taxes are quantifiable. The question is who gains—the taxpayers, the patients, or the hospitals?

Judith G. Waxman of the National Health Law Program comments that the treatment of the indigent patient varies significantly between private and public hospitals. She cites a Johns Hopkins study in which uninsured patients made up 16.8 percent of all public hospital, 7.9 percent of private, not-for-profit, and 6.0 percent of for-profit patients (Gibbons 1984). To Michael D. Bromberg, creaming merely highlights the existence of a subsidy and gives paying patients the opportunity to obtain desired services at less cost. It is a question of how we, as a society, are going to finance indigent care (Gibbons 1984). Clearly, the problem of serving the medically indigent belongs to all of society, with government responsible for devising a solution.

Some strategies are being tested. In New Jersey, all third-party payers and most diagnoses are covered in the DRG plan. The costs incurred in treating nonpaying patients are integrated into the total bill, giving an across-the-board average about 10 percent higher than would otherwise be paid by the payers, but guaranteeing full and equal access to all New Jersey residents. Unfortunately for those hospitals traditionally serving the indigent, their rates are driven up, making them less competitive. A statewide pool is the new recommendation. The other option is, of course, to make up the difference out of general taxes. In either case, there needs to be some spreading of the risk and a universal recommitment to the proposition that health care is a right, not a privilege.

The American Medical Association (AMA) is cautiously distancing itself from some of the more fundamental questions raised by opponents of for-profit hospitals. In fact, the AMA's James E. Davis has said that "the AMA has grave concerns about physicians being put in any situation where their ethics would be called into question. We do not have any evidence of unethical behavior of physicians in the profit setting" (quoted in Gibbons 1984: 37). The AMA did oppose the plan by the Paracelsus Corporation (California) to give cash rewards to physicians who keep the number of services given Medicare patients to a minimum, calling such bonuses kickbacks (Brinkley 1985).

Since the data suggest a fairly substantial growth in for-profit hospital chains over the last 20 years despite what are significant and important arguments against such developments, there are obviously strong forces supporting such growth. It is clear, for example, that hospital complexes (both profit and nonprofit) have better access to equity capital than small, single hospitals (Brown 1983). Since the major growth trend is in for-profit hospital complexes, the major equity advantages will accrue to them.

Certainly, the for-profit objective fits the U.S. capitalist tradition, and investor-owned hospitals, which relieve the public sector of some expense, fit comfortably into the philosophy of the Reagan administration. Furthermore, there is a pervasive assumption that competition is useful to any industry, including health, and that the profit-making sector is more efficient than the public or nonprofit (voluntary) sectors not sustained by the profit and loss standard. Proponents of an enlarged private-sector role also believe that market forces, including competition, heighten attention to quality and effectiveness.

The popular press speaks well of the for-profit hospitals. *Fortune, Time, Reader's Digest* and the *New York Times* and *Washington Post* have all published articles about the advantages of for-profit ownership and management: better planning, better purchasing, better management, and better marketing. The possibility that efficiency can be motivated by anything other than profit or that efficiency may not be the most important goal is too infrequently considered.

CONCLUSIONS

The health industry is in transition. Although the future cannot be forecasted with certainty, present trends suggest that the rapid growth of for-profit hospital chains has peaked and will slow considerably over the next few years. Stock market analysts are even telling investors that "hospital utilization is a declining business" (quoted in Vartan 1986).

The experiences of HCA are instructive. In October 1985, this largest operator of for-profit hospitals announced that its growth had stalled and its earnings were expected to flatten. This event was attributed to the drop in hospital occupancy resulting from tightened federal Medicare regulations and corporate cuts in health costs. HCA reports that its hospital business had dropped 20 percent in just two years, rather more than it had anticipated (Wayne 1985).

The failure of HCA to respond in a timely way to major trends in the health-care industry resulted in a strong stock market reaction. It is estimated that HCA lost over $1.5 billion in market value in one day. Analysts forecast that it will take several years before HCA can regain its status both as an investment and as a company (Wayne 1985). HCA's new strategy is to shift its focus away from hospitals and toward health insurance, particularly prepaid health-care plans (HMOs). Humana has already modified itself similarly and is now solidly entrenched in the HMO business. HCA believes that its current ownership of hospitals will provide it a cost advantage in entering the health insurance market. Thus, although the for-profit hospital chains are not immune to overall trends in the health-care industry and to market forces, their presence in the industry seems unlikely to abate. Instead, their focus will change.

Starr (1982) suggests that the rise of corporate enterprise in health care must be viewed in a context of diminished resources and reduced autonomy of physicians, voluntary hospitals, and medical schools. Also of significance is the loss of control over regulations, standards, markets, and organizations as the health-care industry becomes increasingly politicized and open to widespread intervention. The continued search by government, and more recently by employers and some of the large unions, for ways to limit medical expenditures is also affecting the rise and status of the for-profit health-care system. The net result is a number of severe strains throughout the medical care system. The state will no longer protect and accommodate the medical profession. Physicians are no longer the sole interest group in the medical care complex. The medical profession itself is fragmenting. Professional sovereignty is weakening.

As recently as 1983, Montague Brown saw an optimistic future for corporate health-care enterprise: "Today at least 75 percent of all hospital administrators believe that most, if not all, hospitals and other forms of health care will be operated by a few huge systems by the end of the decade" (p. 74). Brown, of course, is careful not to declare that these "huge" systems will necessarily be profit-making.

Brown's remarks were not atypical. Well into 1985, many observers were equally confident that the hospital chains would soon dominate the hospital business. Most of them limited their observations to the for-profit sector.

There are many other conceptions of the future of the for-profit health-care system. The various forecasters are inclined to believe neither that the profit-making sector will continue its rapid growth nor, especially, that a near monopoly or oligopoly will arise within the next few years. The nursing home industry provides a case in point. It accumulated its nationwide and international profit-making organizations much earlier than did the acute-care hospitals. Even now, over 80 percent of the industry is for-profit, but it still does not have a single chain controlling more than a small portion of the market. Beverly Enterprises, the largest nursing home company in the country, controlled nearly 8 percent of the 1.6 million nursing home beds in mid-1986. Its goal is to control 15 percent by the mid-1990s (Greenhouse 1986). It is thus one matter to move into the for-profit sector. It is another to build a few truly large corporations.

To a substantial extent, the favoring by Medicare of the for-profit hospitals and nursing homes through tax breaks and return-on-capital allowances is vexing to Congress and may very well be eliminated. By mid-1985, the House Ways and Means Committee had approved a provision that would do just this. It estimated the savings in three years to be $415 million. The chairman of the Subcommittee on Health described the AMA and the for-profit hospitals as maintaining "a greedy attitude" (quoted in Pear 1985: A14). Thus, the advantage tenuously held by for-profit health-care providers for over 20 years may be at high risk.

As the use of diagnostic related groups (DRGs) continues to expand and, in so doing, places limits on the rate of reimbursement for health care services, the unique opportunities for profit-gaining will be moderated. The potential cost savings that may accrue from DRGs is of obvious interest to health insurance companies, but of equally negative concern to hospitals and other health-care providers. The trend, however, is clearly in the direction of controlling health-care costs through policies, regulations, or practices that place limits on physician and/or hospital discretion. In New Jersey, all insurers are now included in that state's DRGs. The reimbursement limits placed on Medicare are but the beginning of a national version of DRGs. There will be many more versions, more sophisticated in nature, leaving less margin for manipulation.

Access to medical care for the uninsured and underinsured will remain important. Already, coalitions are actively lobbying Congress for legislation that would provide incentives to states to provide health insurance coverage for high-risk populations. Two bills under consideration include an essential role for the private sector, much like high-risk pooling among automobile insurance companies. Whether they pass or not, systems will soon be designed and implemented to include those 35–40 million people, many of them very young, who currently fall outside the insured population (see, for example, Nugent 1986).

Contemporary management technology is already well integrated into U.S. hospitals although, according to several published research reports, the efficiency long claimed by the for-profit hospitals has not been substantiated by the data. The issue of scale seems more important; the larger chains are able to buy and apply technology much more successfully than smaller health-care units. Purchasing requires a larger economic base to stimulate maximum competition. Here, the for-profits do not have an exclusive advantage. Nonprofit hospitals also have well-developed cooperative mechanisms to achieve such ends.

The "loss leader" model of charging variable prices for services in order to encourage demand, as currently practiced, will likely be discarded as prospective payment systems are more fully implemented. Thus, those recent studies of comparable costs that show the not-for-profit sector to be slightly more efficient will probably lose relevance, except in spurring questions about for-profit hospital chains.

Pattison and Katz (1983) believe that their research shows that, with respect to patient mix, ownership is a less important determinant than location and staff. Relman (1983b) also believes that with the prospective payment system, the profitability of investor-owned hospitals may be linked more to their ability to control costs than to their ability to manipulate prices and market services. As noted earlier, recent research suggests that the strength of investor-owned hospitals lies in selective pricing rather than in controlling costs.

As matters of values and ethics become articulated and more mainstreamed, the advantageous, income-generating position of the physician will not escape attention. The public will surely seek ways to harness those physicians who profit in a manner opposed to the public interest.

The conflict between making money through other than personal services and adhering to medical ethics certainly deserves careful examination. Ginzberg (1984) believes that several regulatory bodies, including the AMA, need to keep the matter under close surveillance. He feels that under no circumstances can medicine be viewed as just another business like banking or retailing. He comments: "To rely on the market to discipline money-grubbing professionals is to overestimate what the market should be asked to do or is capable of doing" (p. 1164).

The issue of access to capital is a problem that the economic and business literature frequently links to the health-care industry. Lacking adequate finances to modernize large physical plants, some hospitals may have no alternative but to close their doors. Estimates of the demand for capital for 1983–93 range from $106 to $190 billion. Again, it is suggested that simple marketplace solutions can be contraindicated. Donald K. Cohodes (1983) concludes after thoughtful analysis: "Allowing capital formation in the hospital sector to be determined by the market criteria of the bottom-line performance could lead to a serious contraction of the field, to increased financial hardships for the hospitals that remain, to reduced service provision, and to plant deterioration" (p. 171).

Even the marketplace, which works to the advantage of the for-profit chains, has its eccentricities. In April 1985, when the American Hospital Supply Corporation and HCA announced their agreement to merge, their investors reacted by driving down the prices of both stocks. The issue was a fear of lack of profitability. William Hayes, manager of the Fidelity Select Health Care Mutual Fund, commented that "generally, the negative reaction to the proposed hospital merger served as a stark reminder of just how bleak the future is for these industries given the national effort to contain health care costs" (quoted in A. C. Wallace 1985).

Each discipline or profession tends to bring its own perspective to the analysis and definition of the problem. Most matters of cost efficiency and effectiveness are colored by the discipline of economics. Thus, economic analyses tend to search for market forces and, when none are to be found, spend much time searching for reasons. The existence of the not-for-profit sector, to some, is a major cause of the failure of market forces to operate. We disagree. Not-for-profit concerns represent a choice, as in adoption and foster care, about what should be independent of profit-making. Hospitals were similarly formed to serve the public interest for altruistic and humanitarian purposes.

The human services industry is served by a variety of professions, whose members have undergone extensive educational preparation for practice. These professions have formal codes of ethics, professional associations, mandatory continuing education, licensure, and publicly supported, legislatively mandated boards or commissions, among other means, to guarantee minimum competence and accountability to the public. These are not accidental features of contemporary industrialized societies. They reflect a deep distrust of the market forces that operated freely to produce the physicians, lawyers, and social workers of the past, as well as the hospitals and agencies in which they functioned.

The free enterprise marketplace, we are told, promotes efficiency. Whether the for-profit sector is more efficient is a testable question. But since there are several other potential objectives in health and social welfare, it may well be that the continual emphasis on efficiency, to the detriment of other important objectives, partially accounts for the different ecology of the human services industry. Certainly, matters of availability, accessibility, continuity, accountability, and quality of care are hardly insignificant, and to many people may be more important than efficiency.

REFERENCES

Altman, A. K. 1984. "Health Care as Business." *New York Times*, November 27, p. 1, C4.

Anderson, O. W. and N. Gravitz. 1983. "The General Hospital: A Social and Historical Perspective." In *Handbook of Health, Health Care and the Health Professions*, edited by D. Mechanic (New York: The Free Press), pp. 305–17.

Barron, J. 1984. "Humana Focus: Technology." *New York Times*, p. D1, August 14.

Bays, C. W. 1979. "Cost Comparisons of For-Profit and Non-Profit Hospitals." *Social Science and Medicine* 13c:219–25.

Bernard, B. P. 1985. "Private Hospitals' Dumping of Patients." *New York Times*, October 28, p. A19.

Brinkley, J. 1985. "Plan for Cutting Hospital Costs by Rewarding Doctors Draws AMA Fire." *New York Times*, September 24, p. A24.

Brown, M. 1983. "New Payment Policies Spark Query: Who'll Run Hospitals?" *Modern Healthcare* 13:71–72, 74.

Caplan, A. L. 1984. "Should Doctors Move at a Gallop?" *New York Times*, August 17, p. A25.

Castro, J. 1984. "Earning Profits, Saving Lives," *Time*, December 12, pp. 84–89.

Clurman, C. 1983. "Hospital Corp.: Nursing a Monopoly?" *USA Today*, December 13, p. 3B.

Cohodes, D. R. 1983. "Hospital Capital Formation in the 1980's: Is There a Crisis?" *Journal of Health Politics, Policy and Law* 8:164–72.

Egdahl, R. H. 1984. "Should We Shrink the Health Care System?" *Harvard Business Review* 62:125–32.

Engel, M. 1985. "California Conglomerate May Lease George Washington Hospital." *Washington Post*, August 2, pp. B1, B5.

Friedland, S. 1985. "Capital Costs." *New York Times*, August 11, p. 10, N2.

Gibbons, D. L. 1984. "For-Profit Enterprises: A Boom or Threat to Health Care Industry?" *Medical World News* 25, no. 8:35, 37, 39.

Ginzberg, E. 1984. "The Monetarization of Medical Care." *New England Journal of Medicine* 310:1162–65.

Greenhouse, S. 1986. "Riding a Nursing Home Boom." *New York Times*, April 14, p. D1.

"Hospital Executives Consider Operation 'Wise Investment.' " 1984. *New York Times*, November 26, p. B7.

"Hospitals Luring Patients by Marketing Services." 1985. *New York Times*, December 2, p. B1.

Kinkead, G. 1980. "Humana's Hard-Sell Hospitals." *Fortune*, November, pp. 68–81.

Lewin, L. S., R. A. Derzon, and R. Margulies. 1981. "Investor-Owned and Non-Profits Differ in Economic Performance." *Hospitals* 55, no. 13:52–58.

MacNaughton, D. S. 1981. "HCA and the Teaching Hospital." *HCA Annual Report* (Nashville, TN).

Malan, M. 1985. "Hospitals Turn to Advertising." *Washington Post*, December 28, p. A4.

Malinan, S. 1983. "Managers Debate." *New York Times*, November 4, p. A27.

Nugent, R. 1986. *Memorandum of the Coalition for Health Insurance Availability* (available from the Epilepsy Foundation of America, Arlington, VA).

Okie, S. 1986. " 'Dumping' Patients into Public Hospitals May Shorten Lives, Study Says." *Washington Post*, February 27, p. A14.

Pattison, R. V. and H. M. Katz. 1983. "Investor-Owned and Not-for-Profit Hospitals." *New England Journal of Medicine* 309:347–53.

Pear, R. 1985. "House Unit Backs Cuts in Medicare." *New York Times*, July 25, pp. A1, A14.

Purdum, T. S. 1985. "Hospital Company and No. 1 Supplier Plan Huge Merger." *New York Times*, April 1, p. 1.

Relman, A. S. 1980. "The New Medical-Industrial Complex." *New England Journal of Medicine* 303:963–70.

———. 1983a. "Future of Medical Practice." *Health Affairs* 2:5–19.

———. 1983b. "Investor-Owned Hospitals and Health-Care Costs." *New England Journal of Medicine* 309:370–372.

Schrage, M. 1984. "For-Profit Hospitals Boosting Basic Research." *Washington Post*, November 27, pp. D1, D16.

Schwartz, H. 1984. "Cut the Red Tape; Implant at Full Speed." *New York Times*, August 17, p. A25.

Siegrist, B. B. and R. E. Herzlinger. 1981. "Humana, Inc." *HBS Case Services*, rev. April 1983 (Boston, MA: Harvard Business School).

_____ . 1983a. "The Hospital Replacement Decision." *HBS Case Services* (Boston, MA: Harvard Business School).

_____ . 1983b. "Hospital Corporation of America: Financial Analysis." *HBS Case Services* (Boston, MA: Harvard Business School).

Simler, S. L. 1984. "Austin Questions HCA's Loyalty to Town." *Modern Healthcare* 14, no. 6:38.

Starr, P. 1982. *The Social Transformation of American Medicine* (New York: Basic Books).

State of Florida, Hospital Cost Containment Board, 1981–82, 1982–83. *Annual Reports* (Tallahassee, FL: Florida Hospital Cost Containment Board).

Steinwald, B. and D. Neuhauser. 1970. "The Role of the Proprietary Hospital." *Law and Contemporary Problems* 35:817.

"Study Sees 'Growing Danger' in Profit-Seeking Hospitals." 1986. *New York Times*, March 25, p. C13.

Tolchin, M. 1985. "As Companies Buy Hospitals, Treatment of Poor is Debated." *New York Times*, January 25, pp. A1, A17.

Vartan, V. G. 1986. "Hospital Sector Doing Better." *New York Times*, March 7, p. D6.

Wallace, A. C. 1985. "Finding the Right Niche in Health Care." *New York Times*, April 7, p. 10F.

Wallace, C. 1983. "AMI is Guilty in Antitrust Case: FTC." *Modern Healthcare* 13:28, 30.

Watt, J. M., R. A. Derzon, S. C. Renn, C. J. Schramm, J. S. Hahn, and G. D. Pillari. 1986. "The Comparative Economic Performance of Investor-Owned Chain and Not-for-Profit Hospitals." *New England Journal of Medicine* 314:89–96.

Wayne, L. 1985. "The Hospital Corp.'s Stumble." *New York Times*, October 8, pp. D1, D8.

6

The Privatization of Prisons: Panacea or Placebo?

Gilbert Geis

The privatization of penal facilities seems to attract more intense argument than the privatization of most other operations under review for such management change. Many persons wholeheartedly in favor of promoting for-profit entrepreneurship for a broad range of activities now under government control balk when the subject turns to prisons. In part, this is because prison privatization calls for giving the private sector enormous direct control over the lives of a captive human population. Prisoners cannot walk away, cannot resign, from a situation they find abhorrent. They did not elect to be where they are (unless we presume that by their behavior they asked for it), and they certainly cannot elect to go elsewhere because they want to.

Presumably (although this is arguable), government has the interests of such prisoners at the top of its agenda. Private prison managers by definition must operate with two agendas: They must both favor the welfare of the inmates and serve the best interests of their business. This splitting of priorities is likely to be less of a problem with other privatized public services. Nothing awful is lost if garbage collection suffers or rail transportation falters. With prisons, however, a great deal can be sacrificed if involuntary captives are cruelly handled.

Perhaps because of such reservations, there has been little movement toward the privatization of correctional work in the United States. Very recently, however, the issue has attracted much more attention, and intense debate has focused on the few actual instances of prison privatization. The absence of any definitive information about success and failure has, understandably, only heightened the intensity of dispute, since neither side can yet support its suppositions with anything resembling a firm, factual foundation.

This chapter will set the prison privatization movement into the context of the world of corrections by first providing a brief description of that world. It will then discuss the more prominent developments toward prison privatization, covering their origins and aspirations and some of their experiences to date. Finally, it will set forth a more general review and appraisal of arguments for and against privatization of penal facilities.

THE PENAL ENVIRONMENT

Prisons and jails are not very pretty places, although imaginative architecture and decent landscaping can sometimes deceive a casual observer. Legislators intent on capturing media attention chronically dub newer penal facilities "country clubs" and deplore the extravagant waste of taxpayer funds on the unworthy creatures who find their way into them. In earlier times, absent welfare cushions, some members of Britain's Parliament regularly fretted that conditions inside that nation's penal institutions were becoming so appealing that men faced with unemployment and the threat of starvation on the outside had lost any fear of the consequences of whatever crime they might contemplate. In the eighteenth century, Samuel Johnson wryly wrote, "No man will be a sailor who has contrivance enough to get himself into a jail, for being in a ship is being in jail with the chance of being drowned. A man in a jail has more room, better food, and commonly better company" (Clarkson 1975:146).

The truth about penal facilities is rather more sobering. Very few people prefer to be captives inside a penal institution, regardless of how well maintained it may appear or how deplorable circumstances may be in the free world. Prisons are overwhelmingly dull, and they wring from their inmates their sense of dignity and worth. They are apt to be smelly, the food poor, the restrictions petty and galling. They deprive human beings of contact with those of the opposite sex, contacts that contribute enormously to a person's sense of worth, a worth reflected in reciprocated affection and concern.

Above all, penal facilities are notoriously dangerous. They are dangerous because the strong prey upon the weak, partly out of habit, partly out of boredom, and largely to establish some sense of power and importance, two qualities stripped from them by their incarceration. They are also dangerous because they herd together, under tense conditions, persons who have demonstrated their inability to deal effectively with even very mild forms of frustration or affront.

I recall in this regard seeing a very tough inmate at San Quentin, in California, hurriedly draw back his feet, which had been extended in front of him as he sunned himself in the prison yard. By doing so, he barely avoided having another inmate, indifferent to where he was going, trip over him. Although no harm was done, the seated inmate, whom I knew very slightly from a research project I was working on, got quickly to his feet and apologized for his "carelessness." Later, he told me why: "You never know," he said. "There are all kinds of weirdos in this joint. That guy might have a shiv [knife], and he might get some wild idea that I had it in for him, or that I wanted to start something. You can't take those chances here."

Few prisoners are willing to grant that they are in prison because they deserve to be there. Rather, as most of us would, they see themselves as treated unreasonably, as living like caged animals, controlled by the superior force and firepower of those determined to keep them in subjection.

Prisons are not pretty places.

PRIVATE VERSUS PUBLIC

Several significant characteristics of penal facilities have made them particularly ripe targets for privatization, once the general entrepreneurial ethos commanded serious attention. First, prisoners are declassé—they are the outcasts of society, exercising virtually no suasion upon public policy. They cannot vote, for instance, although I have argued that they ought to be able to do so (Geis 1968). Indeed, privatization might itself provide the kind of clout that corrections has sorely lacked. As Fox (1977: 104) has noted: "Probably one of the greatest contributions of private organizations is the political influence they can bring to bear in a field generally devoid of political advantage in appropriations, program improvement and resources."

More particularly, prison inmates are objects upon whom we can righteously heap our own unsettled emotions. They have wronged us by hurting or depriving innocent victims; yet they now live, we presume, in ease at our expense. Freudians maintain, perhaps correctly, that criminal offenders prototypically represent an underside of our selves, and that we tend to fear and despise them as a method of trying to demonstrate our clear-cut distinction from them. Be that as it may, there is no question that the absence of a significant pro-prison lobby has helped to make correctional institutions ripe for privatization.

Second, expense is a recurring theme in discussions of prison privatization: Prisons are inordinately expensive to build and to operate. The usually cited figure is that it requires $16,000 a year to keep one inmate in a state prison. Given its indifference, if not hostility, to the plight of criminal offenders, the public is unwilling to bear current costs. Most assuredly, it is unwilling to take on additional costs to maintain those who are incarcerated. This attitude combines perversely with a growing public demand that more and more offenders be put away for longer and longer periods of time. Despite recent statistics indicating a rather stable, even a declining, crime rate, the public has lost patience with those who commit "street crimes": murder, rape, robbery, burglary, manslaughter, and so on.

The issues of cost and quality of service under public or private control cut to the core of current discussions about penal facilities. A brief comparison between correctional concerns and those in the field of medicine can highlight ingredients of the debate.

In medicine, the U.S. public—and particularly the parties that constitute the health-care establishment—have vigorously fought off attempts to nationalize the delivery of health care, a move that would be in direct contrast to the privatization trend. Their fundamental argument has been that going public would contribute to deterioration in medical care available to Americans. But a staggering national medical bill, combined with poignant stories of elderly persons stripped of lifetime savings by a single catastrophic illness, allowed the government to intrude into the practice of medicine through enactment of the Medicare program in 1965. Medicaid, a form of welfare medicine for the poor, came in on the coattails of Medicare in the same year.

Nobody questions that Medicaid has contributed strikingly to improvements in the health of indigent Americans by underwriting office-based physician services. The notable improvement in infant mortality in the United States (a figure always embarassingly high in international comparisons) has been credited largely to Medicaid. Care for the elderly probably has remained much as before, except that a major part of its expense shifted from private insurers and individuals to the government.

At the moment, a fiscal crisis in health care has increased government intrusion into what has long been regarded as a private realm. Edicts impose restrictions on such matters as the length of hospital stays and the prices that will be paid for particular illnesses and procedures. These developments highlight equivalent paradoxes and perplexities in the movement toward privatization of prison facilities.

For both prisons and medicine, the assumption is that the quality of service will be enhanced in a private, capitalist framework. Doctors and other providers, competing for patients, will do their utmost to give their clients what they desire. Private prison operations would find themselves in a rather more complex position. Presumably, they are trying to satisfy primarily the public, and only secondarily their inmate clientele. They can gratify the public by operating cheap, quiet, and inconspicuous facilities. In the long term, they will find special favor if they bring about a reduction in the number of criminal offenses, perhaps by holding their prisoners longer and thereby keeping them from preying on the public. The crime rate might be reduced more usefully if a prison could persuade its inmates by means of the correctional regimen that they ought not violate the criminal law again.

But if private medicine truly failed the poor, as it did, why will private corrections perform more admirably? A possible answer, and an extremely important one, may be that for some services, particularly those involving human welfare, the best results are obtainable through private enterprise when it is scrupulously monitored by independent public agencies.

A review of cost issues in both medicine and prisons can also prove informative. Nobody doubts that medical costs were becoming unacceptably high under private, uncontrolled auspices. This proved particularly true when providers were able to collect through third-party insurers and were not faced with the discomfiting problem of having to bill patients directly. Today's mixture of private and public medicine surely will ultimately be comparatively cheaper, if only because the government will not be willing to deflect funds from, say, defense spending to the medical sphere. Here again the mixture, allowing private initiative with publicly controlled limits, may prove an effective management scheme.

THE IMPETUS FOR PRIVATIZATION

Jails and prisons constitute the two major places where persons are incarcerated. They are supplemented by a variegated array of facilities, generally community-based, that hold special kinds of offenders, who usually have committed lesser offenses or are deemed minimal risks for further misbehavior. These include halfway houses, congregate foster homes, and short-term detention facilities, such as those operated by the Immigration and Naturalization Service (INS). These last are, more than any other kind of institution, managed today by private companies.

Jails

Jails hold persons who are awaiting trial and cannot raise or are not eligible for bail. They also house persons sentenced for relatively minor offenses, whose terms are for a year or less. Most municipalities and all but one (Petroleum County, Montana) of the nation's 3,000-plus counties have their own jail.

In the seventeenth century, Matthew Hale (1976: 229) pointed out that "anciently the custody of those prisoners taken by the sheriff belonged to the constable of the castle where for the most part they were committed." But by the third year of the reign of Elizabeth I, management of jails had been vested in the county sheriffs, where it has remained firmly until our day. During the Stuart period in England, jail operation involved privatization that could serve as a caricature of what might happen if the jails were now removed from public jurisdiction:

The suspect was usually expected to pay the keep of the jail for fires (when allowed), light, food, drink, and bedding, everything in fact beyond space in which to lie on the jail floor. If he had any money in his possession on arrest . . . the jailer soon found ways to mulct him of it. There might be a fee merely to enter the jail or to be allowed to live in a pleasanter area than custom dictated . . . (Bellamy 1979: 100).

Conditions in jails in both England and the United States have been mercilessly castigated for centuries. One survey (Hoskins 1976–77) described the typical Kentucky jail as "a house of horror." One Kentucky jail had been closed by judicial order because there were no bathing facilities or hot water in the section for juveniles and women. Cells were inadequately ventilated and had dangerous heating systems. Prisoners were so isolated that they could not summon help in the event of an emergency, such as a fire. Sixty percent of the state's 119 jails were more than 50 years old, and 20 percent were more than 100 years old and marked by both physical senescence and total neglect.

In a recent monograph on jails, John Irwin, a professor at San Francisco State University, who himself served five years in prison, notes that all jails share certain characteristics. Many prisoners are crowded together in very small living spaces. "Every personal act—sleeping (and snoring), eating, smoking, talking, bathing, shaving, reading, watching television, playing games, and using the toilet—will be done in a group, even a crowd, sometimes with a deputy (perhaps unexpectedly) looking on" (Irwin 1985: 60).

Nonetheless, as Robertson (1974: xx) has pointed out, the jail system has shown "amazing intransigence" in resisting change, despite scandals, constant media exposure, and periodic reform movements. Undoubtedly, part of the reason for the jails' unaltered survival lies in public abhorrence of their clientele—gutter drunks, prostitutes, and similar detritus of the criminal justice system. Another element of resistance resides in vested political interests. Jails are part of the sheriff's turf, valuable for patronage and budget. It is not surprising that the major group formally on record against privatization is the National Sheriffs Association.

Jails, almost since their inception, have been desperate for reform. Privatization may lead or at least impel toward such reform. But a 1920s illustration also shows how sheriffs, operating jails as private fiefs, have behaved in a manner embodying the worst forebodings of those opposed to jail privatization:

In one county the cost of feeding a prisoner was eight cents a day while the sheriff received forty-five. In many counties, the sheriff is permitted either directly or through concessionaires, to sell special articles of food, tobacco, or other so-called luxuries, to prisoners. He is thus permitted to starve them to the point where they or their friends purchase food to supplement the daily ration. He thus enjoys the extraordinary privilege of reaping a profit not only from starvation but from the relief of starvation (Smith 1960: 143).

Prisons

Prisons are state operated and hold felons, persons who have committed the more serious criminal offenses. In addition, municipalities or counties sometimes see to it that their offenders end up in prisons rather than jails, since they thereby are relieved of the incarceration expense.

The state of U.S. prisons can be summarized by noting that in 32 states they have been under court order to relieve overcrowding and to do something about inhumane conditions, *with similar suits pending in eight other states* (see Giertz and Nardulli 1985; McConville 1985; "Prison Overcrowding" 1984). The state prison in Folsom, California, for instance, built in the 1880s, was designed to hold 1,782 persons; at a recent count, it had a population of 3,036 inmates. There are an average of 19 stabbings inside the Folsom walls each month, and the facility has been branded "a squalid, antiquated mess," a characterization equally applicable to many other U.S. prisons. Criminologist Richard Korn summarized the situation aptly. "Prisons," he says, "animalize people" ("Mayhem in the Cell Blocks" 1985).

At the end of 1984, 463,866 persons were being held in federal and state prisons, in addition to the 130,000 in jails. Since 1980, prison populations have grown by 134,000 inmates, an increase of 40 percent in a four-year period. The growth has been accompanied by an equally dramatic growth in spending; state and correctional authorities paid out nearly $7.2 billion in direct and capital outlays in 1984 ("Prisoners in 1984" 1985: 1). To relieve overcrowding, prisoners are now released on the average in 16 months, the shortest time on record.

The major difficulty connected with operating a state prison, either publicly or privately, inheres in the contradictory missions that are set for it. The problem was clearly noted by Gresham Sykes (1958: 30–31) after his study of the maximum security prison at Trenton, New Jersey:

> The administrator of the maximum security prison . . . finds himself confronted with a set of social expectations which pose numerous dilemmas when an attempt is made to translate them into a concrete, rational policy. Somehow he must resolve the claims that the prison should exact vengeance, erect a specter to terrify the actual or potential deviant, isolate the known offender from the free community, and effect a change in the personality of his captives so that they gladly follow the

dictates of the law—and in addition maintain order within his society of prisoners and see that they are employed at useful labor. If the policy of the prison sometimes seems to exhibit a certain inconsistency, we might do well to look at the inconsistency of the philosophical setting in which the prison exists.

The Entry of Privatization

Events in Tennessee in 1985 offer a powerful example of how current prison conditions, especially overcrowding, can provide a possible entree for privatization. In July, Tennessee convicts set buildings ablaze and seized hostages in uprisings at four penal facilities. Before the rioting ended, one prisoner had been stabbed to death and $7.5 million in property damage had occurred. The inmates' complaints focused primarily on overcrowded conditions, but they also dwelt on poor food, lack of rehabilitation programs, and the design of new prison uniforms, which had stripes along the pants legs to provide easier identification of inmates.

That fall, in the wake of a federal court order mandating upgrading of the state prison facilities and a reduction in prison populations, the Tennessee governor, Lamar Alexander, proposed to the legislature that the state's mandatory sentencing law be weakened and that local jails be given fiscal encouragement to hold state prisoners. He also wanted funds for new prison construction.

Simultaneous with the governor's proposals, the Corrections Corporation of America (CCA), the most prominent group in prison privatization (although itself only two years old), offered to pay the state $250 million ($100 million in cash and the remainder in notes) for a 99-year lease on the entire Tennessee prison system. The company proposed to operate the state's 17 facilities for a fee based on the number of prisoners it would hold; the CCA thought it could do a better job than the state was accomplishing for about the same $170 million budget that correctional services received annually.

The governor indicated that he thought the CCA proposal well worth further exploration: "Anytime someone in effect offers $250 million to do the same amount of work as a state would have to do, we're obligated to take a look at that," he said ("Governor Offers Plan" 1985).

The CCA solicitation came only a few days before the annual conference of the National Association of Criminal Justice Planners, a group made up of prosecutors, judges, corrections officers, and criminal justice system planners in 75 metropolitan areas. It was the main topic of conversation, and it provided an opportunity for establishment officials to air their views thoroughly. Sample responses offer a sense of the grounds for opposition to privatization in at least one segment of the population:

With a 99-year lease, they're going to see to it that people are sentenced. They're going to lobby against alternative programs, including probationary programs. It's big business. [Richard J. Elrod, sheriff, Cook County, Illinois]

With that kind of investment, they're going to promote less turning over to halfway houses [Robert A. Edmonds, assistant sheriff, Los Angeles County]

The private sector has an enormous investment in stimulating demand. They could start political and advertising campaigns aimed at making Americans even more fearful of crime so as to fill the jails and prisons [Michael E. Smith, executive director, Vera Foundation, a New York City-based research organization]

Smith granted that he was not aware that any such campaigns had been inaugurated, but he said that he could not envision private industry not using marketing tactics to promote its own interests.

The only reported encomium for privatization came from the director of the Ramsey County Community Corrections organization in St. Paul, Minnesota. He said that both popular and political support had led his jurisdiction, in consort with six others, to turn over the operation of a jail for women offenders to the New Orleans-based Volunteers of America, an organization whose roots in correctional work go back to 1896. The Volunteers hold a five-year lease on the 42-bed jail facility, located in Roseville in Ramsey County, and charge $50 per day per prisoner, $10–15 less than their incarceration had been costing the counties. Under its new management, this jail has earned the sobriquet of the "Holiday Inn of Jails" (Bartlett 1985).

The Ramsey County correctional official insisted that the Volunteers had provided "more efficiency and flexibility" than could otherwise have been achieved. This comment drew strong rebuttal at the conference from Herbert Williams, president of the Police Foundation: "I don't like to hear criminal justice arguments predicated on efficiency and effectiveness," he said. "Being efficient does not mean that justice will be served" (Tolchin 1985c).

CAN PRIVATIZATION WORK?

In a thorough, balanced review of the movement of private firms into the correctional world, Joan Mullen, Kent J. Chabotar, and Deborah M. Carrow (1985; see also Mullen 1985) divided their subject into three major components: the involvement of private concerns in prison industries, their participation in the construction and leasing of correctional facilities, and the operation of penal facilities by private nonprofit and for-profit organizations. Let us consider each of these components in turn.

Prison Industries

The problem of idleness has plagued the operation of correctional facilities. The traditional sentence of a certain number of years of incarceration at "hard labor" is usually an empty formula. There is very little labor, difficult or easy, available within prisons or, especially, within jails. Vast stretches of unscheduled time often create management and morale problems of monumental proportions. Perhaps worse, what labor that is available does little to prepare inmates for lawful employment after their eventual release.

I recall, in this connection, watching sulky inmates at Oklahoma's McAlester State Penitentiary "working" at their assigned task of paging through mounds of elementary and high school textbooks and erasing the notations and other marks the state's students had placed there. McAlester, like many penitentiaries, also kept a number of inmates at work making license plates, an occupation for which there is not a howling demand in the free world.

The outstanding record of U.S. prisoners in producing materiel during World War II provides strong evidence for the potential of prison labor if sufficient motivation and reward is involved (England 1955). By far the most significant barrier to the installation of satisfactory programs of work has been the opposition of labor unions, fearful of competition from poorly paid workers. A series of federal laws (the Hawes-Cooper Act in 1929; the Sumners-Ashurst Act in 1935) so narrowed the marketplace for prison-made goods that they made meaningful work programs virtually impossible to mount. Recently, however, the trend has been reversed, and as Auerbach (1982: 25) notes, upwards of 20 states now have legislation authorizing access to the open market and private-sector involvement with prison industries. She summarizes the matter in these words:

> . . . the new federal and state statutes . . . represent significant change for prison industries for the first time in almost 50 years. . . . The open market for prison-made goods is developing in tandem with a growth in protective measures for prisoner workers. The new statutes prohibit the kind of low wages and involuntary servitude which typified earlier experiments with prison labor. There is little doubt that the inclusion of wage floors as well as measures to protect free world labor made it possible for such legislation to be enacted. It is less clear, given the current

economic climate, whether the private sector will find sufficient induce-
ment in statutes to cause them to join with [prison] industries in significant numbers. The future of the public/private partnerships made possible by these statutes may well depend upon the creation of financial incentives to encourage more private sector businesses to explore the
possibilities available through prison industries (p. 35).

Several ventures already are under way involving private organizations
in prison industries. Both Florida and Oregon have turned their entire
prison work operation over to outside managers. The PRIDE (Prison
Rehabilitative Industries and Diversified Enterprises) program in Florida
represents a nonprofit business that manages more than 22 types of prison
production, including an optical lab, print shops, furniture manufacture,
metal fabrication, and a range of agricultural projects. PRIDE has its own
marketing division. Florida state agencies must purchase from the corporation any needed goods that it has available (Mullen et al. 1985: 22).

Businesses of more modest reach have begun in a number of other state
facilities. For example, since August 1981, Best Western International Inc.
has been employing 25 prisoners at the Arizona Center for Women in
downtown Phoenix to handle overflow calls to its reservations system. Best
Western bore the start-up costs, including equipment, and continues to pay
for training and supervision. Workers are screened for any history of credit
card fraud; successful applicants are chosen because of typing ability,
knowledge of geography, and sales-oriented personality. The company pays
the imprisoned women at the same rate as its headquarters' reservations
agents. In its first five years, the program had generated more than $30
million in room reservations, and it had handled about 6 percent of the
company's U.S. call volume. To date, 146 women have worked in the program, and after release, 31 percent have taken jobs with Best Western. The
contract was arranged after Best Western had experienced difficulty hiring
persons as needed for its reservations overflow ("A Good Way to Do Bad
Time" 1985).

TransWorld Airlines' Los Angeles office is setting up a similar program inside the California youth correctional institution in Camarillo. The
work will pay minimum wage, and a portion of the employees' income will
go to the state and to crime victims ("From Over Prison Walls" 1985).

There is as yet no reliable evidence regarding the utility of pioneering
efforts such as these, but at least on their face they seem to be sensible innovations. Emphasis on the ethic of work in prisons, as Cullen and Travis
(1984: 47) have noted, "is one of the few reforms capable of securing
broad-based ideological support" and "one of the few reforms holding the
potential to refashion the prison social order in a manner that will be conducive to both inmate and custodial interests." Labor unions remain wary

of the replacement of free workers by cheaper and more malleable institutional labor. There also are difficulties associated with the constant turnover brought about by release from confinement, problems with training, and possible complexities associated with discrepant wages for different groups within a penal facility. But these do not appear to be unresolvable issues and, pending contrary evidence, the movement toward privatization of prison industries seems likely to flourish.

Construction of Penal Facilities

Prisons are inordinately expensive to build and the public tends to resist strongly financing such construction through bond issues. It is also difficult in fiscally lean times to include the large sums necessary for prison building in a regular operating budget. Nonetheless, prisons are morbidly overcrowded and decrepit, and the need for new construction is pressing.

To deal with this matter, a number of novel private financial arrangements have arisen (Mullen et al. 1985). Typical is the approach used in New York. The legislature authorized the state Urban Development Corporation, a public authority, to sell $380 million in prison construction bonds. The state Department of Corrections would then have leased the completed prisons at an annual fee equal to the debt service of the bonds. But the plan was challenged in state courts as an attempt to circumvent the earlier defeat of a $500 million prison and jail bond issue. More successfully, the supervisors of Jefferson County, Colorado, momentarily handcuffed by the voters' rejection of a proposed increase in the sales tax to finance the building of a new jail, issued $30.2 million in "certificates of participation" for sale to private investors in order to build the jail (Cory and Gettinger 1984: 21).

The most disturbing aspect of such endeavors is that they represent camouflaged campaigns to short-circuit long-established procedures for public financing of state facilities. Mullen and her colleagues, who tend to be admirably fair-minded in their review of prison privatization, reserve their most critical language for such private construction plans. They note that they allow jurisdictions to "evade debt limits" (p. 9) and point out that "debt limitations and referenda requirements are intended to have more than cosmetic value in regulating [public] expenditures" (p. 90).

In many ways, lease/purchase arrangements depend on favorable tax laws. As Mullen et al. (1985: 38) note: "The tax shield afforded by energy and investment tax credits, accelerated depreciation charges, and interest paid on borrowings may be more valuable to the lessor [that is, the private prison construction organization] than the asset itself." In the final analysis, though, through its tax bills, the public always pays the cost of the prison facility. With lease/purchase it never adequately comes to appreciate this. The movement toward private financing of penal facilities, however expedient for beleaguered public jurisdictions it may be, seems the least defensible of the new developments.

Operation of Penal Facilities

Less movement toward privatization has occurred here than in the other two areas, although this realm represents the key element of any drive toward privatization in the correctional world. It also is the issue around which the most intense dispute centers.

Table 6.1 provides a comprehensive portrait of facilities throughout the country that now are or are scheduled to come under private management. The RCA facility in Weaversville, Pennsylvania, the first private program, dates back to 1975, when the company established a 20-bed, high-security, dormitory-style training school. It was another seven years before a second exemplar arose. The Okeechobee School for Boys, located in south-central Florida, is generally regarded as the most important testing ground to date for the principle of privatization, although it deals with juveniles, not adults. The Eckerd Foundation, which operates the facility, is the nonprofit arm of the Eckerd Corporation, a drug-manufacturing firm. Eckerd took over when the state of Florida was contemplating closing the Okeechobee facility because it was run down. The 1983 operations budget was $4.8 million, while the educational budget was $1.1 million. Most of the residents are regarded as tough juvenile offenders; they remain in the facility an average of six months.

Mullen and her colleagues (1985) note that Eckerd rehired the former superintendent, but that about half the staff elected to remain employees of the state and transfer elsewhere. At first, Eckerd decided to reduce the staff, while increasing efficiency, but the facility now has more employees than it did when the state ran it. Eckerd clearly has increased the range of training programs, and it claims to have done so while operating for $600,000 less than the cost at the state's other training schools. New staffing patterns, which eliminated high-priced persons doing low supervisory level work, and which transferred medical personnel to on-staff status, are said to have contributed to reduced costs. At the same time, the Foundation put $250,000 of its own funds into the operation (Mullen et al. 1985).

The American Correctional Association (ACA) in College Park, Maryland, has been responsible for a comprehensive evaluation of the Eckerd Foundation work. The ACA report, prepared by Robert Levinson, a special projects director, has not yet been released by the National Institute of Corrections, but a senior ACA official agreed to share some of the

TABLE 6.1
Summary of Privately Contracted Penal Facilities

Public agency	Private contractor	Facility	Cost ($/yr/inmate)
State of Pennsylvania	RCA	Heavy security training school for delinquents, Weaversville; 20 beds; 1975	40,000
State of Florida	Eckerd Foundation	Okeechobee School for Boys; secure; 425 beds; 1982	14,588 (based on $6.2m/yr, total)
INS	Behavioral Systems Southwest	Detention centers for illegal aliens in AZ, CA, CO (proposed: NM); 350 beds; 1983	5,110 (based on $14/day)
INS	Corrections Corporation of America (CCA)	Detention center for illegal aliens, Houston; 350 beds; 1984	8,670 (based on $24/day); covers construction ($5m) and operation
Hamilton Co., Tennessee	CCA	Medium security corrections facility; 250 beds; 1984	7,665 (based on $21/day); includes $1m renovation
U.S. Bureau of Prisons	Palo Duro Private Detention Services	Medium security prison for convicted immigration offenders; 575 beds; 1984	16,425 (based on $45/day)
Counties in WY, TX; CO, NM	Southwest Detention Facilities	Jails owned and run in TX, WY; negotiating same for CO, NM	19,710 (based on $54/day)
U.S. Bureau of Prisons	Eclectic Communications, Inc.	Prison for youthful offenders; near San Francisco; 1983	—
INS	CCA	(Contracted) alien detention facilities; 175 + beds; 1985	10,585 (based on $29/day)
—	Buckingham Security Ltd.	(Planned) maximum security prison near Pittsburgh; 720 beds	24,000 covers $15m construction
U.S. Bureau of Prisons, Fayetteville Co., NC	CCA	Community treatment	18-20 persons, $29.99 per day
Bay County, FL	CCA	County jail	Approx. 220 inmates at $24 per day
Kentucky	?	200-bed community correctional facility	Contract pending, due early 1986

Source: Logan and Rausch 1985: 309, updated.

major findings for this chapter. Eckerd, he said, had taken over the facility more as a venture in philanthropy than as an effort to make money. As time went on, it became increasingly evident to Eckerd that "just because you treat kids good they will not act good." Facility employees were described as "restless and apprehensive." Balking at longer shifts on fewer working days, they had forced the company to abandon the plan. It was not that they distrusted Eckerd, which was said to be a good employer, but they preferred a "stable" environment. "The state of Florida is going to be around for a long time; they were less certain about Eckerd."

In terms of cost, the ACA evaluation concluded that the operation "did not show great savings or more expenditures." Eckerd, it was said, seemed to be doing a job that was "really no better, no worse" than anybody else's. "There are good public facilities and good private ones. We went into this evaluation with a slight bias toward privatization but, if this can be taken as a true example, privatization will not prove a panacea" (Logan and Rauch 1985).

Detention facilities operated under private auspices by contract with the Immigration and Naturalization Service (INS) represent the most prominent and seemingly successful of various privatization efforts. They service somewhat less than half of the total number of illegal aliens apprehended by the INS, and usually house them for less than a week while they are processed for return to their own countries. In Pasadena, California, for instance, Behavioral Systems Southwest took over a former convalescent home and now holds a daily population of about 125 aliens. Previously, at three times the cost, the aliens had been kept in the Los Angeles County jail, and families had been separated. Now parents and children are housed together in the Pasadena facility.

An earlier INS use of a private company in Houston to detain stowaways provided one of the few court considerations of an aspect of privatization. Danner Inc.'s primary business was transporting crew members and freight to and from the docks. It also provided security for ships in the port of Houston, and it maintained a two-cell detention facility. In late January 1981, the captain of the *Cartagena de Indios* notified INS that he had 26 Colombian stowaways aboard his vessel. They were taken ashore, and the first night 16 of them were placed in a city jail. After that, however, they were transferred to the Danner facility, where all 16 were put into a single windowless 12′ by 20′ cell designed to hold a maximum of six persons. Two days later, some of the men tried to escape while an untrained guard was taking a telephone call. When he caught them, the guard used his shotgun as a prod; it went off, killing one person and wounding another (*Medina v. O'Neill* 1982, 1984; Tolchin 1985a).

On behalf of the victims, the American Civil Liberties Union sought damages as well as a ruling that "in allowing plaintiffs to be placed in a private detention center defendants violated plaintiffs' rights as secured by the 5th Amendment to the United States Constitution." Chief Judge John Singleton of the Houston Division of the U.S. District Court ruled, among other things, that illegal aliens are entitled to constitutional rights, that their detention by Danner clearly rendered government agents liable if such rights had been violated, and that those rights had indeed been violated (*Medina v. O'Neill* 1984: 104; cf. Becker and Stanley 1985). The court quoted a recent affirmation that "the relevant question is not simply whether a private group is serving a 'public function'. . . the question is whether the function performed has traditionally been the exclusive prerogative of the state" (*Rendell-Baker v. Kuhn* 1982).

Ultimately, Danner had to pay substantial damages. But the court did not accede to the plaintiffs' argument that the INS did not have the constitutional right to contract with private groups for detention of aliens. Indeed, it implicitly rejected that argument at several points in the decision. For its part, the INS, to deal with the more than 1.2 million aliens it annually apprehends, plans additional privately run facilities in Las Vegas, Phoenix, and San Francisco, as well as Laredo and El Paso, Texas.

Stefan Presser, the ACLU's *Medina* attorney, indicated in a brief telephone interview that privatization represented "a morally repugnant practice." On the facts of the Houston case alone, however, it seems impossible to support such a conclusion. As noted earlier in this chapter, inmates are often killed or injured in correctional facilities. The important question is whether this is more or less likely to happen in privately run facilities; a definitive judgment should not be based on a single instance. It is also possible that, although far from adequate recompense for death or injury, the ability to collect damages may be easier when a facility is privately operated than when it can seek cover under the (now much limited) doctrine of sovereign immunity.

On another INS front, the San Francisco Lawyers Committee for Urban Affairs has filed a lawsuit on behalf of the Committee of Central American Refugees, challenging INS transfer policies. The suit maintains that aliens often are sent away from their local communities, where they have ties and access to free legal counsel, to remote detention centers (Silverman et al. 1985; Tafoya 1985). If successful, a suit such as this might well prompt the INS toward further privatization in order to provide a wider array of facilities in local communities and to be able to open and shut such operations rapidly and as needed.

The fifth facility noted in Table 6.1, CCA's medium-security jail in Hamilton County, Tennessee, also has been in the news recently. The modern Silverdale Detention Center has a diverse complement of prisoners serving long murder terms, short misdemeanor sentences, and mandatory 48-hour drunken-driving sentences.

Difficulties arose when there was a boom in the facility's population. Before CCA took over its management in the fall of 1984, it had cost the county about $24 a day for each prisoner, with a normal population of about 250. CCA contracted to do the job for $21 per person. When the population rose, to everyone's surprise, to about 300 persons, the cost to the county ran in excess of $200,000 more than it had anticipated. County officials maintained that the additional inmates should have cost only $5 a person, since the overhead expenses remained fixed. But they were paying CCA $21 under their contract. The county seemed inclined to blame its lack of foresight when negotiating the contract with CCA for the cost overrun. Meanwhile, prisoners were being accommodated with double-decker bunks, and CCA was offering to take over the construction and management of a new $1.5 million facility to handle what was anticipated to be a continuously growing population (Tolchin 1985d).

Two important observations are essential to any summary of developments in the private management of correctional facilities. First, there has been a dramatic recent increase in this sphere, even though only an exceedingly small proportion of the nation's facilities are under private management. Second, the kind of facilities run by private organizations to date tend to be peripheral to the mainstream of correctional work. They are apt to be small and to handle short-termers, juveniles, or aliens.

In addition, as the table illustrates, a handful of organizations dominate the privatization field in corrections. By far the most active, in alphabetical order, are: Behavioral Systems Southwest (Pomona, CA); Buckingham Security, Ltd. (Lewisburg, PA); Correctional Corporation of America (Nashville, TN); and the National Corrections Corp. (Denver, CO). Unless a number of other firms enter the field, some of the competitive advantages claimed for privatization will be lost.

CONCLUSION

The privatization movement in corrections rests on two basic facts: The public demands protection from crime, yet it is chronically unwilling to pay the high price necessary to warehouse convicted criminals. Studies indicate that present incarceration policies fail to rehabilitate criminals (Lipton et al. 1975), and they often do not succeed in keeping them quiescent. Inmates rebel against what they see as repressive prison conditions and turn institutions into cauldrons of violence and destruction.

This situation has been vital to the emergence of actual and planned private prisons in the United States. The key question, though, cannot truly be answered at the moment: How likely is the new, private-sector approach to reduce costs, placate inmates, cut crime rates, and calm public concerns and fears? On the basis of slim evidence, it does not seem likely that privatization will prove a panacea. At the same time, privatization can become more than a mere placebo; it could inject vitality and imagination into a situation that through the centuries has been notoriously leaden and inadequate.

At the moment, correctional privatization is a tentative and barely nascent movement. It remains unclear how far the process will proceed. Fortuitous circumstances can have incalculable consequences. A dramatic prison riot, as in Tennessee, can focus public and political attention on privatization as a reasonable alternative. Conversely, a catastrophe in a privately run facility (and inevitably there will be some) could irremediably crush the hopes of those who support privatization.

There is no question but that a private presence in prison industries offers strong advantages, and except for the unions, which will have to be conciliated, there is no deeply entrenched opposition to such developments. Conservatives like to see prisoners working and paying for their keep, and liberals favor marketplace wages and meaningful job training and experience.

The involvement of private enterprise in construction arrangements, such as through lease/purchase, seems more questionable. These usually represent roundabout maneuvers to achieve what cannot be realized in a manner set out by law, through referenda, and with bond issues responsive to jurisdictional debt ceilings. If private efforts are to go forward in this arena, it must be only after thorough public and legislative scrutiny.

Privatization has made some small but significant inroads on the margins of the management of correctional enterprises. The Immigration and Naturalization Service's situation is ideal for private contracting. The INS flow of "customers" is apt to be erratic, and it behooves the agency to avoid long-term investments in facilities and in custodial and service personnel.

Specialized facilities would seem to have a strong likelihood of meshing well with the privatization movement because they call for a unique kind of expertise and deal with a delimited, well-defined clientele. But the much-publicized project of the Buckingham Corporation to construct a $20 billion, 715-cell facility for child molesters and similar offenders remains stalled. It had been planned for North Sewicky Township, Beaver County, Pennsylvania, and would have housed protective custody inmates from a cordon of Eastern states. A similar facility was to have been built by Buckingham in Gooding, Idaho, for the Western states. However, "hundreds of angry residents stormed the town hall in protest" ("Public Service" 1986), wanting to know, among other things, who would be responsible for chasing down escapees. Buckingham's answer, that the task would fall to regular law enforcement officers, did not altogether calm fears, and there was no way to respond to objections that a multi-state prison population would involve importation of offenders from other jurisdictions. The entire issue of the public's opposition to facilities being located in any area remains a difficult one; at the moment, it is arguable whether private or governmental groups would be most effective in dealing effectively with such resistance.

How deeply will privatization be able to penetrate the hard core of state prison operations? The wretched conditions of these facilities clearly favor such a development. Once (or if) some comprehensive programs are launched at the state prison level, it will become possible to judge points that are often pressed in favor of or in opposition to prison privatization. At the moment, the best that can be done is to set forth a plateful of items that will need descriptive and empirical attention before a satisfactory verdict can be returned.

These are some of the points made by opponents to privatization:

- Operating costs eventually will rise beyond those of government prisons because, once entrenched, corporations will prove difficult, if not impossible, to dislodge and will be able to write their own ticket. This will be particularly true because there are so few competitors in the field.
- Monitoring private operations will add heavy and hidden costs for the government.
- Privately employed persons are not acceptable for the work of classifying and controlling inmates.
- Privatization will make correctional work less visible to the public, because business firms traditionally use their resources to avoid careful scrutiny of what they do.
- Privatization violates fundamental constitutional rights.
- Private corporations, once in the field, will generate great political and public pressures to feather their own correctional nests, primarily by pushing for more incarceration and longer sentences.
- Private organizations will be loath to parole deserving inmates because they would stand to lose money.
- Reduced costs, if any, will mostly be realized by use of part-time employees and decreased pension and other employee benefits; this is regarded by some as exploitation and a form of union-busting.

On the other side of the issue, there are those who are persuaded that privatization is the only sensible course to take. They argue, minimally, that public efforts have been a dismal, long-time failure and that new arrangements are overdue. In addition, they claim that:

- Private facilities will be more efficient, because it is in their own self-interest to do a good job.

- They will reduce recidivism because they will have a motive to show results. Ted Nissen, director of Behavioral Systems Southwest, has maintained that he would be willing to have his contracts canceled if he couldn't bring down repetition of crime by those released from a facility his group operates to at least ten percent what it was under public operation.
- Private management will bring into corrections, which is now a back-alley enterprise, new faces and techniques and a spirit that will revitalize the work.
- The clout of businesspeople will enable them to advance the cause of corrections with the public and with legislative bodies.
- By eliminating civil service roadblocks, private managers will be able to hire and use personnel more effectively.
- Costs will be reduced. Proponents cite, for instance, the case of the Bay County Jail in Florida. The sheriff's proposed yearly budget for operating the jail was $3.2 million, but after soliciting bids and receiving nine offers, the county commission was able to let its contract to CCA for $2.5 million (Clendinen 1985).
- Costs will be fixed so that states will not be plagued with constant fiscal emergencies.
- Overcrowding, a chronic correctional problem, will be avoided because private operations will not allow themselves to be pushed into potentially explosive and self-defeating situations.

Kenneth Schoen (1985), a former director of the Minnesota correctional system is among the privatization critics:

> Private prison operators will work the crime trends both ways. Any drops in the crime rate will be attributed to long prison sentences. An increase will add weight to the call for more prisons. And the taxpayers will finance the profit-makers while double-locking their doors at night.

Others adopt a more wait-and-see attitude. Norman Carlson, director of the federal Bureau of Prisons, says, "It's not going to solve our problems. But we ought to go ahead and look at it" (Tolchin 1985a). Similarly, Abner Mikva, a judge on the U.S. Court of Appeals in Washington, D.C., argues, "When you're dealing with people's problems, you ought to look at all conceivable ways to solve them" (Tolchin 1985a).

Finally, there are those more staunchly pro-privatization. Philip E. Fixler, Jr. (1984), director of the Reason Foundation's Local Government Center, puts his argument this way:

> Private companies have proven their capabilities by first providing housekeeping and support services, such as prisoner medical care and transport, then progressing to halfway houses, detention centers, and now accepting responsibility for operating high-security facilities, and soon prisons themselves. It would be unfortunate indeed if unprogressive forces of the status quo were able to arrest the privatization solution.

Senator Arlen Specter of Pennsylvania has called private corrections "the major unexamined new social policy of the 1980s" (Tolchin 1985a). This chapter has attempted to reduce this inattention and to set forth in some detail developments and discussions of the prison privatization movement.

REFERENCES

Auerbach, B. 1982. "New Prison Industries Legislation: The Private Sector Re-Enters the Field." *Prison Journal* 62: 25–35.

Bartlett, K. 1985. "Privately Run Prison Mixes Strictness, Homey Comforts." *Orange County (CA) Register* (AP), May 12, pp. F1–2.

Becker, C. and A. D. Stanley. 1985. "The Downside of Private Prisons." *Nation*, June 15, pp. 728–29.

Bellamy, J. 1979. *The Tudor Law of Treason: An Introduction* (London: Routledge & Kegan Paul).

Clarkson, L. 1975. *Death, Disease and Famine in Pre-Industrial England* (New York: St. Martin's).

Clendinen, D. 1985. "Officials of Counties Discuss Private Operation of the Jails." *New York Times*, November 14.

Cory, B. and S. Gettinger. 1984. *Time to Build? The Realities of Prison Construction* (New York: Edna McConnell Clark Foundation).

Cullen, F. T. and L. F. Travis III. 1984. "Work As an Avenue of Prison Reform." *New England Journal on Criminal and Civil Confinement* 10: 45–64.

England, R. W. 1955. *Prison Labour* (New York: United Nations Department of Economic and Social Affairs).

Fixler, P. E., Jr. 1984. "Behind Bars We Find an Enterprise Zone." *Wall Street Journal*, November 29.

Fox, V. 1977. *Introduction to Corrections* (Englewood Cliffs, NJ: Prentice-Hall).

"From Over Prison Walls: Inmates May Be Taking Your Reservations." 1985. *Wall Street Journal*, November 12.

Geis, G. 1968. "The Right to Vote for Prisoners." *Presidio* 35 (July–August): 9–10.

Giertz, F. and P. F. Nardulli. 1985. "Prison Overcrowding." *Public Choice* 46: 71–78.

"A Good Way to Do Bad Time." 1985. (Phoenix, AZ: Best Western International Corporation Communication Department).

"Governor Offers Plan for Prisons." 1985. *New York Times* (AP), September 18.

Hale, M. 1976. *The Prerogatives of the King*. Edited by D. E. C. Yale (London: Selden Society).

Hoskins, W. A. 1976–77. "An Analysis of the Questions of County Jail Reform in Kentucky." *Kentucky Law Journal* 65: 130–67.

Irwin, J. 1985. *The Jail: Managing the Underclass in American Society* (Berkeley, CA: University of California Press).

Lipton, D., R. Martinson, and J. Wilks. 1975. *The Effectiveness of Correctional Treatment: A Survey of Treatment Evaluation Studies* (New York: Praeger).

Logan, C. H. and S. P. Rausch. 1985. "Punish and Profit: The Emergence of Private Enterprise Prisons." *Justice Quarterly* 2: 303–18.

"Mayhem in the Cell Blocks." 1985. *Time*, August 12, p. 20.

McConville, S., ed. 1985. "Our Crowded Prisons" (symposium). *Annals of the American Academy of Political and Social Science* 478.

Medina v. O'Neill. 1982. "Plaintiffs' Motion for Partial Summary Judgment against All Federal Defendants." *Civil Actions no. H-81-2928 and 3242* (Houston, TX: Southern District of Texas, U.S. District Court).

Medina v. O'Neill. 1984. *589 F. Suppl. 1028*.

Mullen, J. 1985. "Corrections and the Private Sector." *NIJ Reports*, May, pp. 2–7.

Mullen, J., K. J. Chabotar, and D. M. Carrow. 1985. *The Privatization of Corrections* (Washington, D.C.: National Institute of Justice, U.S. Department of Justice).

"Prison Overcrowding" (special symposium). 1984. *University of Illinois Law Forum*, pp. 203–421.

"Prisoners in 1984." 1985. *Bureau of Justice Statistics, Bulletin* (April).

"Public Service, Private Profits." 1986. *Time*, February 10, pp. 64–66.

Rendell-Baker v. Kuhn. 1982. *457 U.S. 830*.

Robertson, J. A., ed. 1974. *Rough Justice: Perspectives on Lower Criminals Courts* (Boston, MA: Little, Brown).

Schoen, K. F. 1985. "Private Prison Operators." *New York Times*, March 28.

Silverman, M., and R. Rubin, and I. Bau. 1985. "Committee of Central American Refugees v. Immigration and Naturalization Service: A Challenge to the Transfer of Refugees to Remote Detention Facilities." *Immigration Newsletter* 14 (August): 8–10.

Smith, D. 1960. *Police Systems in the United States*, 2nd ed. (New York: Harper & Row).

Sykes, G. 1958. *Society of Captives* (Princeton, NJ: Princeton University Press).

Tafoya, F. 1985. "Immigration, Detention and Public Policy." *Jericho* 39: 1,4.

Tolchin, M. 1985a. "As Privately Owned Prisons Increase, So Do Their Critics." *New York Times*, February 11.

———. 1985b. "Private Concern Makes Offer to Run Tennessee's Prisons." *New York Times*, September 12.

———. 1985c. "Private Operation of Prisons Debated." *New York Times*, September 19.

———. 1985d. "Privately Operated Prison in Tennessee Reports $200,000 in Cost Overruns." *New York Times*, May 21.

7

The Realities of "Profitization" and Privatization in the Nonprofit Sector

Robert P. Corman

If you look honestly about you, . . . you may come to share my belief that the service motive is at least as powerful as the desire for profit or power.

Richard C. Cornuelle
Reclaiming the American Dream (1965)

AN ORIENTATION TO NONPROFITS

The depth and breadth of the nonprofit sector[1] positions it to play key roles in the privatization of public services. Various nonprofit organizations will observe, monitor, participate in, criticize, challenge, and/or ignore the activities that mark the trend. This chapter will offer a perspective on the nonprofits' role in and reaction to the changing relationship among government, the private sector, and nonprofit corporations. Privatization of public services, defined in terms of private business involvement in the public-needs market, is an important component of a new and developing balance.

Many essential public services, now the targets for privatization, once lay in the province of the private nonprofit sector. That sector has exemplified the community spirit of America longer than either government or business. Consider Tocqueville's (1840) well-known characterization of this feature of our history:

> The Americans make associations to give entertainments, to found seminaries, to build inns, to construct churches, to diffuse books, to send missionaries to the antipodes; in this manner they found hospitals, prisons and schools. . . . Whenever at the head of some new undertaking you see the government in France, or a man or rank in England, in the United States you will be sure to find an association.

Such associations are so deeply entwined in the welfare of the American community that their activities now cut a huge swath across our social, educational, cultural, scientific, economic, and religious landscape. For most of our history, these voluntary agencies "cornered the public service market." It is little remembered (by anyone, including nonprofits) that government entered this market long after voluntary agencies (with the obvious exception of prisons). The Depression first and then the "Great Society" of the 1960s altered this course.

In 1915 and 1961, two commissions, for different reasons, addressed the proportions of public needs satisfied by the efforts of nonprofits and government. In the process, they pointed up the interesting historical reversal that took place between those two years. In 1915, Congress' Walsh Commission encouraged the ongoing "monopoly in welfare services" by nonprofits. The 1961 commission, funded by the Rockefeller Foundation, signaled a broadening of governmental service delivery: "An *ad hoc* commission on voluntary welfare agencies . . . wrote the new case for a public service cartel—this time with the independent agencies reduced to limited subsidiaries of government: 'It is important for voluntary agencies to recognize that they are allies, not competitors [with government] in providing . . . health and welfare services. It is important . . . that voluntary agencies not be used as a means to oppose the development of government services'" (Cornuelle 1965: 67–68). It was not long before government became the senior partner in the delivery of public services.

The pendulum is now swinging back, and it can be said that much of the government delivery of public service that is now becoming "privatized" is more of a "re-privatization," especially in the area of human services. The difference is that for-profit corporations are now joining in, both as entrepreneurs and as champions of privatization.

An interesting example of the latter is the Alpha Center for Public/Private Initiatives, Inc., a nonprofit established by corporations to promote the privatization of human services via new businesses and for-profit subsidiaries of nonprofit corporations (both the president of Control Data, Robert M. Price, and the former senior partner at Goldman Sachs, John C. Whitehead, now Undersecretary of State, were founding board members of the Alpha Center). With plans to set up a for-profit venture capital fund to help pursue this goal, Alpha's prospectus (*Pragmatic Visions* 1985: 2) captures well the attitude of the founding corporations:

> For decades, we have assumed that solving America's social problems entails an endless one-way flow of resources. We have characterized these problems (e.g., unemployment, crime, alcohol and drug abuse) as bottomless pits into which we pour billions of public and private dollars, with little hope of a return on the "investment." Often, it seems the best

we can expect from our human services sector is to maintain an uneasy status quo.

What would happen if we changed our expectations?

Nonprofit Corporate Motivations

As national, state, and local corporations, nonprofits have traditionally operated in a marketplace not attractive to profit-seeking companies. In doing so, they added a rarely acknowledged breadth to the phrase "corporate America."

Both nonprofit and for-profit corporations engage in a diverse span of activities. Both have boards of trustees. And both may legally buy and sell assets, borrow, earn and spend money, and enter into contracts. Increasingly, state laws that govern corporations of both kinds are being structured, wherever possible, to make the activities of the two consistent with each other.

Nevertheless, there is a critical difference. Nonprofits exist first and foremost to serve the public good, not to accumulate capital for private gain. Indeed, they are literally owned by the people of the state in which they are incorporated. Their assets and earnings always remain in the public domain and return to the public when they dissolve. The nonprofits are thus not mandated to give first priority to dividends and capital gains for stockholders; they are obliged to act to maximize public benefit.

Nonprofits also differ from public-sector governmental units. Under contract to government (a form of privatization), many nonprofits deliver services to needy citizens. While they resemble government service deliverers, private citizens are responsible for creating these agencies. Volunteers, not elected politicians, comprise their boards of trustees, which adopt policies, set directions, and select senior personnel.

Nonprofits come into existence when a group of citizens determines that a legal charitable (educational, cultural, etc.) concern exists that requires sustained attention in order to benefit the people of the state, and that that objective can best be met through a nonprofit, tax-exempt corporation.[2]

The nonprofit sector is one of the great assets of the U.S. economy. In his grand call to all sectors to appreciate its role as a third force working with the government and commercial sectors, Cornuelle (1965: 26-27) asserts that this

. . . third force deserves a name. It is a distinct, identifiable part of American life, not just a misty area between commerce and government.

I have come to call it "the independent sector". . . [N]o other word seems to express its unique, intrepid character as well as the word "independent." . . . De Tocqueville saw the American impulse to act independently on the public business as our most remarkable trait. He marveled not so much at our economic success and our political machinery as at our tendency to handle public business directly and spontaneously.

The suggestion is clear that these independent-sector organizations were, and still are, pioneers of our social technology.

In 1983 the vital national organization of nonprofits, the Independent Sector, provided fresh statistical data on the substantial economic stake the nation has in the sector. Hodgkinson and Weitzman (1984: 11) reported that nonprofit corporations contribute 6 percent of the total GNP in the United States.[3] That did not include the enormous in-kind contribution to which it is difficult to assign a dollar value. In New Jersey, more than 9 percent of civilian full-time employment is in the nonprofit community (Lang 1985: 27).

The Many Faces of Nonprofits

Nonprofits vary widely in their origin, size, and methods of securing income. In New Jersey, a full 70 percent of all nonprofits describe themselves as service providers in the areas of health, education, housing/community development, and social services (Lang 1985: 33). Seventy percent of New Jersey nonprofits have annual budgets below $200,000; 80 percent have budgets below $400,000 (Lang 1985: 30).

The bulk of the almost 800,000 nonprofit corporations in the country serve the low- and moderate-income populations, the mentally and physically handicapped, ex-offenders, the elderly, and children.

The larger "establishment" nonprofits were also created by individuals, families, and groups of citizens or religious organizations to provide public services. Hospitals, universities, and private schools are clear examples. Many cultural and arts institutions such as museums and theaters also fall into this category.

Most national, state, and local advocacy organizations have relied on nonprofit structures. They promote a viewpoint that they consider in the public interest, trying to alter current government and, occasionally, private practices or policies. Examples include consumer, environmental, peace, gun control, and housing organizations; child and senior advocacy organizations; abortion and "right to life" groups; and others.

Private nonprofit research organizations that produce and disseminate findings have some of the deepest roots in the history of the independent sector. Think tanks such as Brookings, the Heritage Foundation, and others fall into this category at the national level, and one example at the state level is the Center for Analysis of Public Issues, a New Jersey nonprofit.

Some nonprofit corporations are created by government agencies, especially local ones. Examples include the Newark Economic Development Corporation and the Council on the Environment of New York City. Some state agencies also create autonomous fund-raising organizations to support state programs or to help maintain recreation areas.

In addition, literally thousands of other nonprofit corporations are involved in activities that provide support, friendship, stimulation, entertainment, preservation, enlightenment, self-help, and much more.

Forces Affecting Nonprofits

Both cash[4] and non-cash contributions[5] are insufficient for nonprofits to do their work. Medium-sized and smaller nonprofits in particular are struggling to meet general operating expenses.[6]

The struggle is worsened by the perception common among grant-makers that nonprofits are poorly run. Many corporate givers who want to ensure that their companies' funds are not being wasted pressure nonprofits to improve their organizational and management skills and to establish and upgrade long-range planning procedures. Although this pressure has been intense and largely beneficial, the standards of performance set often exceed those that corporations apply to themselves.

Such pressures, even if taken seriously and acted on in good faith, cannot compensate for the traumatic federal, state, and local budget cutbacks directly and indirectly visited upon the nonprofits in the early 1980s. Costs for operations, rents, insurance, and salaries have been increasing drastically. Nor do these pressures help nonprofits accommodate the changing needs of their agencies' clienteles, competition with other nonprofits, or a host of other challenges. Middle-sized and smaller representatives of the independent sector have come close to losing their ability to respond to the needs of those they have chosen to serve. For most nonprofits, then, the writing is on the wall: Unless they find other sources of revenue, they will go under. Even among those that have managed to secure funds, a combination of their disinterest in becoming too dependent on private sources, a shortfall in dollar needs, and a general desire to become more self-sufficient has produced for them a rather challenging era.

NONPROFITS IN THE MARKETPLACE

The Profitization of the Nonprofit Sector

Alluding to the "intense joy" that comes from "personal involvement," Cornuelle (1965: 61) comfortably risks asserting: "If you look honestly about you, . . . you may come to share my belief that the service motive is at least as powerful as the desire for profit or power." He argues persuasively that, as *the driving force of business is profit,* and as *the driving force of government is political power, the driving force of the independent sector is, indeed, public service.*

The desire of the sector to achieve greater independence, its interest in surviving massive funding cuts, and a fresh acknowledgment by those within the sector that management and financial skills are crucial, have led many nonprofits into the for-profit market. There, through the sale of products and services to a paying market, they are able to generate revenue. While many nonprofits have been competing in the marketplace for years, for the reasons stated, the interest and activity in this option have increased significantly in the last few years. I refer to this business-venturing trend as the "profitization" of the nonprofit sector. Profitization represents a quantum step in maturity for the independent sector, and in turn a time of transition and growth for the American society and economy.

> As a nation grows richer, services which the independent sector once had to supply can be supplied commercially. As their incomes rise, people can pay for more of the services they need. Independent groups should be eager to pass responsibility to the commercial sector and put their own activities on a business basis. People don't resist paying for things they need . . . independent groups now fight to governmentalize their work; they should look for ways to commercialize it. . . . any burden efficiently accepted by commerce is a net gain for the society (Cornuelle 1965: 132).

Profitization is well under way. Particularly among larger and medium-sized nonprofits, which have relied on the traditional sources of funding, some have started business within the framework of their nonprofit organizations, while others have established new nonprofits to run a business whose profits return, to the extent possible, to the parent organization. Still others have launched independent profit-making corporations, and some have even established joint ventures with existing for-profit companies.

Some corporations and foundations have been very actively supportive of these efforts. The businesses launched by nonprofits, often with the support of private-sector dollars, range from the sale of air rights to weather vanes, from bakeries to secretarial services, from energy conservation consultancies to parking lots.

Many of these businesses are clearly not public-needs enterprises. Others are. Early research suggests that 50 percent succeed, which about equals the small-business sector's start-up performance. What is notable here is that some of these ventures represent privatization of public services while others do not.

Privatization

As this trend toward profitization continues in the nonprofit sector, for-profit corporations are embracing privatization. What is motivating businesses to invest privately accumulated capital in markets and activities that have traditionally been monopolized by government (schools, prisons, and other institutions) and the nonprofit sector (day care, health delivery, halfway houses, and so on)? The answer has at least four components:

1. "Corporate social responsibility" is no longer to be considered an oxymoron. Increasingly, corporations are realizing that it makes good sense to invest in the community from which their employees come. Many larger companies are investing even beyond the region that hosts their headquarters or factory. Such activities may well improve both the community and work life in the local setting (which in turn produces corporate benefits in productivity, attractiveness, commitment, and so on) and serve the public relations agenda far beyond the corporate home office.

2. The private sector's view that its expertise is needed now more than ever is motivating some companies to address the "failure" of government to deliver public services in areas such as public education. They may choose to address such failures through their corporate contributions (no. 1 above) or through identifying and filling a gap in the market.

3. For some companies, tax-supported financing of public services ensures a reliable market. It makes good sense to consider that market as part of a diversified portfolio for the corporation. This would suggest a profit-motivated decision rather than a socially conscious interest in a community. Prisons are a fine case in point. Incentives found in federal legislation and regulations also promise subsidies that attract private investment. Examples can be found in youth services and other human services, particularly in Medicare-reimbursement-related businesses.

4. Finally, there are market opportunities independent of government subsidy. Such is the case, for example, in certain health-care industries, child care, and educational services such as software development.

A corporation's choice to do business in a "public benefit" market requires first a business decision like any other: Are the financial risk and effort reasonable relative to the expected level of return? Does the competition seem beatable? Do the regulations and barriers not seem overly imposing? Does the company have the skills and knowledge to succeed in the business? Where the primary decision is a straight "business" choice, as it is in many cases, social consciousness is often an afterthought. The belief that a business concept can compete successfully is enough to make many a private for-profit firm at least explore a business opportunity—even a privatized human service opportunity. Other firms find their prime motivation in the social impact of their business activity. No private firm can ever ignore profits, but it can modify its standards or establish new policies to promote ventures that only indirectly serve the company.

Corporate involvement today ranges from social investment in projects related to public education improvement and correctional reform, to direct prison management and operation, to hospital management and the operation of day-care centers. In some of these markets, government, nonprofits, and for-profits are all involved. Although we see a variety of ways that the business sector is involved in serving "public ends," the question arises: Is it all privatization?

Corporate Involvement in Education: Is This Privatization?

An examination of the effects on nonprofits of the corporate sector's involvement in public education provides an opportunity to make the very important distinction between corporate social philanthropy and privatization.

Recently, corporations have become very active in public education. Education provides them with a great opportunity to reap long-term economic advantages from socially minded activity. Key corporate concerns for the future include: the rise in the percentage of minority children in the urban school population, the high dropout rate, the unequal education opportunities provided, and the resulting declining labor pool. In both non-urban and urban areas, corporations are preparing students now for the workplace's rapidly changing demands, generated largely by new technology and the shift to a service economy.

One of the strongest private-sector actors in the arena of corporate responsibility shows these concerns. Aetna Life and Casualty's Public

Involvement Department produced *Contemporary Issues in Public Education and Opportunities for Corporate Initiatives* (Coolbrith 1985). In the policy statement accompanying this information document, the company clearly states: "Aetna is also a prime beneficiary of a strong public education system."

For Aetna, this translates into many Aetna-sponsored programs designed to help schools to become more effective. Significantly, the publication shows a keen understanding that a high "return on investment" in public schools requires both a partnership with individual schools and delineation of and respect for the separate obligations of the partners.

> Though achieving a true collaboration between business and educational leaders may be a difficult process, it is a vital one. If schools continue to approach business with a "tin cup" mentality, second-guessing corporate interests, they will shut themselves off from the skills and insights true collaboration can bring, as will the private sector if it tries to impose on education a narrowly defined self-interest or business standards of economy and efficiency (Coolbrith 1985: 10).

Coolbrith adds that any corporation interested in exploring ways "to make a responsible difference needs to examine honestly the ways in which its short-term, profit orientation may conflict with the rhythms and goals of education."

Aetna is not alone in pronouncing the importance of public education to the private sector's well-being. For years, the Pittsburgh corporate community has been leading the way in launching innovative private/public-sector collaborative efforts to address many of the region's social and economic ills. One major priority of the Allegheny Conference on Community Development (as the effort is known) is the relationship between corporations and the urban public education system. Using private-sector contributions, the Allegheny Conference established the nonprofit Public Education Foundation, which has cultivated numerous community-based strategies for improving teacher/student effectiveness (Bergholz 1985).[7]

Whatever the method for increasing corporate involvement in public education, the motivation seems most often to be the legitimate, pervasive concern with the competence of the future work force.

It is interesting to note that a number of corporate-inspired efforts (such as the Allegheny Conference) that focus on education have relied on independent nonprofit corporate structures to do their bidding. The nonprofit community provides a vehicle for the broad dissemination of information as well as a viable structure for assisting the corporate community in "getting the message out." This shows a corporate appreciation of the social motivations of not-for-profit corporations. It also suggests a credibility that corporations often acknowledge they lack with the public in areas outside their main business.

Corporate and independent-sector cooperation will probably continue in areas such as education. Their end goals are very much united: a better educated citizen who is more able to participate in the mainstream of the U.S. economy. But these examples of corporate public involvement are *not* the same as privatization of the public education apparatus. In public education, a distinction must be drawn between a motivation based on the long-term interests of the private sector in America's work force and an investment by corporations, large or small, in a promising profit-making opportunity in the public education sphere.

Indeed, there are numerous venture opportunities where for-profits can compete to serve the public school system. Here they may run into competition from the nonprofit sector as well. Examples include counseling services as well as software development and hardware sales. This competition is all to the good.

Nevertheless, at present, school districts, local schools, and government agencies are not selectively promoting privatization of public education as much as they are encouraging corporate involvement to improve public schools.

Criminal Justice Enterprises: True Privatization

In the criminal justice enterprise market, government is the only consumer. The annual costs of maintaining a prisoner in a modern corrections facility[8] (double the tuition for a year at a prestigious college) have prompted corrections officials to seek alternatives. Two main focuses have been the privatization of prisons and increased reliance on community-based alternatives, especially for the nonviolent offender.

Government can reduce its own role in actually operating prisons, but it cannot reduce its role in paying for someone else to do it instead. Short of operating successful prison factories[9] (which cover annual operating costs of the prison and the prison factory), any operator of a prison will require nearly full government subsidization.

For-profit and particularly nonprofit organizations have long been involved in this public service conundrum of prisoner management. Taft (1982) states:

> Private agencies, both profit and non-profit, have had a long and sometimes tempestuous relationship with the court and prisons. According to some historical sources, the first proposal for a halfway house appeared in Massachusetts in 1817; one of the first formal contractual

relationships between public and private agencies has been between New York City and the Society for Reformation of Juvenile Delinquents, which in 1825 leased barracks on Madison Square to run a house of refuge.

It is estimated that in the early 1970s more than a quarter of the juvenile delinquents diverted from public institutions were sent to private agencies (profit and nonprofit). In fact, some states, "including Massachusetts and Florida, passed legislation mandating the use of private vendors as a way to save money" (Taft 1982). Such programs come into and go out of favor. Government reactions to them are rarely in terms of their effectiveness but more in terms of their political acceptability. Nonprofits have been advocating alternatives and pressing the economics issue, since it among all arguments seems to carry some weight in our pro-incarceration society.

The fact is, however, that whether operated by government, profit-making, or nonprofit corporations, the recidivism rate will likely remain the key criterion by which a prison's "success" is measured. Halfway houses represent a good social technology for controlling costs and providing alternatives to prisons in much the same way that home health care helps to keep health-care costs in check. The prison operator, whether government or a private business, will find good reason to rely on halfway houses to wean the offender from the prison setting and prepare him or her to re-enter the community, hopefully to stay.

If state and federal governments conclude that these community-based alternatives continue to make sense economically and politically, then the business opportunity that comes with government subsidization of these community facilities will increasingly create competition for and among nonprofit groups providing such services. This would be a serious challenge only where a clear, long-term commitment is made by the government authority.

The privatization of the half-way house system is a good example of the role nonprofit corporations play in the marketplace. Through their advocacy and pioneering, the nonprofit sector has created a new market that the private sector can now take advantage of. Through their service mission, nonprofit correctional organizations have performed the R&D functions corporations require for entry into a new field.

There are problems in this business, however. Just as a society as a whole may value the benefits of community-based alternatives to prison and of halfway houses, the local community has been opposing the siting of such facilities on the grounds that they are dangerous or that they should be in someone else's neighborhood. Interestingly, in at least two towns, the government itself is fighting the placement of a residential facility for ex-offenders (*New Jersey Association*).

The experience of the nonprofit sector in dealing with communities and offenders should make cooperation between any private prison operator and a community-based nonprofit correction corporation a high priority for any enlightened operator. Nonprofits could even sell services to help prisoners to such a prison management firm. It should be noted that it is much less likely that nonprofits will get into the business of operating and/or building prisons than that for-profits will get into the business of operating halfway houses.

Market forces (the public and the government) will ultimately decide what services will be provided. If there is no support for rehabilitation of ex-offenders, particularly those from low- and moderate-income communities, the marketplace may well be satisfied with a private corrections system judged solely on its ability to operate less expensively than the publicly operated system. In this market, the traditional nonprofit sector would have a limited role. Yet if the marketplace chooses to support rehabilitation, many opportunities exist for collaboration, not competition, between the sectors. The private sector is able to contribute to the collaboration its knowledge of management and operations. The nonprofit sector, which often has roots in the communities from which offenders come, may work through its own range of corporate procedures to develop opportunities for housing, economic advancement, social interactions, and educational skills enhancement.

In any event, no matter who the operator is, the nonprofit advocacy community will continue actively to monitor and study the criminal justice system.

Health-Related Businesses—Expanded Privatization

The nonprofit sector has been providing health care to the public for years (via hospitals, nursing homes, and so on). In doing so, nonprofit hospitals have operated in a market primarily supported by third-party payments (Medicare, Medicaid, Blue Cross, private insurance). These third-party payers are the same income sources that have increasingly attracted for-profit health-care providers on a large scale across the country. At the same time, federal laws and regulations, as well as many reimbursement formulas, are encouraging privatization. These corporations bring management systems and economies of scale that even nonprofit hospitals have found attractive enough to seek via paid management.

In order to survive in this highly competitive and potentially lucrative field, nonprofits are employing a variety of creative strategies. Many nonprofit hospitals have entered into mergers with other nonprofits. This helps them secure more capital, streamline management, and find economies of scale necessary to compete not only with the profit-making health delivery enterprises, but also with other nonprofits.

Nonprofits are also entering into joint ventures with for-profits so that each can take advantage of the other's offerings (perhaps cash will attract nonprofits to the for-profits, and prime nonprofit-hospital-owned land in strong market areas will attract for-profits).

The differences between the two sectors will ultimately matter less than the opportunity they see to collaborate. At the same time as these trends are occurring, a 1986 *New England Journal of Medicine* article (Watt et al. 1986) comparing the efficiencies of for-profit and nonprofit hospitals concluded that for-profit hospitals were costlier, while nonprofit institutions were no less efficient. While for-profit hospitals are fewer by far than nonprofit hospitals, for-profit home-care firms have recently exceeded in number their nonprofit counterparts.

Certainly competition will be rigorous as our health industry continues to appeal to healthier patients who are less expensive to serve and as each sector struggles to find its niche. While Hill-Burton legislation ensures the policy that health institutions give at least a minimum of attention to the poor, it is nonetheless likely that, to the extent that the poor, uninsured, and under-insured are served, they will be served more by government and nonprofit than by for-profit organizations. Studies suggest that for-profit hospitals have taken the same amount of Medicare and Medicaid beneficiaries as nonprofit hospitals (Watt et al. 1986). The real questions relate to who will ultimately serve those not covered by third-party payers.

For-profit and nonprofit hospitals, home-care agencies, and other health-related services all will pay more attention to the bottom line in making decisions. In addressing their competition, they will care very little whether or not they are competing with for-profits or non-profits in their market area. Nonprofits have long competed with other nonprofits in the health arena and will continue to do so, just as they will continue to seek new ways to generate revenues.

(The grant-making community—corporations and nonprofit foundations—which has long supported nonprofit hospitals, has focused substantial attention on these issues recently. In 1986, Grantmakers in Health, a group of national funders, dedicated a program of activities to "The Future of the American Hospital." One of the primary issues this group raised is the extent to which "notions like 'service' and 'community need' become secondary to concepts like 'strategy' and 'market penetration'" [McDermott 1985].)

CONCLUDING OBSERVATIONS

The Public's View of Privatization

The citizen, student, client, consumer, or patient in the American marketplace cares only incidentally about the legal boundaries that separate the three sectors. They will rarely distinguish between the local bakery (private), the local boys' club (nonprofit), and the local library (public); or, on a larger scale, an airline (private), a hospital (nonprofit), and a state university (public). The fact is that the public cares more about choice, quality, price, and equal opportunity than about the sector that provides it.

"Public Business": Competition between Sectors

Largely because of this, and because of forces visited upon nonprofits as well as corporations, competition exists in a variety of places. For instance, nonprofits compete with each other for funding at all times, and in the marketplace even when neither or just one of them is involved in a revenue-generating business venture. There are numerous examples of nonprofits competing with for-profits, regardless of whether either or both are subsidized or whether they are involved in public service business efforts. Finally, nonprofits may in some cases be competing with government agencies.

On a more focused scale, the simultaneous moves toward "profitization" (by nonprofits) and "privatization" (by for-profits) create interesting opportunities for overlap between the sectors. Any attempt to measure the negative or positive effect of privatization of public services on nonprofit entrepreneurial ventures, however, requires that one determine which of the businesses started by nonprofits are simultaneously addressing their own revenue needs *and* public service needs.

The following profit-making ventures, actually started by nonprofits, represent a good sampling of such public service business activity. Here the for-profit sector may find strong competitors: architectural planning, catering, counseling, economic development businesses, employment services, meeting accommodations, laundry services, moving companies, parking lot management, social service planning, renovation/contracting/construction work, school material development, software, secretarial services, and snow removal.

Reactions of the Business Sector

In their reactions to the nonprofit sector, large and small private businesses are hardly uniform. On one hand, the large private-sector corporations (and their foundations) have been supporting the nonprofits not only to enable them to serve the public more effectively, but also to encourage them and even fund their entry into entrepreneurial ventures.

Simultaneously, some in the small-business community have indicted nonprofits for entering into "their" area of business activity. Corporate and private philanthropic supporters of these ventures are, from the standpoint of many in the small-business community, having a negative effect on small-business enterprise.[10] The complaint is that nonprofits have certain tax advantages that smaller businesses do not. This would not apply where a nonprofit creates a for-profit subsidiary to generate revenues. The charge of unfair competition is made regardless of whether the nonprofit is engaged in a traditional marketplace venture or a public-needs business.

One rationale for accepting this competition is that the public interest is served when a nonprofit uses an entrepreneurial venture to stabilize its funding base, especially when the for-profit community has no attraction to the nonprofit's underlying service to the community. If a service is subsidized while a profit-making venture is satisfactorily providing the same service to an equivalent clientele without subsidy, such government funding is at least questionable and probably should not be provided. (Of course, some nonprofit entrepreneurial efforts may just as easily compete with a government-subsidized service.)

The public interest is served by the entry of the for-profit sector into the public-needs areas they have historically avoided. We need a strong independent sector and an expanding business sector that will tap the viable connection between public needs and private gain. There are risks to both, and to the public, that are manifesting themselves in this time of transition. The formulation of sensible policies and practices will take time, and patience is required as we frame new legal and marketplace relationships.

The Province of Nonprofits

Many in the voluntary sector are concerned that, with this attitude, they will be left to serve only the most indigent of society's members, who are also the most difficult to assist. This is a realistic, unavoidable concern, not because nonprofits would not be a valuable presence in the effective delivery of service to the moderate- and middle-income population, but because government regulation and market forces always did and, in my opinion, always will favor the private sector's competitive role in meeting human-service needs of those who can afford to pay.

The nonprofit sector must address its own issues of privatization relative to its own entrepreneurial ventures and the ongoing role of the nonprofit corporation. It is possible that the tax advantages that now benefit nonprofit entrepreneurial ventures may not last. I would risk speculating that nonprofits that spin off for-profit ventures will have much greater success in the long run in meeting human-service needs than nonprofits that operate an entrepreneurial venture within their own structures. Moreover, as has already been the case in many areas, state legislatures and local contract agencies will be hard pressed to permit, without some equalization formula, the public service bidding for contracts by nonprofits, which have tax advantages over for-profit ventures.

Whatever future legislation may bring, it is clear that privatization holds potential, and nonprofits will have to become more aggressive to stay competitive, particularly in human-service delivery. Indeed, in some instances where private business can operate at lower costs and equal effectiveness and efficiency, and achieve public acceptance, the nonprofit may not be needed. This is not something to be regretted, but is purely the maturation of a service area in terms of market attractiveness for private capital.

Competition with the private sector from nonprofits remains desirable if for no other reason than to ensure the maintenance of quality. It is possible to make money and do good, and if this is the case, both nonprofits and for-profits will do the best they can to get into the act. One should also anticipate an increased number of joint ventures between nonprofits and for-profit corporations.

Certainly, some service activities will not prove attractive or marketable for the private sector. Here the nonprofit sector will continue to serve citizens and citizen interests regardless of the arrival of, or trend toward, privatization in other areas. Funding for these types of activities will come in part from government and in part from private grant-making institutions. This is likely to be the case in providing specialized social services to under-politicized constituency groups as well as the grass-roots enterprises that are so important to revitalizing neighborhoods and addressing local public concerns. We will also see this in arts and cultural activities. While the future will witness more efficiency in management and the operation of revenue-generating ventures, these areas will not experience privatization.

Nonprofits Serving Other Sectors

Nonprofit grass-roots groups can actively assist either for-profit or nonprofit corporations working in a particular community. Corporations commonly run into roadblocks erected by concerned local residents who see "outsiders" doing business in their neighborhoods. Indeed, it will become important to the private business sector to understand the community setting better and to establish relationships with the "tone-setters" often found among the local nonprofits. Collaboration with competent grass-roots organizations in hiring workers, gaining public support, and preserving a good public image will remain important to any private-sector business choosing to do public-sector work.

Nonprofits as Watchdogs over Privatization

Nonprofit organizations rely increasingly upon umbrella organizations to serve their segments of the independent sector. Examples include coalitions of day-care centers, youth service organizations, environmental groups, mental health agencies, and even entities to serve all nonprofits. At the national level, we find the Independent Sector, mentioned earlier; the Center for Non-Profit Corporations exists at the state level in New Jersey; the Camden Human Services Coalition in Camden County, New Jersey, exists at the county level; and the Non-Profit Coordinating Committee of New York City serves the agencies of that city. Such agencies are each bound to develop a method to monitor the effects of privatization on their respective constituencies or concerns.

Hospitals and university bookstores have already begun to do so. The increasingly sophisticated skills some of these independent agencies have shown in their influence on state and local policy certainly will be brought to bear on the politics of the privatization process. This is not meant to suggest the inevitability of opposition, but rather the active presence of the advocacy arm of the independent sector.

What will these politically powerful presences be looking for? They will undoubtedly be searching for a handle on what really motivates the private sector to pursue contracts with government, making every effort to determine whether service quality and profit are compatible. They may ask whether the reasons for rising costs are rooted in Civil Service personnel practices, organized labor, purchase procedures, bureaucratic red tape, political corruption, and so on. They may ask whether the saving of tax money by government units through privatization is a better alternative than increasing taxes. This will involve an evaluation of whether government services and public efforts actually require, and if so, are worthy of, a larger investment from the public coffers.

Aside from these questions raised in context with the trend itself, they may look at least as closely at the issues that will emerge should privatization take hold. One key concern will certainly be whether the strategic decisions made by the private sector in allocating its capital to any new business could just as easily lead to withdrawal from an investment. That is, are there "escape clauses" that could leave people suddenly unserved? Citizen monitoring by organizations of these government/private business ventures (subsidized or unsubsidized) will look for contract language that ensures that the public is protected from "service delivery closings." A parallel can be drawn here to the contemporary concern, particularly in older urban areas, with plant closings.

It is safe to say that these umbrella organizations will also take advantage of, and even encourage, public hearings whenever privatization is being seriously considered and where the implications of it are bound to be unusual or serious. Some of the strongest opinions and positions will be advanced by these agencies themselves. All of the above is one way to express the very definite, very clear prospect that a public advocacy component of the nonprofit community will not tolerate privatization without providing its input, criticism, and muscle in the decision-making process.

What motivates these larger nonprofit advocacy groups in this regard is nothing less than their skills and commitment to public service. They do this on behalf of their constituencies and try to reflect their understanding of their respective clienteles. Indeed, it is their very closeness to the community that makes their participation in the discussion of privatization valuable. They have long tried to be sensitive to the needs of their constituencies, and while often faulted for failing to keep their own houses in order, they have not been kept from learning how to articulate a constituency's viewpoint to the public.

Many nonprofits have a wealth of research and understanding of what it takes to work with and for government agencies. As indicated above, they have long been monitoring them, overseeing the public policy process, cooperating with them in joint projects, entering into purchase-of-service contracts, and even suing them as circumstances "require."

Clearly, the nonprofit sector has offered society some of its more important research and development into the social technologies on which we have come to rely. Supported particularly by private philanthropy, it has operated social and scientific laboratories, designed pilot programs, even (in some cases) for the benefit of industry, and it could be argued that they indeed opened up some markets to the private sector by relying on grant-making capital to take the risks that the private entrepreneur or corporation simply would not assume. This no doubt will continue as long as there are independent funders, individuals, or institutions willing to support the imagination and discipline that go into social research and development enterprises.

It would make enormous sense for the government and commercial sectors to acknowledge the richness and importance of the public-service motive that drives the nonprofit sector. Its deep commitment to serve the public without guarantees of financial, technical, or moral support from government or private business has instilled in it a useful appreciation of our political and economic institutions. In turn, the voluntary spirit in the United States has helped ensure the fluidity of the other two sectors as they tested their strengths, limits, and opportunities. As we test privatization's mettle and observe its social consequences, it is imperative that the independent sector be viewed with parity by these counterpart sectors. Both will need advice, seek trust, desire partners, and benefit from criticism, all available in high quality from the nonprofit community. If this dynamic relationship indeed develops, the major issues facing the health and welfare of our citizenry, our environment, and our economy will surely benefit.

NOTES

1. For purposes of this chapter, the "nonprofit sector" comprises those tax-exempt organizations determined by the Internal Revenue Service (IRS) to fall within Section 501(c)(3) of the Internal Revenue Code. This is by far the largest category of nonprofit corporations, but it is only one of the Code's more than 24 categories of tax-exempt organizations.

2. A tax-exempt corporation results when, after the necessary papers and applications have been filed, the IRS determines that the activity that citizens propose to address collectively is an acceptable charitable and legal purpose as described in Section 501(c)(3) of the Internal Revenue Code.

3. The Independent Sector's President, Brian O'Connell, has produced a literary companion to this important data base. His *America's Voluntary Spirit* is a collection of selected writings by persons deeply appreciative of the stake the United States has in its volunteer community.

4. While on the rise, contributions from contracts and grants from government, foundations, corporations, and individuals have not kept up with the current expenditure levels of nonprofits (Hodgkinson and Weitzman 1984: 21-23).

5. The organizational strength of the business world far exceeds that of nearly all foundations, and corporate non-cash giving—donated products, services, and facilities; loaned executives; employee voluntarism; matching gift programs; and program-related investments (below-market-rate loans, grants, or other investments in economically under-financed projects directly of benefit to the larger public need)—is now a key part of a growing number of corporate contribution programs (Mittenthal 1983: 3-13).

6. Hodgkinson and Weitzman (1984) provide ample evidence of the degree to which various components of the nonprofit sector rely on government dollars and contributions from corporations, foundations, and individuals: health services, 43.2 percent; social service agencies, 64.2 percent; civic, social, and fraternal organizations, 61.9 percent; arts and cultural organizations, 86 percent. In each case, the remaining revenues come from such sources as dues, fees, and sales.

7. The Public Education Foundation, formed after a number of years of experimental program development in Pittsburgh and San Francisco, has now exported its Mini-Grant Program of Small Grants for Teachers to over 20 cities in the United States.

8. Estimated at $15-20,000 per year. Prison overcrowding has exacerbated the problem to the point where some county jails housing state prisoners are using the system of *per diem* fees paid to them for the state felons as a new revenue source (Ladd 1985).

9. Relatively common in China and a few other countries (Miller 1982).

10. Foundations in particular have begun supporting nonprofit business ventures with both grants and loans. For example, The Fund for New Jersey, with approximately $20 million in assets, has supported revenue-generating ventures for organizations with little hope of otherwise securing their full operational budgets. These include a loan to a new community foundation for marketing software (developed with federal government assistance) to county government human service agencies, as well as grants to an urban community arts school and a health-law organization to do product and service development respectively. The prospects for competition are strong, but no stronger than the capacity to develop partnerships.

REFERENCES

Bergholz, D. 1985. *The First Two Years—The Public Education Fund, 1983-1985* (Pittsburgh, PA: Public Education Fund).

Coolbrith, A. G. 1985. *Contemporary Issues in Public Education and Opportunities for Corporate Initiatives* (Hartford, CT: Aetna Life & Casualty Foundation).

Cornuelle, R. C. 1965. *Reclaiming the American Dream* (New York: Random House).

Crimmins, J. C. and M. Keil. 1983. *Enterprise in the Nonprofit Sector* (Washington, D.C.: Partners for Livable Places and the Rockefeller Brothers Fund).

de Tocqueville, A. 1840. *Democracy in America*, vol. 2, Second Book, Chapter 5 (thereafter, translation by Henry Reeve, Oxford University Press, London, 1959, p. 376).

Elgin, D. 1981. *Voluntary Simplicity* (New York: Morrow).

Hodgkinson, V. and M. Weitzman. 1984. *Dimensions of the Independent Sector—A Statistical Profile* (Washington, D.C.: Independent Sector).

Investing in Our Children: Business and the Public Schools. 1985. A statement by the Research and Policy Committee of the Committee for Economic Development (New York: Committee for Economic Development).

Jones, B. and J. Laurie. 1985. *An Alternative Approach to Business—Hiring the High Risk Worker* (Denver, CO: Artisan Services).

Ladd, S. 1985. "Passaic Turns a Profit from Overcrowded Jail." *Sunday Star Ledger*, March 3, Section 1, p. 44.

Lang, M. H. 1985. *New Jersey Non-Profit Profile* (Trenton, NJ: Center for Non-Profit Corporations).

McDermott, C. E. 1985. "The Future of the American Hospital: Challenges and Opportunities Facing Health Philanthropy." National Program announcement insert. *GRANTSCENE—A Newsletter for the Health Philanthropy Community* (New York: Grantmakers in Health) 2, no. 2 (December).

Miller, E. E. 1982. "Prison Industries in the People's Republic of China." *Prison Journal* 42, no. 2: 52-57.

Mittenthal, S. 1983. *Non-Cash Corporate Philanthropy: A Report on Current Practices* (Tacoma, WA: Weyerhaeuser Company Foundation).

New Jersey Association on Correction et al. vs. Gupko et al. (On Appeal—Docket L-064702-85) (New Brunswick, NJ, and in Paterson, NJ).

O'Connell, B. 1983. *America's Voluntary Spirit* (New York: The Foundation Center).

Pires, S. A. 1985. *Competition Between the Non-Profit and For-Profit Sectors* (Washington, D.C.: The National Assembly).

Pragmatic Visions. 1985. (New York Alpha Center for Public/Private Initiatives).

Private Sector/Public Services Newsletter. 1985 issues. K. Feider, managing editor (New York: Council on Municipal Performance).

Skloot, E. 1986. *Handbook of Nonprofit Organizations* (New Haven, CT: Yale University Press).

Smith, D. H. and J. Van Til. 1983. *International Perspectives on Voluntary Action Research* (Washington, D.C.: University Press of America).

Taft, P. B., Jr. 1982. "The Fiscal Crisis in Private Corrections." *Corrections Magazine* (December): 27–32.

Watt, J. M., R. Derzon, S. Renn, C. J. Schramm, J. Hahn, and G. Pillari. 1986. "The Comparative Economic Performance of Investor-Owned and Non-Profit Hospitals." *New England Journal of Medicine* 314: 89–96.

8

Strategic Marketing of Social Services

Diane J. Garsombke and Thomas W. Garsombke

The key issue in the privatization of social services is profit. The private sector will seek to compete with or displace government in any service or product where a profit seems likely. It has already done so with mail delivery (Federal Express, United Parcel Service, and so on), hospitals, and even prisons.

Privatization is already a trend on a large scale. How far is it likely to go? The answer is that profit-seeking entrepreneurs try any activity from which they are not barred by law or regulation. They venture into public-service areas that have always been operated and subsidized by government and that therefore lack any history from which to judge potential profitability. Yet they venture only where they think they can find profit.

At the same time, public administrators have long sought more appropriate means for providing public services. The motivations for this search have ranged from elimination of corruption, to making governmental services more responsive and accessible to all people, to achieving greater cost efficiencies. Today, this last motive seems strongest, and it feeds neatly into the claims of the private sector. Yet the private and public sectors are not the same. They differ notably in their major areas of concern. They also differ in the obstacles they face—the demands of other public agencies and voters, and the demands of customers—although they both approach those obstacles with their versions of marketing.

Marketing is an essential aspect of delivering any service or product. It is crucial to privatization for two reasons. First, the entrepreneur who wishes to take over a public service must sell government decision-makers on the idea that he can provide the service efficiently and reliably. Second, he must persuade the public to choose the private version of the service.

Marketing is second nature to the successful private entrepreneur, and it is not entirely a stranger to public-sector managers. But there are crucial and often unrecognized differences between the marketing methods of profit-oriented entrepreneurs and those of service-oriented public agencies. The latter do not have to think about profit when they are trying to make contact with—or serve—their clients. They do have to think about the political context of their services. The private entrepreneur has to think about profit, but he may not be accustomed to the political conflicts that characterize the public-service marketplace.

CONFLICT IN THE MARKETPLACE

Public bureaucracies are so used to political conflicts that they take them for granted and deal with them in set, preprogrammed ways. Even the sharpest confrontations are met with institutionalized responses. Private entrepreneurs who have succeeded in the public-service arena have also learned to cope with the political problems there.

The aim of this chapter is to explain the types of conflicts that occur in the public sector and, in light of these conflicts, to determine why marketing techniques and strategies that are common in the private sector must be adapted to work well in the public arena. Without such adaptations, the differences between the public and private sectors can provide insuperable roadblocks to privatization. It is thus appropriate for a book on privatization to contain some suggestions on how to build on the differences between the two sectors and respond constructively to the inevitable conflicts between them.

What are the special problems faced by the private sector when it steps into the public arena? There are conflicts among external constituencies, conflicts among internal constituencies, limited ability to control revenue generation, and the public relations problem of changing society's view (and expectations) of social services provided by the private sector.

These issues influence considerably the entire nature of marketing in the public sector. They change many aspects of marketing planning, from the distribution system and promotional tools used to the description and pricing of the service. Marketing social services such as health care is not the same as marketing more traditional private-sector products such as hamburgers and TV sets.

CONFLICT OF EXTERNAL CONSTITUENCIES

The consumers of any service or product, private or public, are a varied group, yet they all share a single identity, that of "consumer," or customer. In the private sector, managers need to consider only their needs or desires.

In the public sector, on the other hand, there are other external constituencies as well. They comprise all the various "third parties" that have a voice in the provision of any public service, sponsors, regulators, legislators, funding agencies, and taxpayers. Perhaps unfortunately, these third parties remain very much in the picture when a public service is shifted into the private sector. They then place numerous constraints on the delivery of the service; they may also seek to control the level of profit a private supplier of public services may reap.

The private-sector manager who must market social services must balance the desires, needs, and wants of each of the many constituencies she must serve. The same thing, of course, is true for marketers in the private sector as we have always known it, for they too face constraints of law and regulation. However, in marketing manufactured products and for-profit services, the focus is on the needs, wants, and desires of one external constituency, the consumer.

This difference means that it can be much more complex to initiate a marketing concept in the public sector. We can see how this must work in an example that, while it is not truly public, is not truly private either, for it is a not-for-profit operation funded by both public and private agencies. We are talking about the Boston Symphony Orchestra. The orchestra's market manager must strive to satisfy not only the interests of the orchestra's beneficiaries, concert-goers, and broadcast listeners, but also those of donors and supporters such as foundations and holders of season tickets. He must also counterbalance the goals and values of the enabling publics—the community, government agencies, and the media—with the desires of distributors of the orchestra's services, including broadcasters and schools.

Traditionally, profit-making organizations have been able to concentrate on the needs and wants of the purchasers of their product or service. These people are usually the users of the product as well. But in the marketing of social services, the users and the purchasers are often two separate groups of people. The first group is those served, the users of the service; the second is those elected or appointed officials who pay the bills, and less directly the taxpayers. The differences between these two groups are the root of the conflicts over the type and quality of the service (or product) and the reason why adaptive marketing techniques are crucial.

In publicly subsidized transit systems, managers (public or private) must deal effectively with local government officials as well as transit riders. In this case, the subsidies add the concerns of local authorities to those of the riders. The size of the subsidy is determined by a weighing by public decision-makers of priorities among all the other services for which local government is responsible. The question public officials must ask themselves is what level of subsidy the public treasury can afford and what level of tax support the electorate is willing to provide. From the user's perspective, the transit system should be inexpensive, fast, and reliable, and it should go wherever the user wishes.

Regulators, cognizant of the riders' concerns, are reluctant to grant higher fares. At the same time, local government feels that other demands for funds are more urgent. In the twin competitions for public subsidy and the approval of the voters, transit systems fail to get all the funds they need for upkeep. The system deteriorates severely. The need for money becomes obvious, but now the system seems unworthy of a subsidy and it does not get it. Regulators, forced by obvious need, approve higher fares, but this is not enough. The deterioration continues, while little-used routes are cut and vehicle maintenance is deferred, and fares rise again.

This sad result, so visible in New York, Chicago, and other cities, supposedly balances the needs of funders against those of users, but hardly to anyone's delight. And it is hard to see how to change the outcome. Private entrepreneurs who venture into the politically charged arena of public bus and rail transit, especially within urban areas, need to develop marketing strategies that address all of the active constituencies. With skill and insight they may be able simultaneously to identify and to satisfy everyone's needs, and thus to succeed in finding the profit they need. We hope that this chapter will help.

Not-for-profit organizations such as town libraries, theaters, and symphony orchestras experience a great difference in the marketing techniques that work to attract customers (users) and funding support (comparable to products and revenues for profit-oriented organizations). This is because the constituencies are different. Users and contributors may be the same people, but in their separate roles they respond to different appeals. The problem of motivating people to give money is very different from that of motivating people to use or benefit from an organization's offerings.

Competent managers of not-for-profit organizations know this problem well, and they structure their marketing techniques to match each of their several target constituencies. They tailor their appeals for funds to activate altruistic motives or to offer a benefit in return for a gift. To bring in users, they appeal to the benefit their service holds for this person. With town libraries, for example, the appeal to contributors might say, "Help spread literacy!" while the call for users might say, "Read for fun and profit!" The user appeals may also differ when aimed at children, young adults, housewives, businesspeople, college students, and senior citizens.

Another aspect of external conflict that bears on marketing strategy is the close scrutiny to which public services are routinely subjected. Most public services, including those operated by the private sector (such as nursing homes), are closely regulated and periodically reviewed. The entrepreneur who is considering offering a service that traditionally lies in or is monitored by the public sector should be forewarned that marketing practices that are acceptable—or even taken for granted—in the private sector may be unacceptable or intolerable to the public constituencies associated with the service. For instance, human rights organizations would surely object if a private prison advertised its guards as "Rambo" types, no matter how secure that image might make the public feel. And many people would consider it offensive to advertise a family-planning service with photos of child-abuse cases, or with claims that *"Our* teenagers don't become unwed mothers!"

If the sensitivity to marketing practices is rooted in the standards of the profession involved in the public service, the marketing manager should be aware of this fact and take it into account in choosing a marketing strategy. For example, many medical people feel that comparative advertising and price wars are techniques debasing to their profession. Marketing of medical services thus requires special attention to the breadth of services offered and to professionalism and ethical standards. The marketing manager of any public-service organization should carefully assess the standards of the industry and be sensitive to the political ramifications of any marketing-related plans.

As El-Ansary and Kramer (1977) noted in their discussion of Louisiana's statewide family-planning program, the marketing process can involve many participants. In Louisiana, the funding sources included the community, the church, the Department of Health and Human Services (then HEW), and the Ford Foundation. Other participants included local hospitals, the American Medical Association, and other family-planning advocates such as Planned Parenthood and the March of Dimes. Because of the sensitivities of several of these participants (black leaders raised the question of genocide at the time), the Louisiana program managers took the strategic precaution of avoiding a mass media communications approach to the program's target publics. Instead, they promoted (marketed) their service through personal contact with prospective "customers." This was their way of recognizing and dealing with the external controversy that surrounded the project. Marketing strategies and techniques that take into account significant external conflicts can be the key to profitable, effective privatization of public services.

Hospitals are now reevaluating marketing strategies. Their problem is that they now face numerous consumers who are more knowledgeable and assertive about health-care alternatives. In addition, many employers are actively suggesting to their workers such more cost-efficient services as health maintenance organizations (HMOs) and preferred provider organizations (PPOs). In the past, hospitals have encouraged their staff physicians to hospitalize their patients, even pushing them to use a particular hospital. This "push" strategy is now being replaced (or joined) by a "pull" marketing strategy, whereby the hospitals sell their images and services to patients and employers (Kuraitis 1985).

This strategic shift in the marketing of one social service highlights the importance to marketing of continually monitoring an institution's external constituencies and assessing their changing attitudes toward the institution and its service. In this regard, the marketing manager should take an active, anticipatory stance when planning a social service marketing program. He or she must analyze the trends of constituency power and influence in the industry and strive to predict the forces to which they will give rise. Marketing techniques which, based on current trends, are in place to meet future developments, can lead to more successful private marketing of public services, just as they have led to more successful marketing of private products and services.

CONFLICT OF INTERNAL CONSTITUENCIES

External constituencies are not the only sources of conflict for privatized public services. Every institution, public or private, also has its *internal* constituencies, its managers and employees, and they too have demands that must be met and motivations that must be satisfied. Successful marketing of public services by a private operation therefore requires understanding these internal constituencies.

Motivations

Historically, those entering public organizations have sought security of employment. They have also possessed a higher level of altruism than those in the private sector, according to the *Economist* ("Privatization" 1986). The *Economist's* writer differentiated managers in the public sector from their private-sector counterparts by the altruism of their goals. Public-sector managers want to deliver services regardless of the price, to employ surplus labor and, where necessary, to provide services below cost. Private-sector managers most often see maximization of profits as their highest goal.

This difference in motivation has obvious implications: the key to effective management in either sector is knowing what motivates people and using that knowledge to increase their effectiveness and, ultimately, the quality of service they can deliver. Because of the differences in needs and goals of public and private managers, the private-sector manager of public-sector employees (or of private-sector employees on public missions) may need to vary his or her methods of motivation. There will be times when traditional private-sector methods will be adequate, but at other times, something else will be necessary.

Some companies that sell private versions of public services may find a useful model in Japan. The Japanese private sector has long used long-term job security and participative management as motivational techniques. Japanese employees are included in organizational goal setting and planning and hence are made to feel a part of the organizational "family" for life. Similar methods may be eminently appropriate for companies that represent and serve society as a whole, to which employees already belong for life (Kotler and Fahey 1985).

Some experts argue that the long-term job security inherent in the Japanese approach to motivation is not realistic for U.S. firms. This may be true, for in the new Nissan plant opened in Tennessee last year, the Japanese management substituted as incentives increased job training (both task-related and managerial) and employee participation in goal and strategy setting. They also offered their employees increased salaries, bonuses, a smorgasbord of benefits, and profit sharing, together with training and acculturation techniques designed to enhance employee commitment and loyalty (Cook 1984). In the privatization of the public sector, the guarantee of life-long job security may be neither productive nor practical. Substitutes for this motivational technique may be essential if efficiency and effectiveness are to be promoted.

Changing motivational techniques can transform the organizational culture, climate, and atmosphere. This is precisely what happened in the case of the Houston Metro (the Metropolitan Transit Authority of Harris County, Texas), whose policies had by 1981 led it into serious trouble. Buses were breaking down every 513 miles, the accident rate was four times the national average, and costs were double the national average.

In 1982 the Authority's general manager said, "Houston was at or near the bottom of the pile." Public opinion and community confidence were at their lowest ebb, and that in turn had impaired the employees' morale. To change this situation, Metro management engaged two private consulting firms (McKinsey and Co., Inc., and Daniel J. Edleman, Inc.). The consultants convinced management and labor to hold joint planning meetings to set measurable goals of improving the accident rate, costs, and schedule accuracy. Salaries and bonus plans were tied directly to accomplishing these goals. A public relations program emphasized goal-related improvements as they occurred, focusing on the concept of the "super crew"—the dedicated personnel who came up with innovative plans to make the Metro faster, cleaner, and safer.

As the new program developed, the corporate culture transformed into one that encouraged innovation, outstanding performance, and a sense of pride and identity with the Metro (Kiepper and Baker 1985). In this instance, the change in motivational techniques reversed the negative consequences of previous management policies. This success seems in large part due to the ability of *private*-sector managers to assess the needs and goals of the workers and to choose the incentives and motivational methods that best matched those needs and goals, while creating an organizational culture that built cohesiveness and synergy within the organization.

Resistance to Marketing

Not all the difficulties with internal constituencies have to do with differences in motivation between the public and private sectors. Another problem lies in the simple fact that public-sector managers and employees are not accustomed to "selling" their services and products and may, in fact, be actively antagonistic to the use of formal marketing techniques. When the topic of marketing comes up, they disdainfully say, "We certainly don't want to sell our service like a used car salesman!" If asked, "Do you use personal selling techniques to promote your service?" they may immediately cry, "No!" Private entrepreneurs who are getting into public service areas for profit will surely face this difficulty, for they will have former public employees on their staffs and they will have to deal with public-sector people as regulators and monitors. They may find it useful to point out that the people within any organization serve as public (or external) relations officers, which amounts to the same thing as a personal sales force for the public service.

Some public-sector workers may say, "Well, we may do some personal selling, but we certainly don't advertise. Nor should we!" Yet if the army can advertise for doctors, why shouldn't hospitals do the same? If the Catholic Newman Center found it acceptable to use a Wall Street advertising firm to emphasize the nonmaterialistic lifestyle of possible priesthood candidates, why shouldn't public-service organizations feel free to use appropriate and tastefully done promotional approaches?

Environmental Factors

Outside environmental changes often influence organizations, both private and public, to become more marketing oriented. These factors, all beyond the organization's control, include demographic trends, increasing competition, new waste-disposal regulations, and others. They differ greatly from each other, but they all make it more difficult to deliver products and services at a profit and hence make marketing more obviously necessary.

In any rapidly changing, unstable business environment, there is likely to be a "great deal of innovative marketing" (Peter and Donnelly 1985: 209). In higher education, demographic changes have been forcing just such adaptations. Ever since the decline in the numbers of high-school graduates began in the 1970s, colleges and universities have gotten into the unfamiliar territory of aggressive student recruitment. The more successful institutions in this effort have been those that went all out with professionally developed recruiting programs aimed at the student markets they wished to reach.

Such efforts are marketing efforts. They sell the school to its customers, and they are now much more extensive than the traditional yearly catalog and school-touring recruiter. On most modern campuses, there is a public relations department that endeavors to keep the school's public image bright. There is also a marketing department behind the door labeled "Admissions." The people there perform industry and market research analyses, and the staff—as well as the alumni—are extensive users of personal selling. Modern promotional and advertising techniques are also used more extensively, and in many instances, marketing consultants and advertising firms have been engaged to develop sophisticated marketing programs.

Colleges and universities that understand the need for marketing easily take the next step of expanding the services they offer. In such schools, the curriculum has changed to include more attention to computers, weekend and night courses, current topics courses, and "internship" experiences. Student services such as day care, health care, student clubs, orientation programs, and financial aid packages have also expanded. The result has been a broadening of the appeal of higher education to new groups of students; campuses today have more commuter students, more older students, and more single parents, among others.

Another environmental factor is the rising demand, from legislatures and activists, for healthy living and working conditions. This takes the form of numerous measures designed to protect the world in which people must live. One of these measures has been the outlawing of open-burning dumps and their replacement by sanitary landfills. However, landfills have problems too—one of the greatest is water pollution—and the search for alternatives has provided a number of private companies with opportunities.

One of these companies is Signal Environment Systems (SES). In 1985 it signed a contract to build and operate a 200 ton-per-day refuse-to-energy facility in Claremont, New Hampshire (Nelson-Horchler 1985). The company did *not* have to respond to environmental forces with any special marketing efforts, for the dissatisfaction with landfills had already created a demand for an alternative. What it did have to do was to create a proposal for the alternative and present (market) itself as the best one to implement it. It thus reacted to its environment. A more proactive or anticipatory company might have seen the problems with landfills earlier, devised an alternative solution to the waste disposal problem, and then used marketing to build demand for its services.

The contrast between the reactive and the proactive manager may be especially great when we consider the ways public-service managers accept the need to use the "marketing concept." It is the people of any organization, the managers and employees, who create and implement marketing innovations. The reactive manager, however, sees the need for marketing, innovative or no, only when the organization can no longer insulate itself from environmental changes. In the privatization of the public sector, effective managers anticipate changes in external forces and work toward satisfying the needs and wants of their customers; that is, they plan their service program in light of a total "marketing concept."

LIMITED CONTROL OVER REVENUES

The problems of dealing with external and internal constituencies are likely to consume much of the time, energy, and resources of the private-sector manager of public-sector services. Yet the acid test for success will be the ability to turn a profit. Unfortunately, public-service operations usually have limited control over their revenues. Their budgets are set by government authorities, and the number of customers may be limited by such factors as jurisdictional boundaries. Nevertheless, there are ways for public-sector operations to control expenses, to gain new customers or clients, and even to increase revenues.

Streamlining

When private-sector managers take control of public-sector services, the first step is usually to cut operational expenses—to trim the fat. Nonproductive employees are released, competitive bidding for equipment and supplies is introduced, and expendable tiers of management and staff positions are eliminated.

Do public enterprises really have excess employees? Consider that many cities employ separate construction inspectors for structural safety, electrical and plumbing standards, mechanical systems, and zoning codes. Phoenix, Arizona, has one inspector for all these areas and saves over a million dollars per year (Poole 1980).

After the 1981 air controllers' strike, the FAA gave permission to local authorities for private contracting of air traffic control services. One of these private contractors, Kansas' Midwest Air Traffic Control Services, has been able to cut costs in half, saving $120,000 per year. The secret of its and other contractors' success lay mainly in using fewer controllers and paying them lower wages ($16,000–18,000 versus FAA rates of $24,000–31,000). The FAA says that these private contractors have had an excellent safety record to accompany the savings and plans to increase the use of private contractors in the future (Main 1985).

The federal and state governments have taken another leaf from the private book in the area of overdue loan payments. These "lost" revenues have been costly, amounting to some $21 billion owed by students, businesses, and farmers, but private debt collection agencies have put a sizable dent in the sum and allowed some reduction in staff (Foltz and Hughey 1984; Grover 1984; Holmes 1985).

Recognizing that competitive bidding can lead to "bargain basement" deals that reduce the quality and reliability of services, experienced public officials prefer the "request for proposals" approach or "setting bid standards at higher levels" (Main 1985). They may soon have other options as well, for proposed legislation would let government units contract with private agencies for five years at a time, instead of only one, as at present. Such changes will encourage more private companies to bid for government work; they should work well if they are accompanied by tougher guidelines for the bidding process ("A Plan to Increase Privatization" 1985).

In addition, many public-sector services can save large amounts of money by closing excess or duplicate distribution centers. Several state universities have consolidated campuses in response to declines in enrollments. Wisconsin closed three campuses in its state university system after initiating a "marketing concept" approach and hiring private-sector managers to administer the system. While the initial public outcry in the affected communities was considerable, the savings to the state thoroughly justified the change.

In the long run, the distribution of Wisconsin's educational programs was enhanced as each campus was required to, and did, develop a "distinctive competency" in a particular educational area. Like Kentucky Fried Chicken, the University of Wisconsin Educational System found that it could create more centers of excellence by doing "one thing right" at each campus ("How Academia Is Taking a Lesson from Business" 1984).

Although much excess expense can be trimmed from public-sector programs in the form of facilities, programs, personnel, and equipment, there comes a point where no additional cuts can be made without impairing the quality of the services offered. Here lies the true strength of the private-sector approach to the marketing of public-sector services—the application of the "entrepreneurial mentality."

Marketing

The entrepreneurial mentality focuses not only on internal operations, but also on the external environment. It searches for opportunities outside the organization—opportunities that can affect the system in a positive manner. This proactive approach requires the manager to look to the future, anticipating demands for new products and services and the growth and establishment of new markets.

The proactive manager uses time and resources to assess relevant political, cultural, social, legal, technological, and demographic factors that can affect the revenues of the company. This attention to critical external factors can result in information on which sound planning can be based. For example, new services or products can be developed to respond to discovered needs. In the private sector, this process of monitoring the external world is what market analysis is all about.

Seeking out and developing new markets allows economies of scale that can be exploited to hold and generate more revenue. This in turn can lower the cost of services to the customer and result in greater organizational effectiveness. Businesses that have been successful in providing social services under contract to state and local governments are finding lucrative new market opportunities in other states and municipalities, and even other countries. For example, Waste Management Inc. has grown from a Wisconsin-based firm to a holding company with numerous state subsidiaries, and is fast becoming a multinational conglomerate. Its efficient management and disposal of chemical and solid waste is its trademark ("Trash means Cash" 1983; "Waste Management, Inc" 1985; Main 1985).

There are many similar stories of private businesses that have succeeded in traditional public-service areas. The hospital and health-care industry is one of the fastest growing of all. With the increased competition for health-care dollars and the growing concern of employers about rising costs of health insurance, public hospitals are experiencing a growing need to adopt professional marketing programs to attract both patients and physicians. In addition to staff directors of marketing, hospital management firms, working under contract to public health agencies, have improved the management of public hospitals and other health-care facilities while minimizing costs. With success, these management firms have been able to expand and establish a nationwide role in the health-care industry (Bacas 1986; Marion 1983; Rudnitsky 1983).

Fund Raising

Raising funds from sources other than clients and customers can be an attractive way to bring more revenues into public-service organizations. Likely sources are parties who do not use the service but are involved in the goals and administration of the organization. This is a traditional tactic for foundations, charities, and institutions of higher education, who call it "fund raising." It is not traditional for public-service agencies, but that is no reason why these agencies should not learn to use it.

In California, some public schools are tapping local and national businesses to set up educational funds for developing new programs and services and acquiring new personnel, equipment, and facilities (Smith 1985). These educational funds function as an "endowment"; that is, the schools use only the interest the fund earns, maintaining the principal. While these endowments are presently not large enough to make monumental changes, they are growing and providing a base for future improvements in the California schools. They also set an example, showing how other public-service operations, in either public or private hands, might increase their resources. Fund raising promises to have a significant impact on the operation and management of public-sector services.

THE NEED TO CHANGE SOCIETY'S VIEWPOINT

Many people are accepting the idea that the private sector can effectively manage social services. Yet the prevalent American view is that the dirty, thankless, and supposedly unprofitable jobs must be done by the government. Among these are care of the indigent, warding of criminals, and performance of services for which demand is limited. Government organizations such as symphony orchestras, prisons, and public hospitals furnish society with special services that the private sector could not guarantee. For the performing arts, public-sector control ensures "art for art's sake" rather than only the most profitable performances.

Advocates of government-run prisons often warn of privatization problems. The problems, they say, are likely to include increased security breakdowns due to economy-motivated cuts in staff, or making prisons so comfortable for inmates that they have no incentive to reform and reenter society.

Indigent health care has aroused controversy. Americans feel that indigents should receive necessary care and that government has a duty to furnish the facilities and personnel to provide this care. However, indigents do not always go only to the public facilities that have been established for their benefit. In emergencies, they often show up at private hospitals. A number of deaths have occurred because some of these hospitals have turned indigents away. As a result, public opinion is now pressuring private hospitals and other private-sector health-care facilities to accept indigents (Provan 1984).

The interplay of societal values and public regulation can bring out anomalies. The utilities industry is an example. Increasing regulation and competition have made privately owned utility companies encourage their consumers to reduce energy use and search for alternative energy sources more aggressively than have publicly owned utilities. The reason seems to be that the private utilities feel more keenly regulatory and societal pressures. Public ownership seems to insulate a utility's management from such pressures. Public utilities often are "rewarded not for maximizing the long-term economic well-being of the organization but rather for protecting the organization's political autonomy" (Butler 1984; Wilson and Richardson 1985).

The issue remains: Can society accept a stronger role of private business in the public sector? Or will the skepticism be so great that no matter what private-sector managers accomplish in efficiency and effectiveness, society will condemn their efforts as profiteering and therefore as detrimental to societal values? Or will there be an enlightened acceptance of privatization on its merits? Advocates argue persuasively that privatization will bring to public-services marketing innovation, increased variety and quality of services, lower social service costs, and more efficient delivery of services to better meet customer needs, while keeping regulatory and societal pressures strong enough to minimize user risks, problems of security, and denial of services to indigents.

SUMMARY

We have focused on the private marketing of social services, asking such questions as how marketing must be different in the public-service sector. We have also considered the leading demands on private-sector managers who strive for the effective, profitable marketing of social services.

The marketplace for the privatization of public services is rife with pitfalls for the private-sector manager. These pitfalls include conflict among and between internal and external constituencies, constraints on revenue generation, and confrontations with societal viewpoints. If they are not addressed in the overall marketing and management plan, the very survival of the public-service organization can be threatened.

The private-sector manager must balance the needs of different groups and communicate appropriate promotional messages to each. Yet the marketing techniques that work for one group may not work for another. Unique appeals must be created to satisfy the particular needs of each constituency, each group of "customers."

Careful attention must also be paid to the controversial nature of the service itself. If advertising a sensitive service such as family planning on national television fuels the fires of controversy, then more professional and cautious communications such as one-to-one personal selling and educational approaches may make more sense.

The major issues to be addressed with regard to internal constituencies are the motivational values of managers and workers in public-service organizations. Do their values differ from those of private-sector employees? Can private-sector motivational techniques be successfully substituted for existing public-sector incentives? Can personal and organizational goals, which often seem mutually exclusive, be effectively dovetailed in the privatization of the public sector?

Another problem area for the private manager of a public service is how best to make a profit. Cost-cutting measures are the first line of attack, but a better tactic is likely to be seeking opportunities in the dynamic external environment that can take advantage of the organization's strengths.

The final area of concern to the privatizing manager is the bias that society has against business partnership with government. Social services have been the exclusive purview of public organizations because their values seem more closely aligned with those of society as a whole. Business has been tainted by its pursuit of profit, and the sincerity of business' newfound "social responsibility" is suspect.

REFERENCES

Bacas, H. 1986. "Health Care Costs: Cooling the Fever." *Nation's Business* 74 (January): 68–70.

Butler, S. M. 1984. "Privatization: The Antidote to Budget-Cutting Failures." *USA Today* 113 (July): 22–24.

Cook, J. 1984. "We Started from Ground Zero." *Forbes*, March 12, pp. 98–106.

El-Ansary, A. I. and O. L. Kramer, Jr. 1977. "Social Marketing: The Family Planning Experience." In *Marketing in Private and Public Nonprofit Organizations*, edited by R. M. Gaedeke (Santa Monica, CA: Goodyear), pp. 356–66.

Foltz, K. and A. Hughey. 1984. "It's a Crying Shame." *Newsweek*, December 10, p. 70.

Grover, R. 1984. "The Private War of J. Peter Grace." *Business Week*, November 26, pp. 54–55.

Holmes, P. A. 1985. "Taking Public Services Private." *Nation's Business* 73 (August): 18–24.

"How Academia is Taking a Lesson from Business." 1984. *Business Week*, August 27, pp. 58–60.

Kiepper, A. F. and W. R. Baker. 1985. "Houston Metro's Turnaround." *Management Review* 74 (December): 33–35.

Kotler, P. and L. Fahey. 1985. "The World's Champion Marketers: The Japanese." In *Strategic Management of Multinational Corporations: The Essentials*, edited by H. V. Wortzel and L. H. Wortzel (New York: John Wiley & Sons), pp. 295–306.

Kuraitis, V. T. 1985. "Push vs. Pull Marketing for Hospitals." *Marketing News*, January 18, p. 10.

Main, J. 1985. "When Public Services Go Private." *Fortune*, May 27, pp. 92–100.

Marion, L. 1983. "Prescription for Robust Growth." *Financial World*, March 31, pp. 32–33.

Nelson-Horchler, J. 1985. "CEO 'Privatizes' Himself—and Public Services." *Industry Week*, 225 May 13, pp. 40–41.

Peter, J. P. and J. H. Donnelly, Jr. 1985. *A Preface to Marketing Management*, 3rd ed. (Plano, TX: Business Publications, Inc.).

"A Plan to Increase Privatization." 1985. *Nation's Business* 73 (October): 14.

Poole, R. W., Jr. 1980. *Cutting Back City Hall* (New York: Unicorn Books).

"Privatization: Everybody's Doing It Differently." 1985/1986. *The Economist* 297 (December 21, 1985/January 3, 1986): 71–78.

Provan, K. G. 1985. "Implementation of Effective Management Policies in Not-for-Profit Hospitals." *Academy of Management Proceedings* (45th Annual Meeting, held in San Diego, CA, August 11–14, 1984), pp. 309–313.

Rudnitsky, H. 1983. "Health Care." *Forbes*, January 3, 190–91.

Smith, C. 1985. "Private Help for Public Schools." *Foundation News* 26 (September–October): 42–48.

"Trash Means Cash at Waste Management." 1983. *Sales and Marketing Management*, January 17, pp. 36–38.

"Waste Management, Inc.: Rooney's Garbage Empire." 1985. *Industry Week*, 225 May 13, pp. 79–80.

Wilson, J. Q. and L. Richardson. 1985. "Public Ownership vs. Energy Conservation: A Paradox of Utility Regulation." *Regulation* 9 (September/October): 13–77.

9

Privatization: A Game-Theoretic Analysis

Justin F. Leiber

Game theory is an intellectual X-ray. It reveals the skeletal structure of those social systems where decisions interact, and it reveals, therefore, the essential structure of both conflict and cooperation.

Kenneth Boulding (Rapoport 1966)

Those who favor privatization share an important assumption: that private businesses, spurred by competition and the profit motive and operated with entrepreneurial flexibility and ingenuity, can provide superior goods and services more inexpensively than government. However, it is not difficult to imagine circumstances in which the private sector would be a far less effective and more expensive provider of public services than the public sector. It is therefore crucial that we ask: Under what conditions can privatization fulfill social needs more effectively and cheaply? A related question is how government may best help this privatization to succeed.

Our answers to these questions necessarily hinge on certain other, subsidiary assumptions. One of these assumptions is that consumers can make good judgments about what they need. If we agree with this assumption, as people did in the nineteenth century, when consumers could freely buy opium or indeed any available drug at their local pharmacies, we pursue the absolutely free market. If we do not, we choose to regulate the market, as we do today, when government bans some drugs entirely and restricts most others to physicians' prescriptions.

Another assumption is that consumers can make good judgments about the optimal mix of quality and cheapness. In some cases, we have delegated such decisions to professionals (doctors, lawyers, engineers, and so on) subject to peer and governmental review. In others (the food industry, for example) government requires quality levels, standardized measures, informative labels, and so on.

A third assumption is that the product or service is one that can be supplied to individuals. Yet this assumption too does not always hold. Good air is a basic need, but I cannot pay the local factories enough to make it profitable for them to stop pollution—and if I could pay enough, the air would be made clean for everyone, not just me.

A fourth assumption is that several businesses can compete in supplying a particular product or service. The privatization of our armed forces seems impractical. The notorious inefficiency and overpricing of the armament industry suggests how difficult effective privatization can be when real price competition is nearly impossible to achieve and collusion is both tempting and all too easy.

A fifth and most important assumption is that *cooperation*, rather than *defection*, characterizes the transactions between suppliers and consumers. We assume that supplier and consumer make independent, self-interested judgments: if it makes economic sense, either one may *defect* (deliver faulty goods, fake weights, pass counterfeit money, default on payments). An important role of government is to foster *cooperative* behavior in transactions that will efficiently deliver social goods. Recent game theory has given us an analytical model for understanding how cooperation can evolve among independent, self-interested agents (Axelrod 1984). I shall use this analytic model to indicate both when privatization ought to succeed and how government, as regulator, can foster this success.

PRIVATIZATION—A SLIDING SCALE

Before I lay out the analytic model, two reminders are in order. One is that complete privatization is unrealistic in the vast majority of cases. Another is that our concern with privatization is limited to cases where genuine needs can be better met through private enterprise. We are not concerned with ideological privatization, where the claim is that "needs" that cannot be met through private enterprise and private philanthropy simply cannot and should not be met at all. We shall return to the distinction between pragmatic and ideological justification.

As to the first point, it is difficult to think of any aspect of our economy that is, or should be, totally removed from any government regulation. Our food industry, from farms through retail sales, is thought to be on the whole a triumph of free enterprise. But it is, of course, a thoroughly regulated industry, and much of this arose through well-justified public fears of unregulated food production and marketing. Aside from reciprocal cooperation in sharing chores and entertainment among neighbors and friends, our analytical model will show why complete privatization is impractical.

The food stamp program is a test case for the difference between realistic and ideological privatization. In reality, the food stamp program is an example of relatively successful privatization. Before this program, government provided "surplus food" directly, inefficiently, and ineffectively to the poor. Expensive butter and cheese, a by-product of price support programs and, on the other hand, inedible and unmarketable food products were provided; needs were not well met, although they were papered over.

The food stamp program is a realistic effort to deliver food to the poor through the free enterprise system. Opposition to it flows not from its inefficiency but more from the ideological conviction that the poor will and should find work when the only alternative is starvation.

GAME THEORY: ONE-TIME "PRISONER'S DILEMMA" TRANSACTIONS

Let us ignore for the moment the distinction between supplier and consumer (both provide something of value to the other and both can defect, as opposed to cooperate, in transactions). In our own society, an act of private barter is one close approximation of the situation we are to imagine.

Imagine two players, then. At a particular time they have a transaction, one in which either has a chance to cooperate or defect. Just to fix it in our minds, we will make the situation still more concrete.

Jack and Jill each have something the other wants. At a given time each will place the desired object in a spot known only to the other. Then each will go to make a "pick-up" of the desired object. (The reason why this situation sounds even more like an illegal drug deal than neighborly private barter will soon be clear.)

There are four possible outcomes (payoffs) for this situation: (A) Jack and Jill both leave the appropriate object (both cooperate). (B) Jack does but Jill doesn't (Jack cooperates, Jill defects). (C) Jill does but Jack doesn't (Jill cooperates, but Jack defects). (D) Neither Jill nor Jack leaves the appropriate object (both defect).

As Table 9.1 makes clear, Jack rates the outcomes CADB (his best payoff comes when he "suckers" Jill, second is if they both cooperate, third is if neither cooperates, and the worst is if Jill "suckers" him). Jill rates the outcomes BADC. In other words, from the point of view of either player, the most desirable payoff is to "sucker" the other, next best is cooperation, then mutual defection, and the worst is to be "suckered." (I have put specific dollar payoffs in Table 9.1, but subsequent remarks apply to any situation with this general structure.)

This payoff structure is characteristic of transactions between independent, rationally self-interested individuals. Why? Because it defines the

TABLE 9.1
The Prisoner's Dilemma

| | | *Jill* | |
		Cooperate	*Defect*
	Cooperate	Jack gains $20	Jack loses $10
		Jill gains $20	Jill gains $40
Jack			
	Defect	Jack gains $40	Jack gains $5
		Jill loses $10	Jill gains $5

situation in which both sides would profit from a deal (cooperation is better than mutual defection), but also a situation in which each has some temptation to "cheat" the other. The reason game theorists call it "dilemma" is that individual rationality suggests defection *even though* both would be better off with mutual cooperation.

Look at it from Jack's viewpoint. If he thinks Jill will cooperate, his best strategy is obviously defection, which will give him $40 rather than $20. If he thinks Jill will defect, his best strategy is also defection, which will give him $5, as opposed to a loss of $10. So whichever strategy he thinks Jill will adopt, defection is his best strategy.

Obviously, Jill will reason about the situation in a similar way. So both will defect. But then both will get $5 rather than the $20 which mutual cooperation will bring. Nonetheless, since the formulation of game theory and the prisoner's dilemma in the 1950s, defection has seemed the only rational strategy, for it is a "minimax" strategy, one which maximizes the minimum result (Von Neumann and Morgenstern 1964).

In nonmathematical formulations, recognition of the dilemma of cooperation among rational, selfish individuals is not new. Over two thousand years ago, Plato, in *The Republic*, Book II, suggested that government arises just because rational individuals will defect unless restrained by custom. Similarly, in *Leviathan* I, Chapter 13, Thomas Hobbes writes of

> . . . the time, wherein men live without other security than what their own strength and their own invention shall furnish them. In such condition, there is no place for industry; because the fruit thereof is uncertain: and consequently no culture of the earth; no navigation; no commodious building; no instruments of moving, and removing, such things as require much force; no arts; no letters; no society; and which is worst of all, continual fear, and danger of violent death; and the life of man, solitary, poor, nasty, brutish, and short.

One may find Hobbes' rhethoric or the minimax analysis of the prisoner's dilemma strategy distressing. It seems too bad to be true. Hobbes, of course, concludes that strong laws and a strong central government are necessary. But, as we all know, continual recourse to legal/governmental solutions can be stifling and inefficient. Others might feel that humans, fortunately, are not as rational and selfish as minimax strategy suggests.

Within the last few years, however, a new game-theoretic analysis has arisen, one that shows how cooperation can arise among rational and selfish players in prisoner dilemma situations. Indeed, under this new analysis, it appears that the most rational, self-interested strategy may well be "nice," "provocable," and "forgiving," *provided certain conditions are met* (Axelrod 1984: 27–54). Aside from direct legal enforcement of cooperation, under what conditions will cooperation arise in prisoner's dilemma situations?

GAME THEORY: THE REPEATED PRISONER'S DILEMMA

By this time the astute reader may well want to say, "Perhaps it is rational to defect if it's a one-time deal, but what if it's repeated? Won't Jack and Jill learn to trust each other?"

The answer seems to be that, provided conditions are right, cooperation can evolve if the transaction will recur an *indefinite* number of times, that is, if the players don't know precisely how many interactions they will have. If they do know this, then they will know which transaction is their last. That transaction will then be like a one-time prisoner's dilemma and both, hence, will defect. But then, when the players face their last-but-one transaction, neither will be motivated to cooperate because they know both will defect on the next transaction. Logically, this reasoning, like dominoes, works back to their first interaction (Luce and Raiffa 1957: 94–102). None of this applies, however, if neither player has any clear sense of exactly how many interactions they may eventually have.

Professor Robert Axelrod recently worked out an ingenious way to determine what is the most rational (the highest-scoring) strategy if we imagine many players engaged in an indefinite number of prisoner's dilemma interactions. He induced many expert game theorists to submit strategies (written up as computer programs) as entries in a tournament. The tournament would be won by the program that scored the most points when playing an indefinite number of transactions against all the other programs. While each program had no information about how many transactions it would have with the others, it could, crucially, "remember" how other programs treated it and react to this treatment differentially (Axelrod 1984).

Economists, psychologists, political scientists, sociologists, and mathematicians submitted the 14 tournament programs. The programs greatly varied in length and complexity; many were quite "nasty," in that they would defect in transactions with apparently cooperative programs.

Surprisingly, the shortest, simplest, and nicest program, TIT-FOR-TAT, won the tournament. TIT-FOR-TAT cooperates on the first interaction with any other program (that's the primary reason it's called "nice"). In subsequent transactions, it just copies the previous move of the other program. In other words, if the other program defects, TIT-FOR-TAT defects on the next interaction (that's why we call it "provocable"). But when the other program goes back to cooperation, TIT-FOR-TAT will return cooperation on its next move (so it's "forgiving").

After the first tournament, the results were distributed and a much larger tournament was arranged. Even though the programmers could plan against TIT-FOR-TAT's strategy, nonetheless TIT-FOR-TAT won again. By this time of course there were many more "nice" programs because the "nasties" had fared badly in the first round, so TIT-FOR-TAT showed it could function with very different competitors.

The primary reasons for TIT-FOR-TAT's success seem to be that it is willing to take risks for cooperation, that it cannot be heavily exploited by "nasties," and that it is easy to understand (other programs can easily see both how to cooperate with it and that it cannot be exploited). The ability to identify other programs and to remember their past actions is obviously vital to the successful evolution of cooperation.

It may have occurred to you that there is one situation in which TIT-FOR-TAT wouldn't win. It wouldn't win if *all* the other players had the simple policy of ALWAYS-DEFECT. Then poor TIT-FOR-TAT would get suckered on the first transaction with each of the "nasties," and after that, all would always defect. Although TIT-FOR-TAT would not do best there, such a world is notably unhealthy; it seems very like the "nasty, brutish" world that Hobbes describes.

But we can draw a very different and more optimistic moral than Hobbes. He argues that only a coercive central government can foster cooperation and put an end to "the war of all against all." But Axelrod's calculations show that if only more than five percent of the nasties become TIT-FOR-TAT players, then the TIT-FOR-TAT strategy will start to win. In other words, cooperation can "invade" a nasty world if only a small portion of the population goes over to TIT-FOR-TAT. And, of course, as soon as TIT-FOR-TATers constitute a sizable portion of the population, the ALWAYS-DEFECTors will, relatively speaking, do very badly.

Indeed, TIT-FOR-TAT also won in five out of six subsequent computer simulations in which various kinds of strategies were made common. TIT-FOR-TAT is robust in that it succeeds when facing "societies" with quite different strategic mixes. So it will have a tendency, given that players have their personal interests at heart, to displace all other strategies.

Now it seems clear why our examples of a one-time prisoner's dilemma seemed more like a drug deal than a "neighborly" act of private barter. If one enters into a one-time transaction, it is good strategy to defect, whereas one has good reasons to cooperate when there may be more deals down the road. For similar reasons, barter is more common and more safe in small towns, while "street deals" in big cities are problematic.

For most of us, the purely private buying or selling of a house is a reasonable approximation of a one-time prisoner's dilemma. Usually the buyer is just coming to the neighborhood and the seller is leaving. The deal is one-time and the stakes are high. There is enormous pressure to misrepresent the condition of the house or one's ability to pay for it. Hence we employ realtors, inspectors, and banks, for whom it is a frequent transaction. They go far to guarantee cooperation.

Indeed, the prisoner's dilemma got its name because the original payoff matrix listed years of prison time, rather than dollars. In the original example, a warden separately interviews two prisoners who are suspected of committing a crime. The "payoff" is three years if both confess (mutual defection), only one year if both keep mum (mutual cooperation). However, since you get five years if you keep mum and the other guy confesses (winning his freedom), the coldly rational prisoner will confess.

Someone might say that in the real world criminals sometimes keep mum under similar conditions, thereby cooperating for mutual benefit. But that is undoubtedly because they do not see the transaction as a one-time matter; both know that "ratting" will cast a black shadow on their future *so long as they stay in the same "neighborhood."* The point of the federal witness program, in which a criminal who confesses is given a new identity, is to ensure that the criminal will see his situation as a classic one-time prisoner's dilemma. Here we see the government acting to discourage cooperation and encourage defection. Similarly, it is very difficult for the government to prevent cooperation in tacit "bid-fixing" among a small number of companies that frequently interact.

(Parenthetically, the success of TIT-FOR-TAT adds weight to a familiar observation about the inadequacies of our criminal justice system. TIT-FOR-TAT's characteristic nice, provocable, predictable, and forgiving behavior strongly promotes cooperative behavior in others. TIT-FOR-TAT immediately "punishes" defection, and a reversion to cooperation is immediately answered by a complete return to cooperation. Quite a different and very much less successful strategy—call it UNDER-OVER-KILL—would be to tolerate a number of defections, and then, unpredictably, switch to the extreme "bully" behavior of punishment and half-hearted forgiveness. Unfortunately, this seems in effect to be how we deal with many potential criminals. By the time we get around to correcting uncooperative behavior, it is firmly engrained. When we do eventually punish, the criminal is never wholly forgiven, for his "record" will mean some degree of mistrust and noncooperation for the forseeable future. The expunging of juvenile records switches UNDER-OVER-KILL in the TIT-FOR-TAT direction.)

A most interesting and cautionary result obtained by Axelrod is that in populations with an identifiable minority, a "bully" strategy may be rational for members of the majority. A "bully" strategy is one in which a player occasionally defects but is totally "unforgiving." The "bully" normally cooperates but "cheats" by defecting every once in awhile, but if you once "cross" the bully (perhaps in response to his cheats), he will defect against you forevermore. Unfortunately, this strategy is reasonably successful if practiced by a majority member against a minority. Correspondingly, the only reasonable strategy by the minority member is to knuckle under to bullying or to avoid interactions with the majority. What this part of the analytic model shows is that bully behavior by members of a majority against minority members can naturally arise without any explicit agreements whatsoever. Indeed, "bully behavior" can be a successful strategy even if the bully has no conscious notion of what he is doing at all. Such strategies can evolve among simple biological organisms (Maynard Smith 1974).

The general question of privatization is this: Under what conditions will cooperation among rationally self-interested individuals arise in such a way that important social needs will be effectively and efficiently satisfied? We have seen, abstractly, that cooperation is fostered if the same two individuals will meet again, if they will recognize each other, and if they will remember how the other has behaved in the past. Government should encourage cooperation to the degree that the payoffs in question meet vital social needs. In particular, government should privatize when such needs can be successfully expressed through particular transactions among self-interested individuals.

REGULATOR–BUSINESS RELATIONSHIPS AS PRISONER'S DILEMMAS

The relationship between a government regulatory agency and a regulated business can also be viewed as a repeated prisoner's dilemma (in two rather different ways).

In Scholz (1983), we find that if the regulatory agent operates with flexibility and restraint, and the business with reasonable, good-faith compliance, both reap the benefits of cooperation. For both sides, costly litigation is avoided.

Two obvious cautionary moves, to maintain this cooperation, are these. One, the cost of compliance for business must not be so high that defection looks like a reasonable risk. Two, correspondingly, the cost of being caught in a violation must be enough to make cooperation profitable.

On the other hand, there is another way to see regulator–business relationships as prisoner's dilemmas. Consider the relationship between individual regulator personnel and the regulated business. Contemplating a long-run relationship, the individual inspector may well find it possible to overlook serious violations if he is permitted to find enough minor violations to satisfy his superiors. Similarly, welfare case workers, pushed to process many cases quickly, may deny a small portion of all claims without further investigation of possible flagrant abuse.

It is important to realize that this pattern of undesirable cooperation can arise without explicit agreement. Axelrod (1984: 73–87) shows that, without any explicit collusion, a "live-and-let-live" cooperation arose between front-line German and Allied troops in the trenches of World War I (Ashworth 1980). Small troop units statically facing each other for months at a stretch would fall into "cooperative" patterns, firing only at predictable intervals, so that soldiers of both sides would have safe periods ("violations" would be met with a carefully limited nasty response). From the command viewpoint, the solution was frequent troop rotation, to produce something more like a one-time prisoner's dilemma, in which cooperation would not have a chance to evolve. In World War II this pattern did not substantially recur because of the lack of static trench warfare. One lesson might be that rotation of personnel can be quite desirable even if one does not suspect explicit collusion.

WHEN AND HOW TO PRIVATIZE: SOME EXAMPLES

Classically, mass transit and mail delivery present two cases that lend themselves to privatization. In many ways they fit the criteria we laid down at the beginning of this chapter. In particular, the customer chooses and can be presumed to know what he or she needs and to be a good judge of which service presents the best mix of cheapness and quality. (It is this feature that is missing from the penal enterprise.)

Difficulties arise, classically, because direct and efficient competition among many providers can be difficult to achieve. Public policy also has been felt to require that uneconomical service be available to isolated, low-use consumers; even small, out-of-the-way towns, it is thought, should have reasonably cheap access to transit and mail. Naturally, a private business will not want to take on uneconomical burdens, and requiring several businesses to service Boondockville, so that competition ensures good service, seems absurdly costly.

What may go unnoticed is that effectiveness of privatization may vary historically. Leaving aside ideology, privatization may make sense at one point, and "publicization" at another. Rail passenger service was originally provided, with profit, by competing, private railways. Technological changes and major government funding for highways came to make the railway passenger business uneconomical. Hence this led to, for example, the municipal takeover of northeastern city subway systems, and the partial federal takeover of long-distance passenger rail service. At the same time, technological developments and, above all, the congressional decision to make the federal mail service more or less pay for itself, have made private mail services much more viable.

Further, it may even be that, over substantial time periods, switches from public to private control and back again may be justified. *Any* enterprise, government, or private, that operates a partial monopoly will be liable, particularly over time, to develop uneconomical practices—in particular, undesirable cooperation of the sort I surveyed in the last two paragraphs of the previous section.

As I have mentioned, the ideological privatizer believes that any service that can be privatized should be. The pragmatic privatizer simply believes that only those services that can be more effectively and more economically met by private enterprise should be privatized. In our concluding section, I shall propose that competition, rather than ideology, is the most efficient way of resolving such questions.

PRIVATIZING PRIVATIZATION

Marlin and Feiden (1986), in part echoing New York Comptroller Harrison J. Goldin, have proposed: "A minimum of a particular service (say 5 percent) should be delivered by the municipality if it is predominantly privatized. A similar minimum should be privatized if service is predominantly provided in-house. The small set-aside provides a yardstick against which to measure relative efficiency." Apart from these minimums, they suggest competition should directly determine the relative proportion of privatization, citing, for example, garbage collection in Phoenix, Arizona.

> Government employees can sometimes learn from private vendors and go them one better. For five years, the Phoenix Public Works Department bid unsuccessfully against private vendors to pick up refuse in the city's northern district. But the last time around, by studying the private firms' efficiencies, the department's tightly audited bid came in $1 million below the nearest competitor.

The logic of this proposal is difficult to escape.

As I have pointed out, proposals for privatization arise in cases where significant features are missing that optimize efficient, competitive service delivery. Typically, the ultimate consumers cannot be given a real, direct, day-to-day choice among a large number of alternative providers. Hence, whether government directly pays for the service or not, the need for heavy-duty regulation arises. But, as our many prisoner's dilemma examples should show, a number of factors, many short of explicit collusion, will breed inefficiency whether the provider is government or private enterprise. Regulation simply cannot be expected to do it all. So the answer would seem to be that privatization itself should be made continuously subject to the review of the marketplace.

May I end with a personal note? Over the past few years, I have experienced considerable improvement in federal mail services. On the other hand, moving to Houston from the Boston–New York area, I am annoyed that I now pay five times as much to travel to my local airport by mass transit. I attribute the first of these experiences to changes that make competition with government more viable. I attribute the second to the City of Houston's ideological decision not to compete with business under conditions in which business itself cannot be sufficiently competitive.

REFERENCES

Ashworth, T. 1980. *Trench Warfare, 1914-1918: The Live and Let Live System* (New York: Holmes & Meier).

Axelrod, R. 1984. *The Evolution of Cooperation* (New York: Basic Books).

Luce, R. D. and H. Raiffa. 1957. *Games and Decisions* (New York: John Wiley & Sons).

Marlin, J. T. and K. Feiden. 1986. "To Avoid Private Firms' Public Scandals." *New York Times*, February 15, p. 19.

Maynard Smith, J. 1974. "The Theory of Games and the Evolution of Animal Conflict." *Journal of Theoretical Biology* 47: 209-21.

Rapoport, A. 1966. *Two Person Game Theory* (Ann Arbor, MI: University of Michigan Press).

Scholz, J. T. 1983. "Cooperation, Regulatory Compliance, and the Enforcement Dilemma." Paper presented at the annual meeting of the American Political Science Association, September 1-14, Chicago.

Von Neumann, J. and O. Morgenstern. 1964. *Theory of Games and Economic Behavior*, 3rd ed. (New York: John Wiley & Sons).

10

Privatization: Carnage, Chaos, and Corruption

Frederick C. Thayer

New York Times, April 3, 1986

The former president of the New York City Health and Hospitals Corporation, appointed to the position by the mayor, has been indicted for allegedly accepting a $150,000 bribe from the private firm awarded a $1 million contract to upgrade the management of Harlem Hospital. The director of the Bureau of Hospital Services of New York State has announced that the firm failed to improve the hospital's operation.

This indictment follows charges levied by other grand juries that Democratic leaders in Queens and the Bronx extorted bribes from firms awarded contracts to assist the city's Parking Violations Bureau in collecting traffic fines. One of those leaders committed suicide during the investigations.

Washington Post, April 1, 1986

The District of Columbia's Public Works Director has acknowledged that he improperly accepted travel and hotel accommodations from Datacom Systems Corp., a company with contracts to assist several cities with their parking ticket operations. Datacom is also charged with making $20,000 in payoffs to a former New York City parking official, and a Datacom vice-president had been charged with extorting $150,000 from a subcontractor.

The director of the D.C. Office of Campaign Finance and Ethics said that the city received "frequent" gifts of property and cash, and that they were legal as long as they were made to the city and it could not be proved that they had influenced the way city officials awarded contracts. Gifts to individual city officials were not legal.

Washington Post, April 1, 1986

Art-Metal-USA Inc., one of the federal government's largest suppliers of office furniture, has been suspended from receiving federal contracts because its president, Philip J. Kurens, had been arrested for alleged bribery. He reportedly paid a General Services Administration quality assurance inspector $5,000 for information about the firms competing with Art-Metal-USA for a $25 million contract for adjustable desk chairs. He had also promised another $50,000 if his company got the contract.

Kurens' arrest came ten days after the conviction of three men for bribery and conspiracy in connection with $2 billion in computer contracts with the U.S. Postal Service and Small Business Administration.

New York Times, January 11, 1981

A federal district judge has granted preliminary approval of the last and largest portion of a $2,424,000 settlement from four dairies in Little Rock, Arkansas. The four firms had pleaded no contest to federal antitrust charges that they had fixed prices to state institutions, wholesalers, and schools. Salesmen for two of the dairies served brief sentences in prison.

Such outcomes are to be expected when operating environments are designed in ways that encourage all those competing for survival in those environments to lie, cheat, and/or steal. In the realm of commerce, businesspeople need not be "natural" or "born" criminals to know that they will lose business if they are not corrupt. It is thus not surprising that the "privatization" of public service delivery—in such forms as "contracting out" services or "public-private partnerships"—is best translated as conspiracies to loot the public treasury. Occasionally, however, illegal activities actually serve the public interest, the Arkansas dairies being a conspicuous example. The laws they broke are open to serious question. Old-fashioned corruption is clearly the worst case.

It is immediately obvious that if a firm feels it must pay out large amounts of money in the form of bribes and payoffs to inspectors and government officials to ensure that it will gain the contracts it needs, this "sunk cost" is likely to prevent that firm from doing an efficient job. If the officials pocketing the handouts are in a position to spend enough public funds on the contract to guarantee first-class performance, of course, the costs associated with the contract will be much higher than they should have been. Since it is reasonable to assume that only a small fraction of those involved in bribes and payoffs are ever brought to justice, the only sensible conclusion is that cheating is more the norm than the exception.

Alfred E. Kahn, the economist who successfully pushed for airline deregulation while chairman of the Civil Aeronautics Board (CAB), has acknowledged that cheating can become so widespread in some competitive markets as to warrant government intervention. Despite his support for airline deregulation, he continued to argue after deregulation that government regulation was necessary in order to prevent the airlines from booking more passengers for flights than there were available seats. In outlining his position (Kahn 1982), he described what he believed to be the source of cheating:

> When consumers are inadequately informed, competition may take the form of providing unsafe or adulterated products, with the least scrupulous among the competitors forcing the more scrupulous to cut corners as well. It shouldn't be surprising that many ethical business people themselves are eager to have the government set limits on this kind of competition.

If, as he puts it, *all* competitors ultimately become cheaters, it seems a waste of time to try to discover which particular competitors were the first to cheat. "Why?" is the question; the answer seems to be that the characteristics of the competitive environment, not innate greed, are the wellsprings of cheating. Intensively competitive markets bring out the worst, not the best, in human behavior.

This essay will first take up the poor "fit" of contemporary concepts of privatization and deregulation, especially the former, with economic principles. Following that, I will argue that competition, and especially competitive bidding, must inevitably produce unethical behavior that can be dangerous to the lives and health of consumers and the general public. I will then use transportation industries and functions (airlines, trucking, urban mass transportation) to show why an increase in competition and reductions in operating costs combine to endanger safety. A summary will then deal with some of the larger reasons why such fallacious economic theories hold sway in this country.

"PRIVATIZATION" ISN'T EVEN GOOD ECONOMIC THEORY

While a case can be made that virtually every principle of free market economics is invalid, this essay can examine only the principles most fundamental to "privatization." The first two such principles are typical in that they directly contradict each other. In its simplest form, Say's law holds that supply always creates its own demand; a substantial excess of capacity or supply over demand, therefore, is impossible. The Keynesian economists who have claimed to disagree with Say's law really do not; all they ever proposed was that if there is a temporary lack of demand ("underconsumption"), government should stimulate demand enough to consume supply. In other words, if Say's law does not work automatically and immediately, it should be made to work. Put another way, the Keynesians did not acknowledge the possibility of chronically excess supply or capacity.

Virtually all economists and policymakers also hold firmly to the principle of unrestricted competition, treating it as both the key to prosperity and an almost sacred right for consumers. From this perspective, "excessive competition" is virtually impossible because consumers can best exercise their "sovereignty" by having as many producers as possible from which to choose. In the view of the Supreme Court as early as 1904, "the unrestrained interaction of competitive forces will yield the best allocation of economic resources, the lowest prices, the highest quality, and the greatest material progress" (quoted in Green 1972). What is often overlooked is that the principle of competition is based fundamentally on the relationship of *one* (or *each*) individual consumer to *all* producers; the principle does not begin with any notion of *all* producers and consumers taken together.

The two principles are wholly at odds. Say's law holds that supply *cannot* exceed demand, but the competitive principle asserts that supply *must* exceed demand (for a longer analysis and argument, see Thayer 1984). Setting aside any consideration of whether the contradiction can be overcome in the free market universe, the case can be quickly made that the contradiction poses an immediate and almost insurmountable problem when the competitive model is applied to the delivery of public services. The problem takes slightly different forms, depending on whether the "consumer" is identified as the government (which is "contracting out") or the individual citizen (who is choosing among competing providers).

Say's law is sometimes expressed as "any market can be cleared at some price." In theory, prices can be reduced enough to enable new buyers to enter the market ("demand elasticity"); presumably, *somebody* can be found to consume *anything*. In the case of a government that sets forth detailed specifications for a good or service that nobody else logically can use, however, government remains the only possible customer. To cite one example, some have argued that the Federal Aviation Administration (FAA) should "contract out" its function of controlling air traffic. If, say, five firms accumulated the equipment and personnel to perform such functions, then four of the five could not possibly find other customers after they had been denied the contract to operate a control system. Say's law, absolutely fundamental to all schools of economic thought (left, right, or center), cannot possibly apply in such monopsony situations, and things get no better when government delegates its authority to choose to individual citizens.

Many have argued that parents and their children should be given the right to choose schools, with government paying all or most of the price through a "voucher system" (Coons and Sugarman 1978). This seems highly attractive until we realize that the number of customers is known to begin with, and that substantial changes are unlikely. Suppose, for example, that 10,000 children are to be given the chance to choose among five competing schools. If each child is to be guaranteed that choice, how many school places and teachers will have to be made available? In the normal "monopoly" situation, a school district would provide only 10,000 places. But 50,000 places would be needed to ensure freedom of choice. Who would pay for the rejected facilities and teachers?

In practice, citizens can be given such opportunities to choose only within carefully restricted limits. With school programs for gifted children, the rule is sometimes "first come, first served." Sometimes only a set number of the most talented children are accepted. Even the most dedicated of free market economists realize that universities could not function unless many students were compelled to register for "second choice" courses when their first choices were already filled.

To drive the point home, I must again emphasize that the Keynesians did not repeal Say's law. They merely asserted that an insufficiency of demand ("underconsumption") could be remedied by artificially stimulating demand. Unlike the concepts of overcapacity or oversupply, which rest on the premise that there are finite limits to effective demand, the Keynesians accept the traditional notion that demand is essentially infinite. In instances such as those above, however, the losing bidders could find new customers only by petitioning other countries for contracts (air traffic control) or by trying to lure children away from other school districts.

A third principle of economics sets the stage for a further analysis of why the impossibility of a textbook market for public services leads inevitably to various types of cheating. The principle is that prices are determined by costs. It is fallacious because prices are *not* determined by costs, but by the degree of competition. As farmers know, production can so far outstrip demand as to cause market prices to drop far below the costs of production. As this was written in the spring of 1986, the inability of oil-exporting countries to agree on precise restrictions on oil production had caused such a sudden drop in world oil prices that profits of any kind were seriously threatened.

The privatization of public services rests on the premise that all bidders for all contracts will set forth "honest" textbook-type prices for the goods or services they promise to deliver. The premise is absurd; any bidder who is serious about winning a given contract knows full well that if he submits a wholly "honest" bid, he is sure to lose. The environmental pressures that produce dishonesty usually have taken their toll long before a government agency even asks for bids.

ALL MUST CHEAT, BUT SOME CHEATING IS HELPFUL

The agency seeking approval for a given project has little choice but to be very conservative in estimating costs in order to gain project approval. The conservative estimates are not *lies* in the technical sense. Nobody knows for sure what unforeseen situations will add to the costs of even the most conventional projects. The agency thus engages in a form of "intentional deception" (Bok 1978). Bidders know that they must stay within the cost projections of the agency, even when the projections are clearly too low, and if one of the bidders feels he must win the contract in order to survive at all, he must deliberately bid prices he knows to be less than projected costs.

Reflecting on eight years of experience in the Department of Defense, two of former Secretary of Defense McNamara's cost analysts concluded that "competition for the contract often drives contractors to bid on the basis of a target cost that is well below what they actually expect the cost to be" (Enthoven and Smith 1971: 239–40). While widely condemned, "cost overruns" really are indicators that attempts have been made to do good work. The projects to worry about are those that are completed without overruns.

In 1978, for example, a contractor submitted a bid of $54.75 million to build an indoor sports arena in New Jersey. On the day the bids were to be opened, the contractor announced that he had underestimated his costs by $8 million. The state's Sports and Exposition Authority, reacting in the normal political way, proclaimed that it would compel the contractor to do the job for $54.75 million. By the time the project was completed a few years later, the costs exceeded $85 million, but other events had given the governing authority a way out of its self-constructed trap. As the arena was being built, the roofs on three other arenas collapsed, and the authority cautiously ordered changes in the specifications (*New York Times*, January 12, 1981, and telephone conversation, New Jersey Sports Authority Public Affairs office). While a 60 percent cost overrun makes the entire planning process seem nonsensical, an arena built for the originally stated price doubtless would have led to disaster.

Some other by-products of privatization are much sleazier. The wave of scandals that disgraced New York City in late 1985 and early 1986 featured the offer of large bribes to government decision-makers and, in some cases, demands by long-time political chiefs for cash payoffs as the price of doing business with the city. These activities demonstrate only that large-scale privatization can involve large-scale payoffs; the $150,000 payoff for the $1 million contract gave the public official, in effect, a 15 percent commission. The New Jersey furniture maker, on the other hand, was offering smaller bribes to lower-level people but, if he had won the contract he was ultimately barred from winning, many more payoffs might have been involved. Obviously, the payoffs are likely to reduce the quality of goods or services actually delivered.

General economic conditions can make the competition for government contracts of any sort so intense that corruption runs rampant. The recovery following the steep recession of the early 1980s resulted in a glut for many industries. Capacity and supply were so greatly in excess of foreseeable demand that competitors could easily conclude that new government contracts were the only possible sources of new business. Because Americans tend to ascribe all human behavior to "free will" decision-making, they tend to ignore the environmental causes of bad behavior in favor of "bad apple" theories. Economists are prime offenders because, preaching the gospel of free markets from tenured positions that are protected from competition, they do not understand the pressures of competition; they may not even understand why referees are needed to detect illegal play in football games.

Aside from the use of cost overruns to make up for the inherent deficiencies of competitive bidding, about the only other good outcomes occur when the competing bidders secretly come together to plan jointly, "colluding" and "conspiring" to "divide the business" and "rig the bids." All such activity is illegal, of course, and executives who are caught in the act may find themselves in jail. Actually, many such "conspiracies" have the effect of saving the public and its misguided representatives from the disastrous consequences of "honest" competitive bidding. The case of the Arkansas dairies demonstrates the point.

The four dairies were considered the "fit, willing and responsible" candidates for the school milk contract. Governments often use such standards to eliminate "new entrants" because such violations of free market principles, they believe, help ensure good performance; the Little Rock school board would be understandably reluctant to award a contract to an individual with no dairy experience, who could only promise to build a new dairy.

If a single dairy had won the entire contract, the award would have represented a 25 percent increase in business. In an "honest" bidding process, each dairy would have sought that revenue spurt for itself, and each dairy would have had to prepare accordingly. It would have needed to acquire more cows, trucks, drivers, and mechanics, and maybe even new plant capacity. It would also have had to buy the 38 refrigeration units the board insisted (in its contract specifications) that the successful bidder install and operate. And it would have had to make the necessary investment ahead of time in order to be ready.

This is a recipe for waste. Altogether, the four firms would have had to buy 152 school cooling units, knowing that 114 of them would not be used. And, to make matters even worse, the school board announced that the contract would be opened annually to rebidding. As one dairy manager rhetorically asked in a later telephone conversation, "What would I do with 38 coolers if I lost the contract after one year?"

The "conspiracy" was uncovered only after a committee found that each dairy had bid the same price. While this was thought highly unusual, it really was a very normal market outcome. In a free market, all competitors must meet the lowest current price. In other words, price differentials are an artificiality not in accordance with free market principles, and they demonstrate again that competitive bidding does not and cannot meet those principles. By arranging to submit identical prices, the dairies made possible the only sensible outcome.

Identical bids led the board to divide the business among the dairies, taking advantage of distances and route structures. The school board then had a ready-made way to compare the performances of the four dairies in different schools, giving itself the data it would need to remove a poor performer. Most important, the price-fixing made it possible for the companies to make sure that the cooling units would be kept in good repair and that drivers entering school grounds would be well trained. This was a far better outcome than occurs with respect to many school-bus contracts; dog-eat-dog bidding leads to poor or nonexistent maintenance and untrained drivers.

Probably the greatest irony associated with the privatization debates is that the actions of the Little Rock dairies matched almost perfectly the recommendations made by perhaps the leading proponent of privatization on how to implement the concept. E. S. Savas, once a member of John Lindsay's New York City administration, began to study garbage removal in U.S. cities when he was at Columbia University. Later appointed to a sub-cabinet position in the first Reagan administration, he was forced to leave that post when it emerged that his book on the benefits of privatization had benefited from extensive work by government employees on government time. While he is yet another example of "over-privatization," his forthright concepts and guidelines remain standards.

From the beginning, one of Savas' main targets has been the "monopoly power" of municipal unions, especially New York's sanitation workers. Labeling this the "most severe management problem extant," Savas campaigned to have a substantial share of the city's garbage removal function turned over to private business (presumably he did not know that private "trash removal" or "carting" operations in New York City are controlled largely by the underworld). Cost comparisons of the public and private operations, he said, would enable officials to find ways to reduce costs (Savas 1971, 1975). The concept has made some headway. In recent years, the union has been forced to accept some two-person trucks in place of traditional three-person vehicles. Ultimate costs are not yet known since, true to form, the new trucks (purchased with competitive bids) were defective in construction and performance (*New York Times*, November 19, 1980; April 9, 1981).

Savas's principal example of new municipal efficiencies in garbage removal, however, is Minneapolis (Savas 1977). Prior to 1971, that city's Sanitation Division collected wet garbage from households, while private firms were available on an individual contract basis for rubbish and trash removal. When city officials decided to combine refuse collections, they chose to divide the business between the Sanitation Division and a new company formed by all the former private contractors. This system has continued ever since, with the corporation and the city each doing half the total job. Savas cites Minneapolis as an example of how the private sector outperforms the public, but his data are open to question. It appears that he and others repeatedly underestimate the costs of supervising contractors and assume that private workers have the same fringe benefits as municipal employees (DeLaat 1982).

More important here is the model Savas outlines for "how to do it." He begins by acknowledging important economies of scale that are often denied by advocates of deregulating such industries as trucking and the airlines: "There are economies in having one truck collect refuse from every house on the block, and one should expect similar "economies of contiguity" in delivering newspapers, mail, milk, or campaign literature; in reading utility meters; or in mowing the postage-stamp lawns of suburban housing developments" (Savas 1977). He then recommends that large cities be divided into districts of no more than 50,000 people each, and that no contractor be awarded more than one district. A public agency would remove trash in one district, thereby minimizing the possibility of collusion among the private firms. The system could then be further purified by using a "process of periodic competition."

Like the Minneapolis example, this is a model that "divides the business," and the only minor change needed to make it completely workable is to have government openly join in above-board negotiations on contract prices. The ongoing comparisons of the private contractors and the one public agency would seem to make it unnecessary to reopen competitive bidding yearly. Unfortunately, it takes a crisis along the lines of finding deadly poisons in pain-killer capsules to make government admit that it should call together the competing firms to design the best system for protecting the public's interest.

Meanwhile, the largest single antitrust investigation in the country's history continues. Hundreds of highway construction contractors have been brought to trial on charges of bid-rigging and price-fixing, and a deputy attorney general has said: "We intend to seek out and prosecute those people who engage in hardcore antitrust violations like bid-rigging and price-fixing. . . . We're not talking about inadvertent conduct in an area where the law isn't clear. We're talking about widespread, collusive, criminal conduct that is literally stealing millions of hard-earned taxpayer dollars'' ("Highway Robbery" 1982). Given the huge, expensive equipment of highway construction, it is wholly illogical to believe that a large number of contractors can be uniformly ready to carry out each individual contract, especially in regions where construction seasons are limited by weather. The need to plan well in advance for the deployment of such equipment, and of its skilled operators, makes it inevitable that some form of collective planning will occur. Government units should plan together with the contractors; lacking this, the contractors must become criminals by doing what the situation requires (for a more extensive version of this argument, see Thayer 1983).

The evidence amassed in connection with the highway-construction cases makes it clear that illegal (but necessary) collective planning has been rampant in the industry for decades. Because this is an era of runaway economic fundamentalism, the orthodox believers have been trying to unearth as much "collusion" and "conspiracy" as possible. At the same time, it can readily be acknowledged that joint public/private planning would require government to restrict new entries in most cases. This seems intuitively reasonable, although economic purists are likely to blanch.

Such restrictions would make government a full-fledged participant in a regulatory process. Other recent experience suggests that this participation is desirable and that attempts to reduce or eliminate it become very costly over time.

TRANSPORTATION: THE PUBLIC/PRIVATE MUDDLE AND DEREGULATION FEVER

For at least the rest of the 1980s, the transportation industries will be as good an example as any of how many issues related to privatization can be studied together. At the national level, to begin with, the airline and trucking industries were "deregulated" to varying degrees between 1978 and 1980. In principle, this meant that the agencies that previously controlled entry into those industries, assigned routes on the basis of "public convenience and necessity," and set rates were wholly or largely relieved of those responsibilities; at the same time, sub-agencies within the U.S. Department of Transportation (DOT) retained the responsibility for overseeing compliance with safety standards. While all this was going on, the DOT's Urban Mass Transportation Administration was lobbying intensively for the increased use of private contractors as replacements for municipally owned and operated systems, principally buses.

One set of issues involves "ownership" itself, and the time-worn debate between Marxists and capitalists over whether "worker" or "shareholder" ownership really makes a difference. Except for municipal transportation authorities, the American tradition has been that carrier transportation systems are privately owned, a tradition that is much weaker (or absent) in other industrial countries. Those who now zealously seek to privatize municipal transportation systems seldom seem aware that many such systems became wards of government only after private operators had failed.

A second set of issues involves competition or the threat of competition. The assumption underlying the deregulation of the airline, bus, and trucking industries was that regulated (restricted) competition was too similar to monopoly operation; the ability of firms to "capture" the regulatory agencies had supposedly resulted in overpriced services. Because the industries were not famous as profit-makers, there were no accusations of "monopoly profits," but many believed that overpricing had produced excessively high wages and salaries. The corollary assumption was that if market forces were turned loose, as in the airline example, more and more firms would enter the business, competitive fares would prevail, and more and more individuals would be able to fly as fares were reduced. The advocates of municipal bus service privatization no longer argue for a permanent private monopoly, but for arrangements that open contracts to periodic rebidding.

It should not be surprising that other issues are swept under the rug to varying degrees by the deregulators and privatizers. One issue is the extent to which intensive competition (in the forms of many firms serving the same routes and engaging in price wars, or of having many firms bid for the same municipal contract) compels firms to cut corners on vehicle maintenance and/or operator qualifications. This issue, of course, has a second side that goes to the heart of government's oversight responsibilities. If there is a relationship between competition and corner-cutting, government must spend much more on safety enforcement when competition is more vigorous. The increased expenditures for safety enforcement can then exceed the alleged "savings" by travelers, shippers, or contracting governments. And, if the incentives to cheat are overwhelming, effective safety enforcement may be impossible.

Similarly, the deregulators and privatizers never mention the waste that can be associated with excess capacity, primarily because their economic principles simply ignore or reject the possibility of overcapacity. The basic cause of bankruptcies, for example, is excessive duplication of capacity, not "inefficiency" per se. Indeed, a major complaint of the airline deregulators was that during the 40-year regime of the Civil Aeronautics Board (CAB), there had been no airline bankruptcies. Since the 1978 deregulation, the number of airlines has tripled, but there have also been 30–40 bankruptcies. Only in theory are the costs of bankruptcies borne by entrepreneurial risk-takers; those costs are spread across society, and they should be seen as costs imposed by deregulation.

Finally, there is the labor–management issue. Before airline and trucking deregulation, only a few isolated observers suggested that one outcome of deregulation would be such substantial reductions in wages and salaries as to warrant the label of "union-busting" (Thayer 1977). Since the drive for deregulation was a "fever" that gripped liberals and conservatives alike, a thorough consideration of the question would have disrupted a coalition that included among its most prominent figures the sturdiest pro-labor senator of them all, Edward M. Kennedy. But there are other reasons why some of these issues were not considered before deregulating some of the transportation industries. These issues are not considered even now by privatizers, for according to economic principles, they cannot exist at all.

As noted throughout this essay, economic theory rules out even the possibility of overcapacity. While Herbert Hoover and Franklin Roosevelt attributed the Great Depression to "excessive," "destructive," and "cut-throat" competition (overcapacity in many industries), the contemporary advocates of deregulation airily dismiss such conclusions as "discredited" (Breyer 1982: 30).

According to economic assumptions, every competitor carefully observes all laws and safety standards (with only minor exceptions) and, if a competitor finds that he cannot meet the market price without large-scale violations of those standards, he merely acknowledges his managerial incompetence, closes down operations, and files for bankruptcy. In principle, the degree of competition has no effect on safety compliance or government's ability to enforce it.

Economic principles are based much more on the notion of "consumer sovereignty" than on "voluntary exchange." Competition is intended to put producers at the mercy of consumers who, exercising their leverage, compel the former to reduce prices; since labor costs are the obvious means of doing this, they always become immediate targets. In fundamentalist economic theology, no price to the consumer can be too low; nor can any wage. Economic theory largely ignores the obvious; the consumer must first earn the wherewithal to buy.

Failure to acknowledge that such problems can exist (let alone make efficient and safe operation nearly impossible) cripples debates on the merits of deregulation and privatization. The very nature of the enforcement problem makes the debates even more difficult. As in the example of the space shuttle that exploded shortly after lift-off early in 1986, one cannot "prove" the existence of a safety problem until disaster strikes. Safety enforcement agencies are supposed to set standards that *prevent* disasters, not merely determine why they happen, as important as the latter function may be to the readjustment of safety standards. Even so, what can be said about the results of deregulation and privatization in recent years—in trucking, the airlines, and municipal transportation?

Trucking

It is not widely known that a substantial fraction of the trucking industry was "exempted" from economic regulation when the industry fell under the Interstate Commerce Commission (ICC) in 1935. The most notable exemption was for produce haulers. Studying as best he could the safety records of different fractions of the industry in the mid-1970s, Wyckoff (1979) turned up some striking evidence. He found that unregulated truckers had many more serious accidents, made many more false entries in the logbooks they had to keep, more often violated driving-time limits (10 hours on the road followed by at least 8 hours' rest), and were cited for many more moving violations. While he stated his conclusions quite tentatively, the picture was clear enough:

> . . . there is substantially better compliance with safety and operating rules in the ICC-regulated sector. . . . Compliance [was] highest among company employees in the highly regulated common-carrier segment and lowest in the exempt segment. Is the relationship between economic regulation and safety compliance causal? Economic regulation does result in larger carriers than exist in the exempt area. Motor-carrier managers believe and act as if the ICC is fulfilling its mandate to ensure that carriers under its jurisdiction are fit, willing and able . . . [although] it is difficult to confirm a causal relationship. . . . (Wyckoff 1979: 120).

Since deregulation (or "regulatory reform") in 1980, some 12,000 new companies have entered trucking, but some estimate that companies are failing at the rate of 1,500 per year. By the mid-1980s, increasing concern was being expressed that safety standards were being violated more and more, and that enforcement agencies were finding it impossible to keep up with all the violations. The president of the Insurance Institute on Highway Safety, for example, asserted that "[Safety is] a major problem and it seems to be growing," adding that if deregulation was not "contributing" to the growth of the safety problem, it was "not helping it." The American Automobile Association said fatigue was the primary cause of about 40 percent of big-truck accidents, while an experienced consultant said that 56 percent of trucking accidents involved drivers who had been on the road more than 16 hours (*Wall Street Journal*, August 22, 1985; *New York Times*, April 8, 1986).

In the absence of truly catastrophic increases in accidents, neither the legislative nor the executive branches will be quick to acknowledge that deregulation may have been an error. At the same time, they can solve the existing problems only by taking actions that will be more costly than re-regulation (such as a federal licensing bureaucracy, actually suggested in legislation sponsored by Senators Danforth and Packwood, and/or a huge increase in the number of safety inspectors). Meanwhile, the industry has been steadily increasing the weight of its trucks in efforts to haul more tons (up to 100,000) per driver; the result is rapid, extensive road damage, and it is widely assumed that many trucks are exceeding legal weights.

This is not to suggest that ICC regulation of the trucking industry was a model of how such industries should be regulated. As in many other cases, ICC regulation was imposed on trucking only *after* there were too many companies and too many trucks competing for the same customers, and the enabling legislation (typically) "grandfathered in" all existing companies. Even when trucking was regulated, therefore, there was a great deal of competition, with as many as 92 firms linking Boston and New York. Both the ICC and the CAB were required to promote competition (duplication) on as many routes as possible, thereby ensuring that overcapacity would be a constant problem. Because economic principles assume that *any* form of restriction on competition is bad, even the ICC limit of 92 firms on that route was interpreted as encouraging monopoly. Thus, the "problems" of the trucking and airline industries were proclaimed to be *too little* competition when in reality there was already *too much*. Adding still more competition was bound to make things worse.

The industry provides yet another paradox. Truckers who are required by their employers to violate safety rules can no longer count on union leaders, who know that if they seek to enforce the rules, the company will surely shift to nonunion truckers. While few mourn the effective "busting" of the Teamsters, few also appreciate how desperate conditions are becoming in this industry.

Airlines

When the air traffic controllers struck in 1981, they believed that since air travel would be almost at a standstill, the government would have to negotiate with them. Yet even though the number of flights was cut in half at more than 20 major airports, air travel was hardly disrupted at all. There could have been no better demonstration of how deregulation had improved the "efficiency" of the airline industry. Since deregulation, more and more flights have been added, the industry has engaged in periodic fare wars, and its financial condition has grown ever shakier.

By mid-1986, this industry had become one of the more interesting examples of mergermania, but most analyses of such activity overlook the major cause of mergers. Firms in industries plagued by overcapacity know that investing money in additional facilities would make little sense, so they turn to buying other firms instead. Each buyer hopes to be one of the largest of the survivors after its industry has been "restructured." Unfortunately, many of the buyers must assume huge new debts in order to consummate the mergers, thereby making themselves simultaneously larger and weaker. To pay off their new debts, firms must become more cost-conscious than ever. The "old" firms, moreover, are gradually compelled to get their costs down almost to the level of the "new" or "upstart" firms that began operations with wage and salary costs about half those of the former. This is precisely what has been happening with the airlines.

Direct and circumstantial evidence has been piling up in favor of those who insist that a major effect of deregulation has been to erode airline compliance with safety standards. There has been no significant increase in accident rates, and perhaps even a decline, but a few major accidents can be directly tied to the by-products of deregulation, and the fines levied by the FAA on safety violators have become so much larger than ever before that airline safety must be declining. FAA fines have grown from $95,180 in 1982 to a whopping $2 million-plus in 1985, a 2,000 percent increase in three years. Early in 1986, I observed that American Airlines, fined $1.5 million for 1985 violations, "cannot possibly be the only large-scale violator" (Thayer 1986). A few weeks later, this unhappy prediction proved correct.

When the FAA announced in March 1986 that it was seeking $9 million in fines from Eastern Airlines for safety violations, this added to the worries of a Department of Defense (DOD) already upset by the loss of 248 American soldiers in an accident involving another airline. Convinced that it could not wholly rely on an overworked and understaffed FAA, the DOD launched its own safety surveys. Combining its own findings with those of the FAA, it decided on a "temporary stoppage" of the use of Eastern by military personnel; the decision was reversed only when the FAA provided written assurance that the airline's compliance had "markedly improved" (*New York Times*, April 19, 1986). A more serious situation can be neither imagined nor remembered, especially since contracting airlines are a form of "air merchant marine" that is presumably available for immediate use in emergencies.

At least two major accidents seem directly connected with deregulation. The winter 1982 crash at Washington National Airport was attributed to young, nonunion pilots with little or no experience in winter flying; the airline had recently expanded its routes, something it could not have done in a regulated environment. A 1979 jumbo jet crash at Chicago's O'Hare Airport was caused by improper maintenance, caused by cost cutting, on the plane's engine supports; the damage to many planes was discovered only after the engine fell off one of them, causing the crash. While a popular book raised many questions about safety in 1986, official Washington was not yet prepared to acknowledge error (Nance 1986).

The FAA did, however, admit that it would have to hire more safety inspectors. Earlier, the supporters of deregulation had promised that deregulation would be a "no-cost" operation, and the FAA had dutifully followed this line in 1978, when the Carter administration was taking credit for the legislation. When the incentives to cheat are so powerful that everyone must cut corners, it is doubtful that enough inspectors can be hired to catch all the violators—even if government were to forget about reducing deficit spending.

Airline cost-cutting, unfortunately, is not the only major culprit where safety is concerned. Airlines have found that "hub-spoke" operations are among the best counter-competitive strategies for keeping passengers on board a single airline from beginning to end (along with "frequent flyer" bonuses and the like). By routing most flights through a central airport, airlines can virtually compel passengers to take connecting flights rather than nonstop ones. In Newark, one airline alone now has 9 million passengers per year changing planes, and none of those passengers has any reason to go through Newark except to change planes. This drastically increases the air and ground congestion in the New York area, already one of the most congested in the world. The National Transportation Safety Board has repeatedly warned that congestion increases the potential for collisions, and there is little doubt that the number of near-collisions is on the rise. (Congestion also forces communities to expand airports and terminals beyond what would be needed in a more logically ordered airline system.)

Since deregulation in 1978, this industry has become a world leader in developing innovative ways to cut wages and salaries. Continental Airlines, for example, filed for Chapter 11 reorganization protection under the bankruptcy laws in 1983 and simultaneously repudiated all union contracts and slashed wages and salaries by half. The firm never suspended operations, even though three unions officially went on strike. They also filed claims of $3.5 billion against Continental, alleging wrongful discharge. By October 1985, the U.S. Bankruptcy Court dismissed all the claims and ordered the pilots' union to end a strike that already had lost all momentum. This effectively set a precedent to the effect that if a firm can establish its financial difficulties to the satisfaction of the bankruptcy court, it can instantly terminate any labor agreement and pay whatever wages and salaries it wishes (*New York Times*, September 11, October 3, 1985).

The airline industry also has been a pioneer in large-scale "two-tier" labor contracts that pay new employees much less than experienced employees doing the same jobs, and that maintain the distinction for many years. Both new approaches are spreading into other industries and are encouraged by the sustained high unemployment rates (7–10 percent) of the last decade. Since it is now somewhat easier for management to ignore labor contracts, and since new employees are likely to resent a union that reduced their pay even before they were hired (whatever happened to "equal pay for equal work"?), both approaches are union-weakening if not union-busting.

The standard argument in favor of such approaches is that wages and salaries should be determined by "free market forces" and that every employee will "naturally" be paid the marginal value of his or her contribution to output. The argument assumes, of course, that "equilibrium" is the natural order of things and that every employee's pay will amount to a "good living." Yet there is every reason to conclude that only minimum wage laws stop wages from falling below designated floors. While the advocates of deregulation have cheered the declines in airline wage and salary levels, they have not addressed such questions as what should be done if sudden steep pay cuts compel employees to sell their houses in glutted markets while seeking cheaper housing.

Urban Transportation Systems

Contemporary efforts to "privatize" urban transportation systems are mislabeled. If "privatization" were the panacea its supporters claim it is, urban bus systems would not have "gone public" beginning in 1964. "Reprivatization" would be a more apt label, but today's advocates of "competitive contracting" insist that the problem of the pre-1964 franchise operations was that they were monopolies. Presumably, the monopolies were "inefficient," although there is no explanation of why they couldn't use their monopoly power to survive. In any event, it is widely claimed that "competitive contracting" will reduce current operating costs by 20–60 percent (Cox 1985: 6).

How does "competitive contracting" work? In the late 1950s, I was an Air Force officer scheduling flights of military passengers and dependents from California to Pacific bases. Some of the flights were on military aircraft, while others were "contracted out" to civil, mostly "nonscheduled," airlines. A typical contract was large enough to use the services of about ten DC-7 aircraft, four-engine prop planes then entering obsolescence. The contract was offered for rebidding each year and, when bids were received, we would dispatch an inspection team to determine if the bidders were "fit, willing and able" to fulfill the contract. What the team found was that except for the company then carrying out the contract, there were no "in-place" firms at all. Each bidder merely produced evidence that if it won the contract, it could immediately lease aircraft and hire personnel; it could do nothing without the contract. All the bidders were prepared to lease the same aircraft, varying only the paint job. As the companies constantly underbid each other, the quality of service gradually declined; no company could accumulate any capital for modernization, and the problems were cured only when the CAB decided in 1960 that a "rate floor" was necessary. Further study has confirmed that a great deal of competitive bidding involves this sort of sham—it must.

The New York City Transit Authority decided in 1984 that 850 buses newly purchased for $99,000–121,000 each from Grumman Flxible were unsafe, withdrew them from service, and parked them on a Brooklyn pier. The Metropolitan Transportation Authority (the parent agency) then sued Grumman for $140 million to replace the buses and $184 million in punitive damages. By then, Grumman had sold its Flxible division, but it counter-sued the city and its transit agencies for $1 billion, charging that poor maintenance and politics had caused removal of the buses. In early 1986, the Flxible Corporation (now a subsidiary of General Automotive) offered to buy back the buses from New York, for $4,900 to $6,500 each, saying that it expected to "do some work on the buses" and then find other buyers for them (*New York Times*, March 8, 1986). Conceivably, it will sell the buses to a leasing corporation that will then rent them to some firm fulfilling a "privatized" and "competitive" urban transit contract.

Widespread advocacy of some forms of deregulation and privatization always seems to accompany the discovery of a huge supply of second-hand equipment. More than 3,000 new airlines tried to start up after World War II, using surplus military transports; quality was low and accidents were high for a few years until the regulatory agencies regained control of the system. The deregulators of the airline and trucking industries openly acknowledged that second-hand vehicles would provide the new competition; the aircraft seemed to be contractor transports left idle when the ending of the Vietnam War also ended many contracts with small airlines. The contemporary drive to privatize municipal bus systems depends on two sources of surplus buses.

The federal government had to provide large-scale capital subsidies to local communities beginning in 1964 because private bus companies had lost their passengers to automobiles and had no funds for buying new equipment. The subsidies have enabled many communities to upgrade their fleets more than once, but some of the buses they "retire" from service then become available for "competitive contracting" operations. Meanwhile, transcontinental bus operators (Trailways, Greyhound) have lost many passengers to the airlines and have pulled operations out of many smaller communities, thereby expanding the fleet of available second-hand buses. It is relatively easy to operate a low-cost bus system, perhaps with non-union workers, for a short period of time, but the municipal bus experience prior to 1964 suggests that old equipment will not be replaced and that the systems will collapse. The privatization advocates seldom address the issues of capital accumulation and modernization.

Careful scholarly research suggests that the apparent efficiencies of some privatized systems are explained in such unusual ways as long-term and municipal subsidies; specialized markets (crowded highways, expensive parking, strong central business districts, and 25–30-mile commuting distances); and the use of "older, possibly more accident-prone buses for longer periods of time. Thus, although the analysis confirms the efficiency of some private firms, it is unclear whether such results can be duplicated on a larger scale given the specialized circumstances surrounding these operators" (Perry and Babitsky 1985).

Contemporary liberal and conservative economic policies prescribe that the federal government must borrow and spend much less to ensure the ready availability of capital for the construction of unneeded office buildings. Among the items fast vanishing into history are the capital and operating subsidies for urban mass transportation systems, and the federal agencies involved with such functions are preaching the privatization gospel. They are not knaves, but merely honest fools who accept the premises of economics. Thus nothing need be said about the need for more and more safety inspectors and the other rising costs of municipal bus service. The same premises enable them to use as evidence data that is easily explained in other ways. The above analysis is not the only example.

The privatizers argue that the operating costs of urban bus systems have risen more rapidly than inflation in the past two decades. The logical explanation is not that monopoly government agencies are by nature "inefficient," as the zealots proclaim, but rather that urban mass transportation had to be rescued from the grave. It was indeed costly to put together a network to link entire metropolitan regions in a coordinated fashion. Add to that a publicly accepted responsibility for top-grade maintenance and professionally trained operators, and the costs were bound to go up. Add to that an absolute commitment to compliance with all safety rules, and costs went up still more. Governments at all levels had to provide the wherewithal to refurbish urban transportation, just as the federal government had to rebuild Conrail. The argument that the "new" privatization will do what the old could not is, as usual, very good economics but foolish.

The case of urban mass transportation suggests to some extent the need for yet other forms of regulation to protect local communities. When a community replaces its old buses with new ones, the sensible thing to do is to make it impossible for those buses to be used again in another city.

Failing that, all such buses should be required to undergo a complete overhaul, and any community then contracting for their use should undertake a detailed study of the mechanical history of each bus. If firms seeking contracts for municipal bus operations were required to comply with such rules, the privatizers could not present the alleged "savings" they do now.

Privatized municipal bus systems, finally, fall victim to the rising costs of liability insurance. Some argue that these costs are rising because juries make exorbitant awards in liability cases; others blame lawyers and their fees; still others point to poor investment decisions by insurance companies. The fact is that rates are growing exponentially and will become more and more prohibitive for the operators of aging buses, trucks, and airplanes. Make no mistake about it—the average age of transportation fleets steadily increases as all-out competition leaves no room for modernization. A firm with a government "certificate of necessity" can use that franchise as collateral for new equipment if future business looks even half promising. In an unregulated market, more capital is needed for equipment replacement, but the firms simply do not have it.

ECONOMIC THEORY: THE CULT THAT PARALYZES AMERICA

Since the noted economist Lester R. Thurow has likened economics to a theology, and one undergoing a return to fundamentalism (Thurow 1983), it is appropriate to say that the true believers are high priests of a cult that distributes a great deal of pain and suffering in the name of altruism. They are sincere, but their tender concerns lead only to lower wages and fewer jobs. The combination of explicit love for consumers and citizens and implicit contempt for workers seems unusual until one recalls that free-market theories were invented by slave-owners. Today's cultists have blinded themselves to any evidence that gets in the way of their articles of faith. The results would be amusing if they were not so tragic.

Willis D. Hawley, long fascinated with the ability of market forces to spur innovation, addressed not long ago the question of how to reform teacher education. His answer was, "To innovate, first deregulate" (Hawley 1986). He used the analogy of the market to make his point:

> . . . we do not know the relationship between effective teaching and preservice teacher-preparation programs.
>
> If one does not know . . . how to build a machine that will produce the product one wants, one experiments with different modes of production, assesses the outcomes, and further refines the processes. Moreover, when it is not altogether clear what product the consumers want and need, the rational planner encourages competition among

> producers and lets the definition of quality derive, at least in part, from market choices. . . . rather than legislate specific processes by which one can become a teacher, we should encourage experimentation with different approaches, evaluate how variations . . . affect teacher effectiveness, and observe how the market for high-quality teaching responds to different models. . . . The solution . . . is not regulatory reform; we need deregulation.

This is a clarion call that virtually any privatizer or deregulator would instantly endorse. After asking, "How should this be done in the absence of government regulation?" however, Hawley reversed himself without even noticing as much. He advocated state licenses for teachers, focusing on standardized national competency testing and accreditation of teacher education programs, through either "approval by the National Council for the Accreditation of Teacher Education, or demonstration that 90 percent or so of the program's graduates regularly receive favorable performance ratings."

Hawley, now dean of the Teachers College at Vanderbilt University, seems to have overlooked a few things. Would *nationally* standardized tests encourage "experimentation with different approaches"? What kind of administrative apparatus would be needed to keep records of *all* performance ratings of *all* teachers in the country? If the graduates of a given program suddenly dropped from 91 percent "favorable performance ratings" to 89 percent, would this cause instant removal of accreditation? If their programs were slipping, would university deans feel compelled to bribe school principals in the hope of getting better ratings for the graduates? How can all this be called a program for "deregulation"?

The example illustrates one kind of economic brainwashing. It is appropriate for government to raise and distribute money, but it is decidedly *not* appropriate for government to *operate* any function at all (except perhaps police forces and armies). Presumably, as many functions as possible should be operated by non-government organizations, either for-profit or not-for-profit. Put another way, proposals such as this use the classical economic view that the authority of government should be diminished as much as possible in the name of freedom, but "freedom" turns out to be only a transfer of authority to those clamoring for that freedom. In Dean Hawley's design, the National Council for the Accreditation of Teacher Education could end up with a strangle-hold on the licensing of U.S. teachers, and who is likely to have more influence there than university presidents and deans?

The problem here has yet to be carefully explored. It is usually assumed that "regulation" involves the assignment of virtually absolute authority to a government agency, and the only alternative to this presumably inefficient form of management is to assign the same authority to some other agency. Seldom if ever can one see proposals for "shared authority" or "team management" or "consensual decision-making." As briefly suggested above, the best forms of regulation might well involve government in openly consensual negotiations with service providers, there being no reason at all to use *different* management methods when dealing with government and nongovernment providers of specific services.

A second kind of economic brain-washing needs much further analysis before privatization debates are settled. The behavioral assumption underlying "competitive contracting" and similar designs is that human beings at work are best motivated by the desire for profit and the fear of losing their jobs. Economics professors with tenure carefully exempt themselves from such assumptions, but otherwise look favorably upon greed and insecurity. It seems to me, conversely, that if I am in such a position, I will do all I can to steal as much as possible while I have the opportunity. The stronger the threat to my security, the stronger the incentive to cheat. The greater the emphasis on competition, the greater the likelihood of corruption.

There is yet another reason for looking at this economic model. In principle, a private for-profit firm is motivated by the desire to maximize profits, but what about a not-for-profit operator? The privatizers hardly ever explore such questions, perhaps because they would be difficult to deal with. The conclusion here is that the privatizers for the most part are not only full-fledged members of the economic cult but consciously aware that they are charlatans. As comedian Bob Newhart once put it, the system encourages such operations as "The Grace L. Ferguson Airline and Storm Door Company." The lowest price, fare, or contract cost is hardly ever the safest price, fare, or contract cost. Cheapness buys lower quality and higher risks. The charlatans cannot help but know this.

Moving to an even more fundamental premise of economic thought, this society is a victim of the belief that government should do as little as possible because it produces nothing of economic value. "Wealth" is thought to be created only when goods and services are produced for sale; since government usually does not sell what it makes, its output is considered "waste." Say's law helps out, of course, by asserting that everything made to sell can, in fact, be sold at or above production costs. While most readers will think this absurd, the privatization of a public function transforms that function (in principle) from one producing only "waste" to one that produces "wealth." It also enables the privatizers to move more and more toward "Kelly Girl Government"—that is, toward permanent staffing not for the "peaks" of high rates of activity, but only for the "valleys" of low rates. If the privatizers ultimately achieve their objectives, almost all public functions may be "contracted out" one by one, day by day, with the remaining government employees becoming pieceworkers.

Privatizing and "competitive contracting," it should be noted, depend on the continued existence of a large pool of "naturally unemployed" workers. The "natural rate" of joblessness, defined as a rate high enough to discourage labor from seeking wage gains in excess of productivity gains, was first listed as 4 percent under Kennedy, but it has gradually moved up to the presently accepted 7 percent (for a brief outline, see Thurow 1983: 82; on the virtues of a "natural rate," see U.S. Congress 1982). This means that policymakers *want* to have at least 8 million people constantly looking for jobs (along with the 5–6 million "discouraged" workers who have given up), a policy that invites privatizers to replace government workers at lower salaries and wages. This is a modern and sophisticated version of what was once called "scabbing" and associated with "strike-breaking" and "union-busting." And the unemployment rates of the past decade are the highest sustained rates of the past century, except for the great depressions of the 1890s and 1930s.

This, along with second-hand equipment, is what passes for "innovation" in this era of privatization and deregulation. Too many Americans have been hoodwinked into believing that the anarchistic principles undergirding free market economics provide the path to prosperous equilibrium. When such principles are put to work, as in largely unregulated free markets and international free trade, they do what they are supposed to do—create chaos and depression. Much of the chaos is very costly, as when extensive litigation is needed to fix legal blame for the shoddy work performed in the name of "efficiency," and when payoffs become the normal method of doing business. The issue has nothing at all to do with ideology. What Americans call "progress" is largely due to the activities of large firms that have been strong enough in important parts of their history to charge higher than minimum prices and pay higher than minimum wages. The purest of free market economists dislike General Electric and General Motors as much as they detest the successes chalked up by government-owned and operated railroads in Japan and France.

CONCLUSION

If private entrepreneurs are to deliver public goods or services and simultaneously make profits while reducing public expenditures, they must achieve substantially lower operating costs than either public or nonprofit agencies. The only ways of reducing costs involve cheaper equipment, fewer employees, and lower pay. If the private operators are to retain their franchise, moreover, they must constantly keep reducing costs in order to avoid being replaced by other providers who promise still lower costs. With prisons, hospitals, and transportation, constant reductions in operating costs amount to ongoing experiments to determine just how much costs can be cut before tragedy strikes. And strike it will—until the loss of the space shuttle *Challenger*, it had long been the astronauts' joke that they rode multimillion dollar machines, each one with hundreds of thousands of moving parts, every one of which had to function with 99.9 percent certainty, and every one of them manufactured by the lowest bidder. Unfortunately, policing the privateers to avoid the problems of cost-cutting is likely to cost much more than any alleged savings—if, indeed, effective policing is possible at all.

Of the cases explored in this volume, education is something of an anomaly. Traditionally, we have regarded quality private education as an enterprise that costs more for the individual user. It seems wholly wishful thinking to assume that the privatization of education will reduce costs. As I have said earlier, education can only function as something of a "natural monopoly" if it is to be operated at the lowest cost; duplication of facilities inevitably adds troublesome costs. I suggest that the problem is not the inefficiency of monopoly per se, but the inefficiency of monopoly *authority*. More participatory forms of management could do much to diffuse the authoritarianism that pervades all too many school boards and educational administrative structures. Regulation does not require authoritarianism.

REFERENCES

Bok, S. 1978. *Lying—Moral Choice in Public and Private Life* (New York: Vintage).

Breyer, S. 1982. *Regulation and Its Reform* (Cambridge, MA: Harvard University Press).

Coons, J. E. and S. D. Sugarman. 1978. *Education by Choice: The Case for Family Control* (Berkeley, CA: University of California Press).

Cox, W. 1985. "Competitive Contracting: Improving Service to the Riders and Taxpayers." Presentation to the Michigan Conference on Public-Private Cooperation in Public Transportation, November 7 (available from P.O. Box 65782, Washington, D.C. 20035).

DeLaat, J. 1982. "Contracting Out for Public Services: Some Unanswered Questions" (doctoral dissertation, Graduate School of Public and International Affairs, University of Pittsburgh).

Enthoven, A. C. and K. W. Smith. 1971. *How Much Is Enough? Shaping the Defense Program, 1961-1969* (New York: Harper & Row).

Green, M. J., ed. 1972. *The Closed Enterprise System: Ralph Nader's Study Group Report on Antitrust Enforcement* (New York: Grossman).

Hawley, W. D. 1986. "To Innovate, First Deregulate." *Education Week*, February 12, pp. 32, 25.

"Highway Robbery." *The MacNeil-Lehrer Report*, June 23, 1982. Transcript no. 1758.

Kahn, A. E. 1982. Letter to the editor, *Washington Post*, June 19.

Nance, J. J. 1986. *Blind Trust: How Deregulation Has Jeopardized Airline Safety and What You Can Do About It* (New York: Morrow).

U.S. Congress. 1982. "The 'Natural' Rate of Unemployment." A staff study, subcommittee on monetary and fiscal policy of the Joint Economic Committee, 97th Congress, 2nd session (Washington, D.C.: U.S. Government Printing Office).

Perry, J. L. and T. T. Babitsky. 1985. "Comparative Performance in Urban Bus Transit: Assessing Privatization Strategies." *Public Administration Review* 46, no. 1 (January/February): 61-62.

Savas, E. S. 1971. "Municipal Monopoly." *Harper's*, December, pp. 55-60.

———. 1975. "Getting on Top of the Problem." *New York Times*, August 6.

———. 1977. "An Empirical Study of Competition in Municipal Service Delivery." *Public Administration Review* 37 (November-December): 717-24.

Thayer, F. C. 1977. "And Now the 'Deregulators': When Will They Learn?" *Journal of Air Law and Commerce* 43, no. 4: 676.

———. 1983. "Regulation Is Inevitable: Legal Planning or Illegal Collusion?" *American University Law Review* 32, no. 2 (Winter): 425-54.

———. 1984. *Rebuilding America: The Case for Economic Regulation* (New York: Praeger).

———. 1986. "The Emerging Dangers of Deregulation." *New York Times*, February 23.

Thurow, L. C. 1983. *Dangerous Currents: The State of Economics* (New York: Random House).

Wyckoff, D. D. 1979. *Truck Drivers in America* (Lexington, MA: Lexington Books).

11

Privatization in Perspective

Norman Elkin

The primary value of this book is that it stimulates us to examine some of our underlying civic values and to question the content of our social policies. The chapters are uneven in this regard: some explicitly or implicitly discourse at that level; some present their positions and/or analyses at the "research/technical" level; and others are in between, generalizing but falling short of theoretical speculation.

The introduction properly alludes to the expansion over time of the government role in an increasing variety of social services:

> Our historical memory is short. Today's generation takes for granted a vast array of federal, state, and local programs that support every conceivable form of social service across the spectrum of health, education, welfare, and even legal and political services. So accustomed have we become to the availability of these services that we find it difficult to imagine a time when most of them did not exist. Yet that time was only a little more than 50 years ago. . . .

Raising the historical question, at least by implication, implores one to ask: If governmental assumption of social services is of relatively recent origin, are we not being hasty in dismantling the existing institutional apparatus? Have we allowed government social services sufficient time to survive the vicissitudes of success and failure that enrich and mature? As institutional histories go, government social service programs are in their infancy. By comparison, the governments of the Western world have been practicing and experimenting with the conscription of popular armies for the past 200 years, ever since the Napoleonic Era, and with constitutional processes for 771 years, ever since the Magna Carta. They have been evolving relationships with institutionalized religion for two millennia. Can we call 20 years of the Great Society, or 50 years of the New Deal welfare state,

171

history? In short, are verdicts premature? Would we be better off trying to perfect our rough beginnings rather than to junk them? Are we sure, and on what grounds, that what we have is not worth saving?

The introduction artfully raises these questions, but the book does not answer them. Instead, it focuses on what may be simply short-term tactical advantages of the public versus the private sector, or vice versa:

> The 1980s brought the Reagan presidency and a strong reaction against the new array of government programs for social services. This reaction seems to be due less to the cost of these programs, or to their contribution to the national deficit, than to *growing doubts about their effectiveness* in improving education, mitigating poverty, reducing crime, and providing efficient public transportation, affordable health care, and trouble-free prisons. *If government is failing* in its efforts to provide essential services, should we not reconsider the role we have given government in these areas? That is what this book is about. (italics added)

This characterization of the public mind raises the issue of the standards by which we are measuring "effectiveness" and "failing." Let us consider these standards, first historically and then technically.

The two major thrusts for expanding government assumption of social services occurred in the 1930s and 1960s. The former was a period of worldwide depression marked by a radical reversal of the democratic progression, expressed in the rise of fascism, Nazism, communism, and militarism. The New Deal, regardless of the merits of its specific programs, may have had the aggregate effect of staving off a revolution (at least an ideological one). The salutary effect of the New Deal may have been largely psychological, as a powerful statement to all citizens that the nation was still a "family" whose members cared for each other. This, the extent to which these programs, as an abstract collective commitment, *bonded the nation*, was the real *standard of success or failure*.

Similarly, the Great Society programs of the 1960s occurred in a revolutionary era, when the headlines were dominated by youth culture, black civil disobedience, the feminist movement, and third world assertiveness. The programs of the Great Society should be judged not by whether any specific program reduced crime or mitigated poverty, but by whether collectively they reduced civil unrest and reassured major segments of society that *the nation cared*, that America was *one community*, not two or more.

In the historical context, the dimension and content of specific social problems, such as poverty, illiteracy, and alienation, change as circumstances change. Therefore, the palliatives and panaceas enacted in one era may prove totally irrelevant in another. This may be what we are witnessing today, as society struggles for more relevant solutions to its problems. That does not necessarily invalidate the struggle, or the efforts of those who came before us. It simply means it's time to reassess, not to dump.

There is also the technical view of the problem of standards. In some cases, the critics imply that government has no business even *trying* to solve certain social problems (or "tinkering" with the system), because such intervention runs against the nature of things. This position brings us right back to late nineteenth century *laissez faire*. In other cases, the critics imply that government operations suffer by comparison to business institutions. This is the general view in this book, some of whose chapters are rife with invidious comparisons and pejorative language. Chapter 3 refers to government's "notoriety for inefficiency and high costs (covered, of course, by personal and corporate taxes)" and says that "business does nothing unless it can see some *benefit* for itself or its investors" (italics added). (Business' inefficiencies would be better documented if, like government, it operated in the goldfish bowl of constant public scrutiny.) Chapter 4 refers to government employees as "bureaucrats." (What are employees of large corporations? Entrepreneurs-in-training?)

The technical problem is that we do not see a wise, logical, knowledge-based approach to the mitigation of our social problems or to the delivery of public services. If the private sector possesses that knowledge, that wisdom, that logic, it is indeed a well-kept secret.

Might government's record be better if it could be more selective of the services it offers or the "customers" it serves? Certainly, almost all privatization has involved some measure of selectivity in choosing the ground on which it operates. Thus, even if we take the more spectacular successes, such as Marva Collins's private school on Chicago's depressed West Side, the fact that her students or their families were self-selected and sufficiently motivated to enroll radically alters the odds of success. Those odds are very different for an open-enrollment school that must take all comers. We may *reduce* the problems via privatization, but the hard core remains whether we are talking about education, transportation, or environmental sanitation. This is explicitly recognized in several chapters that deal with specific subject areas as well as in the chapter on the nonprofit sector.

Are government and the corporate sector both afflicted with the same disease? Is the poor performance in the delivery of social services a by-product of institutional "hardening of the arteries," a condition that seems endemic to all large, and *largely unchallenged*, organizations? The authors of the chapters advocating privatization may be giving too much weight to the profit motive as the disciplining force separating the energetic from the lethargic. The experience of the automotive and steel industries in failing to protect their markets, and the dismal record of some of the more aggressive corporations that have diversified (to their regret) into so-called growth industries, are hardly testimonials to private-sector sagacity and stewardship. Posing the performance problem in terms of privatization versus public service may mask the underlying issue that Justice Brandeis branded more than half a century ago as "the curse of bigness."

What people may be responding to when they hail privatization is the "entrepreneurial phenomenon." American society is so expansive and dynamic that service industries continue to emerge to provide that special cutting edge that corporate enterprises so often lack. Those industries stimulate new activity that in the aggregate results in growth to the economy. These service industries are driven largely by individuals who have split off from the corporate sector or who were never part of it to begin with. They provide much of the creativity and candor that are inhibited in large, structured organizations. The objective reality is that they are capable of *introducing change.*

If this line of reasoning has any validity, then the question becomes more general: What does society need to ensure an environment that will encourage and accept change? If the private sector is as prone as the public and nonprofit sectors to institutional hardening of the arteries, then the need is to formulate a concept that works for all sectors rather than to try to solve problems by transferring them from one sector to another. One can plausibly argue, however, that there is greater corporate, political, and financial flexibility in the private sector, and therefore corrective action is likely to occur sooner there than in the public sector. On the other hand, what happens when a service enterprise that pioneers an efficient and successful public service delivery system becomes the object of a takeover or merger that will make it part of a large corporate entity? Should we try to prevent that? Is it fair to impose such a prohibition? After all, one of the objectives of a start-up enterprise to to create value that can be realized through a sale or buy-out. It hardly seems fair to compel a small, creative enterprise to forego the fruits of success by remaining small and creative.

While entrepreneurship is central to any serious discussion of privatization, its role should not be exaggerated, as Conant and Easton do in Chapter 4, when they say that "Many people . . . look to entrepreneurs to *solve the problems* that face the country today" (italics added) and cite Julian Simon's optimistic view that "there is no physical or economic reason why human resourcefulness and enterprise cannot forever continue to respond to . . . problems with new expedients that . . . leave us better off than before the problem arose." As an article of faith, Simon's opinion is certainly consistent with American optimism. However, translating that worldview into temporal problem-solving is stretching. There is a difference between the *cumulative effect* over time of the results of entrepreneurial dynamics and the relevance of those dynamics to *conscious, deliberative public policy*. The entrepreneur is *not* a problem-solver. Typically, he is a person who doesn't fit comfortably into aggregates of human beings, whether in government agencies or corporations or universities. The only problems he solves are his own. It is his ability to concentrate enormous energy on very specific, narrow tasks that yields the insight and mastery of subject that results in success. That his "breakthroughs" add to the public good is often coincidental. The golden age of the entrepreneur was the latter half of the nineteenth century, a period of great economic progress, but hardly one of civic rectitude, social stability, or great problem-solving. We have to assume that problem-solving requires acute sensitivity to society's underlying civic values, an ability to define or redefine the "public good," and an aptitude for creating collaborative environments among competing interests as a prelude to fashioning some sort of working consensus. These are not the attributes of the entrepreneur or entrepreneurship.

The book's first three chapters, all of which speak to a special affinity between business and education, approach the subject from a slightly different perspective. That perspective seems to rest on a *noblesse oblige*, a sense of obligation and responsibility on behalf of business toward society. This approach would have greater validity if in fact we could convince ourselves that there is a self-conscious business class or community "out there." The contrary seems more true. There may be many explanations for this perception (lessened class-consciousness generally in society, lessened labor-management polarization, and so on), but that is outside the scope of this book. It is difficult to achieve civic consensus on problems such as public education and economic development because the "players" are players in name only. Nobody speaks for anyone anymore, and nobody can "deliver the votes." Nobody has found a way to mobilize the businessperson around a coherent philosophy and to generate the necessary commitment. There is a sense of powerlessness (inability to get anything done) and, more basically, a lack of conviction as to what *the* problem is and what the *priorities* are in dealing with the problem. This is evident in the survey of businesspeople reported in the first three chapters. The "business community" exists only as an abstraction. *If* it were a real community, it would *know* what its shared values and needs are and it would be able to act with conviction and influence.

Chapter 10, while polemic in tone and intent, raises some interesting challenges to many of the basic theses in this book. Chapters 10 and 4, if juxtaposed, reprise the basic argument that has coursed through public debates since the 1870s—*laissez faire* versus public regulation, free enterprise versus the welfare state, and, in our own time, economic development versus corporate responsibility.

Dr. Thayer asserts that progress results not from aggressive competition but from monopoly or from significant market dominance:

> What Americans call "progress" is largely due to the activities of large firms that have been strong enough in important parts of their history to charge higher than minimum prices and pay higher than minimum wages. The purest of free market economists dislike General Electric and General Motors as much as they detest the successes chalked up by government-owned and operated railroads in Japan and France.

He challenges us to define "progress," or at least to defend our definitions against his. Perhaps it is not so much a matter of definitions as it is of assessment of the historic moment. If one assumes that our economic situation has reached a point where we need to consolidate our gains and *distribute the benefits*, then his position is correct. If, on the other hand, one assumes that our absolute or relative economic situation is declining (enough to jeopardize our standard of living), then one is inclined to define progress in terms of improved productivity. (Take your sides.)

Dr. Thayer sees widespread contracting out of public services, under conditions of easy market entry, as fostering corruption and the debasing of industry-wide standards of marginal, opportunistic business adventurers. Attracting start-up, under-capitalized, inexperienced, and sometimes questionable operators is not unknown where publicly underwritten projects are involved. This is a legitimate concern. However, massive corruption as in the late nineteenth century is not likely to occur for long simply because of the potency of the print and electronic news media. It is much easier to stir up public outrage now than it was then, as witness the impact of TV coverage on public opinion during the Vietnam War and the Iranian hostage crisis.

Finally, Dr. Thayer takes us full circle to the beginning of this critique: How do we create an environment that encourages and accepts change? Earlier we asserted that institutional hardening of the arteries is endemic to all large, *unchallenged* organizations. Thayer makes the same point in connection with education, namely that the basic flaw is a *lack of challenge* to authoritarianism in educational institutions:

> It seems wholly wishful thinking to assume that the privatization of education will reduce costs. As I have said earlier, education can only function as something of a "natural monopoly" if it is to be operated at the lowest cost; duplication of facilities inevitably adds troublesome costs. I suggest that the problem is not the inefficiency of monopoly per se, but the inefficiency of monopoly *authority. More participatory forms of management could do much to diffuse the authoritarianism that pervades all too many school boards and educational administrative structures.* Regulation does not require authoritarianism. (italics added)

In our opinion, participatory management requires a prior condition, namely a receptivity to *criticism*. Tolerance of open criticism is perhaps the ultimate litmus test of a free society. To convert criticism to a motive force for the "good," we have to nurture a predisposition to seek it, weigh it, and *use* it for self-improvement. Instead of focusing so hard on "debate" skills, rhetoric, and psychological defense in our educational systems, we should encourage "listening" and creative cooperation so that we don't view new ideas and criticism as attacks on our egos or as threats to our positions. *Then*, when we serve as managers in business organizations, officials in public agencies, directors in nonprofit corporations, or members of social boards, we will indeed induce environments that are capable of accepting the change necessary for evolutionary progress.

Index

Accelerated Cost Recovery System, 31
Adopt-a-school, 25
advertising, 123, 132
Aetna Life and Casualty, 105
aid, federal, x
air traffic controllers, 159
airline bankruptcy, 156; cost-cutting,
    161; deregulation, 147, 160;
    efficiency, 160; and labor, 161;
    mergers, 160; and pay, 161
Alexander, L., 83
Allegheny Conference on Community
    Development, 106
Alpha Center for Public/Private
    Initiatives, Inc., 99
Altman, L., 57
altruism, in public sector, 124
American Airlines, 160
American Association of Medical
    Colleges, 55
American Automobile Association, 158
American Civil Liberties Union
    (ACLU), 90, 91
American Correctional Association
    (ACA), 88
American Hospital Supply Corp.,
    55, 72
American Medical Association
    (AMA), 68, 70, 72, 123
American Medical International, 55,
    58, 62
American Public Health Association,
    61
Amtrak, 42
antitrust violations, 154
Arizona Center for Women, 86
Art-Metal-USA, Inc., 147
Auerbach, B., 85
authoritarianism, 176

Alelrod, R., 139, 142, 143

Banfield, E. C., 42
bankruptcy, 157, 161
Bankruptcy Court, U.S., 161
Bay County Jail, 95
Bays, C. W., 52, 64
Behavioral Systems Southwest, 89, 90,
    92, 95
Bell, Terrell, 3
Best Western International, Inc., 86
Beverly Enterprises, 70
bid rigging, 152, 154
bidding, competitive, 151, 152, 154;
    periodic, 154, 156
bigness, curse of, 174
Blue Cross, 109
Boston Symphony Orchestra, 121
Boulding, K., 135
Bova, B., 48
Brandeis, L., 174
bribery, 146, 147, 151
Bromberg, Michael D., 60, 65, 68
Brookings Institute, 102
Brown, Montague, 70
Buckingham Security, Ltd., 89, 92, 93
bullies, 141
business characteristics, 13;
    community, 175; creativity 12;
    goals, 1-7; initiative, 12

Camden Human Services Coalition,
    114
capital, 72; equity, 69; need for, 165
capitalism and entrepreneurs, 38
Caplan, A., 57
Carlson, Norman, 95

Carroll study, purpose, 8
Carroll, B. J., x
Carrow, D. M., 84
Carter administration, 9, 161
Center for Analysis of Public Issues, 102
Center for Health Studies, HCA, 56
Center for Non-Profit Corporations, 114
Chabotar, K. J., 84
Challenger, 169
change, role of, 174
charity, ix
cheating, 142, 147, 167; incentives 156
churches, ix
Civil Aeronautics Board, (CAB), 147, 156, 159, 163
Cohodes, D. K., 72
Collins, Marva, 173
collusion, 152, 155
Commission of Private Philanthropy for Public Needs, 2, 6
Committee of Central American Refugees, 91
communication, and incentives, 24
"company store" problem, 47
competence, need for, 30
competition, 132; and cheating, 147; and consumers, 157; and contracts,151; and cutting corners, 156; and deregulation, 156; excessive, 157; and health care, 60, 110; and nonprofits, 110, 113; and privatization, 136; and restrictions, 159; and safety, 157; unrestricted, 149; value of, 69
competitive bidding, 129
competitive contracting, 162, 163, 167
Conant, R. W., x, xi, 174
Conference Board, 14, 24
conflict of interest, 57, 94
conflict, external, 120; internal, 124; marketplace, 119; public sector, 120
Conrail, 164
consensual decision-making, 167
conspiracy, 152, 155
consumer judgments, 135

consumer sovereignty, 157
Continental Airlines, 161
contracting, competitive, 162, 163, 167
Control Data, 99
Cook County Hospital, 59
Coolbrith, A. G., 106
cooperation, 136
cooperation, and game theory, 139; guaranteeing, 141
Corman, R, P., xi
Cornuelle, R. C., 98, 100
corporate culture, 125
corporate responsibility, 104, 175
Corrections Corporation of America (CCA), 83, 89,·91, 92, 95
corruption, 152, 176
costs, cutting, 161, 168; health care, 80; overruns, 151, 152; prisons, 80; and privatization, 50
Council for Finanacial Aid to Education, 14, 24
Council on the Environment of New York City, 102
"creaming" patients, 55, 56, 64, 67
creativity, 12
criticism, value of, 176
Cullen, F. T., 86
culture, corporate, 125

dairies, 152
Danforth, Sen., 159
Daniel J. Edleman, Inc., 125
Danner, Inc., 90, 91
Datacom Systems Corp. 146
Davis, Charles, 60
Dawson, K., 43
deception, intentional, 151
defection, 136
defense, and privatization, 47, 136
Defense, Department of, 47, 151, 160
demographics, 126
Demone, H. W., Jr., xi, xiii
deregulation, 155, 165, 166; airline, 147; and airline safety, 160; as no-cost, 161; and pay cuts, 157, 161; and second-hand equipment, 163; and trucking, 158, and union-busting, 157

detention facilities, private, 90; short-term, 80
DeVries, W. C., 57, 58, 67
diagnostic related group (DRG), 59, 66, 68, 71
discrimination in health care, 58
Drucker, P., 39
dumping patients, 58, 59
Dun & Bradstreet, 39

Eastern Air Lines, 160
Easton, T. A., x, xi, 174
Eckerd Corporation, 88
Eckerd Foundation, 88, 89
Eclectic Communications, Inc., 89
economics, and privatization, 148; as theology, 165
economies of contiguity, 154; of scale, 71, 130, 154, of scale, in health care, 65
Edmonds, R. A., 84
Education, Department of, 2
education, 1, 169; and business, ix, 9, 10, 105, 175; failure of, 1; and investor-owned hospitals, 56; and marketing, 127; need for, 41; and nonprofits, 106; and philanthropy, 14; and privatization, 43, 150; and reform, 10; teacher, reform of, 165; vouchers, 23; and worker skills, 5
effectiveness, standards, 172
efficiency, 73; measurement, 144; and privatization, 5, 50, 164; and shoddiness, 168
Egdahl, R. H., 67
El-Ansary, A. I., 123
Elrod, Richard J., 84
employment, 39
enlightened self-interest, 13
entrepreneurs, xi; characteristics, 38; and education, 44; encouraging, 41; influencing, 40; and jobs, 39; as hero, 38; and imagination, 44; nature of, 175; potential of, 41; and privatization, 37–49; role of, 37
entrepreneurial phenomenon, 174

ethics, 68, 72; medical, 57
extortion, 146

family planning, 123
Federal Aviation Administration (FAA), 128; 149, 160, 161; fines, 160
Federal Express, 119
Federal Trade Commission (FTC), 62
Federation of American Hospitals, 60, 65
Feiden, K., 144
Feinberg, A., 43
Feldstein, Martin, 33
Fidelity Select Health Care Mutual Fund, 72
Filer Commission, 2, 6, 10, 23
fire departments, private, 42
Fixler, Philip E., Jr., 95
Florida Hospital Cost Containment Board, 64
Flxible, 163
Folsom prison, 82
food stamp program, 137
food, surplus, 137
for-profit hospitals, costs, 64
Ford Foundation, 123
forgiveness, 140
foster homes, congregate, 80
foundations, and nonprofits, 110
Fox, V., 78
fund-raising, 131
funding, government, 58

game theory, 135; and cooperation, 139
garbage removal, 153, 154
Garsombke, Diane, xii
Garsombke, Thomas, xii
Geis, G., xi, xiii
General Accounting Office, 61
General Automotive, 163
General Electric, 168
General Motors, 168
General Services Administration (GSA), 147
Georgia Health Planning Review Board, 60

Gibelman, M., xi, xiii
gifts, 146
Gilder, G., 38
Ginzberg, E., 72
goals, 1–7; social, 73
Goldin, Harrison J., 144
Goldman Sachs, 99
government, and entrepreneurs, 41; role of, 2, 5
Grantmakers in Health, 110
grass-roots nonprofits, 113
Great Depression, cause, 157
Great Society, 99, 172
greed, as motive, 167
Greyhound Bus Co., 163
Grumman, 163
guidelines to privatization, xiii

Hale, Matthew, 80
halfway houses, 47, 80, 108; first, 107
Harlem Hospital, 146
Hawes-Cooper Act, 85
Hawley, Willis D., 165, 166
Hayes, William, 72
Health and Human Services Department, 61, 123
Health and Medicine Policy Research Group, 61
health care, and competition, 110; cost control, 71; costs, 66, 80; for-profit, and costs, 67; forecasts, 70; goals of, 61; of indigents, 131; issues, 66; marketing, 63, 123; and nonprofits, 109; private, growth of, 130; and privatization, xi, 43, 79, 109; for uninsured, 71
Health Maintenance Organizations (HMOs), 43, 69, 123
heart, artificial, 57
Heritage Foundation, 102
HEW, 123
highway construction, 154, 155
Hill-Burton Act, 110
Hobbes, Thomas, 138
Hodgkinson, V., 101
Holiday Inn, 43

Hoover, Herbert, 157
Hospital Corporation of America, (HCA), 53, 54, 55, 56, 62, 72; decline of, 69; and education, 56; expenses, 55; and indigents, 56; revenues, 55
hospitals, contracted, 67; for-profit, 53; for-profit, costs, 64, 65; history, 52; investor-owned, and education, 56; investor-owned, and publicity, 57, 58; investor-owned, costs, 64, 65; investor-owned, growth of, 54; investor-owned, prices, 64, 65, 66; physician-run, efficiency, 64; privatization of, 50–75; proprietary, 53
House Ways and Means Committee, 70
Houston Metro, 125
"hub-spoke" operations, 161
human welfare services, 80
Humana, 53, 55, 58, 67, 69; marketing, 63
Humana Heart Institute, 57
Hutts, Joseph, 67

imagination, need for, 44
Immigration and Naturalization Service (INS), 80, 89, 90–91, 93; lawsuits, 91
incentives, 21, 27; and communication, 24; evaluation of, 6; and leadership, 5, 25; and liability relief, 26; lottery, 21; need for, 36; recognition, 5, 23; response to, 13; tax, 5, 6, 22, 35; tax, and philanthropy, 15
independent sector, 101, 114
indigents, care of, 59, 60, 131
inflation, effect on philanthropy, 29
initiative, 12
innovation, 165, 168
insecurity, as motive, 167
Institute of Medicine, 61
Institutional Review Board, 57
insurance, 109; liability, 165
Insurance Institute on Highway Safety, 158

Internal Revenue Service (IRS), 39; policies, 23
International Metals and Machines Corp., 3
Interstate Commerce Commission (ICC), 158, 159
Irvine, Robert, 67
Irwin, John, 81

jails, 80; conditions, 81; expenses, 81
jobs, and entrepreneurs, 39
Johns Hopkins, 68
Johnson, Lyndon B., x
Johnson, Samuel, 77
juvenile delinquents, 108

Kahn, Alfred E., 147
Katz, H. M., 65, 71
Kennedy, A., 39
Kennedy, Edward M., 157
Kentucky Fried Chicken, 129
Kirzner, I. M., 38,
Korn, Richard, 82
Kramer, O.L., Jr., 123
Kurens, Philip J., 147
Kusserow, R. P., 61

lawsuits, INS, 91
leadership, as incentive, 5, 25; role, 29
lease/purchase, and prisons, 87, 88
legal aid, ix
Leiber, J., xii, xiii
Lerner, Arthur, 62
Levinson, Robert, 88
Lewin, L. S., 56, 64, 65
liability, and privatization, 5; relief, as incentive, 26–27
libraries, and privatization, 44
licensing, teacher, 166
Lindsay, John, 153
lottery, federal, as incentive, 21

mail, private, 42, 144
management technology, 71
management, Japanese, 125
March of Dimes, 123
market forces, 69, 72, 109, 156, 162; and innovation, 165

market, free, 38; public benefit, 105
marketing, xi, 129, 132; and controversy, 132; in education, 127; and environmentalism, 127; environmental factors, 126; and health care, 63, 123; and motivation, 124; and prison privatization, 84; and privatization, 119–134; resistance to, 126
marketplace review, 145
marketplace, test of, 66
Marlin, J. T., 144
McAlester State Penitentiary, 85
McDonald's, 43, 58
McKinsey & Co., 125
McNamara, R., 151
MacNaughton, D., 55, 56
media, role of, 176
Medicaid, x, 56, 79, 109, 110; coverage, 59
medical-industrial complex, 56
Medicare, x, 56, 69, 70, 71, 79, 104, 109, 110; coverage, 59; reimbursement, 62; Medicare Trust Fund, 62
Medina, 91
mergers, airlines, 160
metropolitan transit agencies, 125, 163
Midwest Air Traffic Control Services, 128
Mikva, Abner, 95
Milton, John, 63
minimax strategy, 138
minimum wage laws, 162
Minneapolis Sanitation Division, 154
monitoring, need for, 94
monopoly power, 153
monopoly, and privatization, 62
motivation, xi, and marketing, 124; for philanthropy, 20–36
Mullen, J., 84, 87, 88

National Academy of Science, 61
National Association of Criminal Justice Planners, 83
National Association of Free Standing Emergency Centers, 60

National Commission on Excellence in Education, 10
National Consumers League, 53
National Corrections Corp., 92
National Council for the Accreditation of Teacher Education, 166
National Council of Senior Citizens, 67
National Health Law Program, 61, 68
National Institute of Corrections, 88
National Medical Enterprises, 55
National Sheriffs Association, 81
National Transportation Safety Board, 161
neoconservative case for privatization, 51
Neuhauser, D., 64
New Deal, 2, 172
new entries, and trucking, 158
New York State Bureau of Hospital Services, 146
New York City Health and Hospitals Corp., 146
New York City Parking Violations Bureau, 146
New York City Transit Authority, 163
New York Department of Corrections, 87
Newark Economic Development Corp., 102
Newhart, Bob, 67
Newman Center, 126
Nissan, 125
Nissen, Ted, 95
noblesse oblige, 175
Non-Profit Coordinating Committee of New York City, 114
nonprofit sector, xi
nonprofits, 2, 98–118; activities, 100; and competition, 111, 113; employment, 101; future of, 113; grass-roots, 113; and health care, 109; income, 102; marketing, 122; motivations, 100; and prisons, 107, 109; and privatization, 103, 104; reactions to, 111; roles, 101, 112; support of, 111; as watchdogs, 114
North Memorial Medical Center, 63

nursing homes, 70

O'Hare Airport, 161
Okeechobee School for Boys, 88
OPEC, 30
opportunity, fostering, 41
overcapacity, 159; and waste, 156
ownership, as issue, 156

Packwood, Sen., 159
Palo Duro Private Detention Services, 89
Paperwork Reduction Act, 9
Paracelsus Corp., 68
Partnerships in Education, 25
partnerships, business-education, 2
patients, as consumers, 57; "creaming," 55, 56, 64, 67, dumping, 58, 59
Pattison, R. V., 65, 71
penal facilities. See prisons
Pennsylvania Neighborhood Assistance Act, 23
philanthropy, and business, 13; corporate, extent, 27; costs, 31, 33; and education, 14; extent of, 14, 15; goal, 12; as investment, 32; levels, 5; and public relations, 24, 30; and tax incentives, 15
Phoenix Public Works Department, 144
Planned Parenthood, 123
planning, 32; collective, 155; joint public–private, 155; need for, 130
Plato, 138
Police Foundation, 84
Postal Service, 147
Preferred Provider Organizations, 123
Presser, Stefan, 91
price fixing, 147, 154–155
price wars, 156, 160
Price, Robert M., 99
priorities, communication of, 8–19
prison construction bonds, 87; private, 93

prison environment, 77; expense, 80; industries, 84–85, 93; populations, 82

prison privatization, 76–97; basis, 92; difficulties, 92; efficacy, 93; goals of, 79, and marketing results, 90

Prison Rehabilitative Industries and Diversified Enterprises (PRIDE), 86

prison success, 108; unrest, 83

prisoner's dilemma, 137; repeated, 139

prisons, xi, 76–97, conditions, 94; construction, 87; costs, 107; expense, 78; financing, 87; and lease/purchase, 88; and nonprofits, 85, 107, 109; operation, 88; overcrowding, 95; private, 42, 88; private, costs, 92, 94; private, increase in, 92; privatization, 76–97, 107; problems, 82; ripeness for privatization, 78; in Tennessee, 83

Prisons, U.S. Bureau of, 89, 95

privatization, 110; abuses, 42; acceptance of, 132; advantages, 135, and better management, 95; and business's requirements, 12; and choice, 145; and competition, 92, 136; conditions for, 135; constitutionality, 94; and corruption, 147; and cost reduction, 95, costs, 48; and economics, 148; and education, 149; and efficiency, 94, 164; and entrepreneurs, 37–49, escape clauses, 114; and game theory, 135–145; goal of, 41; guidelines, xiii; and health care, 51–75, 109; history, 171; of hospitals, 51–75; jails, 80; and marketing, 119–134; motives, 104, 119; negative influences, 4, 5; and monopoly, 119; neoconservative case for, 51; and nonprofits, 103, 104; objections to, 91; opposition, 94; pitfalls, 132; and policy, xiii; positive influences, 5;

prerequisites, 48; and prisons, 76–97, 107; problems, 131; and profit, 119, 128; and public interest, 112; and quality of service, 79; realism of, 137, reversability, 144; and second-hand equipment, 163; suitability for, 143; and transportation, 156

profit, 128; motive, 20, 173; and private sector, 124

profit-making, in health care, 60

profitization, 111; of nonprofits, 103

profits, as motive, 167

progress, 176

Proposition XIII, 30

prospective payment, 71

provocability, 140

Prudential Life Insurance Co., 55

public benefit market, 105

Public Education Foundation, 106

public interest, and privatization, 112; risk to, 62, violations of, 67

public relations, 24, 30

public sector, excess employees, 128 revenue, 128; and rising costs, 114

public services, rationale, 20

public transit, 121, 143

publicity, 57, 58

publicization, 144

quality assurance, 73

quality of service, 163

Ramsey County Community Corrections, 84

Rand, 43

RCA, 43, 88

Reagan administration, 2, 3, 5, 10, 12, 31, 69; goals 12

Reagan, Ronald, x, 2; and leadership, 29

Reason Foundation, 95

rebidding, periodic, 156

recidivism, 108

recognition, as incentive, 5, 7, 23

reform, in education, 10

regulation, xii, xiii, 72, 79, 122, 131,
135, 136, 155, 166; and game
theory, 142; of health care, 79;
and marketing, 122; need for,
42, 164; role of, 9; trucking, 159
rehabilitation, 109
Relman, A. 55, 56, 57, 58, 61, 71
reprivatization, 162
research and development, 45
responsibility, allocation of, xii;
corporate, 28, 104; in health
care, 61
revenues, 130
Roberts, James, 60
Robertson, J. A., 81
Rockefeller Foundation, 99
Roosevelt, F. D., 2, 157

safety enforcement, 156; inspectors,
159, 161
safety standards, 155, 158, 164; and
airlines, 160; violations, 158,
159, 160
safety violations, 160; and unions, 159
safety, and competition, 157; and
trucking, 158
San Francisco Lawyers Committee for
Urban Affairs, 91
San Quentin prison, 78
Savas, E. S., 153, 154
Say's law, 148, 149, 150, 167
scabbing, 168
Schoen, Kenneth, 95
Scholz, J. T., 142
schools, private, ix
second-hand equipment, and
deregulation, 163; and privatization, 163
security forces, private, 42
self-interest, enlightened, 12; role of,
137
services, cost-benefit, 21; human
welfare, 80; public, ix; public,
marketing of, xii; public, rationale, 20; public, reaction
against, x
Sheps, Cecil G., 61
Signal Environment Systems, 127

Silverdale Detention Center, 91
Simon, Julian, 37, 174
Singleton, John, 91
Small Business Administration, (SBA),
39, 41, 147
Smith, Michael E., 84
social goals, 1
social services, delivery, 17; purchasers,
121; users, 121
society as family, 172
society as Reformation of Juvenile
Delinquents, 108
Southwest Detention Facilities, 89
space shuttle, 157, 169
Specter, Arlen, 96
Sports and Exposition Authority, NJ,
151
Starr, P., 51, 70
Steinwald, B., 64
Strategic Defense Initiative (SDI), 47
streamlining, 128
subsidies, 68, 108; for urban transit,
163, 164
Sumners-Ashurst Act, 85
Sykes, Gresham, 82
synergism, need for, 13

Taft, P. B., Jr., 107
Task Force on Private Sector
Initiatives, 2, 6, 10, 12
tax credit proposal, 6, 9, 18,
response to, 10, 11, 12
tax credits, 31, 34
tax-exampt corporations, 100
tax incentives, 9, 35
tax polity, 18; as incentive, 22; and
incentives, 8; role of, 8; and
voluntarism, 15, 16
Teachers College, Vanderbilt, 166
Teamsters Union, 159
Texas Health Facilities Commission,
63
Thayer, F. C., xii, xiii, 176
third-party payers, 51, 53, 68, 109
Thurow, Lester R., 165
TIT-FOR-TAT, 140
de Tocqueville, 98, 101
town farm, 47

Trailways Bus Co., 163
Transportation, U.S. Department of, 155
transportation, municipal, 155; and privatization, 43, 156; public, 42, 121, 143
TransWorld Airlines, 86
Travis, L. F., 86
Trenton prison, 82
trucking, and deregulation, 158; new entries, 158; regulation, 159
Tulane University, 56
two-tier contracts, 162

unemployment, 162; natural, 168
union-busting, 157, 162, 168
unions, and monopoly power, 153
United Nations, 48
United Parcel Service, 119
United Telecommunications, 44
University of Miami, 56
University of Missouri, 44
University of Wisconsin Education System, 129
urban blight, x
Urban Development Corp., 87
Urban Mass Transportation Administration, 43, 155
urban transit, costs, 164
urban transport, as monopoly, 162
utilities, and regulation, 132

venture capital, 40, 41
Vera Foundation, 84

Vesper, K. H. 39, 40, 41
voluntarism, 16, 17, 115; employee, 15; encouraging, 16; motives, 27; stimulating, 6
voluntary agencies, 99
Volunteers of America, 84
voucher systems, 149

Walsh Commission, 99
Wang, 43
War of Poverty, x
Washington National Airport, 160
Waste Management, Inc., 130
waste, and government, 167
watchdogs, 114
Watt, J. M., 65
Waxman, Judith G., 61, 68
wealth, and sales, 167
Weitzman, M., 101
welfare, ix, 17; cheating, 46; and privatization, 46
White House Office for Private Sector Initiatives, 29
Whitehead, John C., 99
Williams, Herbert , 84
Willis, R., 46
worker skills, need for, 30
workfare, 46
Wyckoff, D. D., 158

Xerox, 43

Young, Quentin D., 61

About the Contributors

Barry J. Carroll holds an MBA from Harvard Business School. He is an officer and director of three groups of companies, Katy Industries, Inc., International Metals & Machines, Inc., and American Machine & Science, Inc., which have a combined total of 88 operating subsidiaries in the United States and Europe. His nonbusiness activities include serving on the boards of trustees of four charitable foundations, Shimer College, and Barat College. In 1983 and 1984, he was a Presidential Exchange Executive serving as a special assistant to U.S. Secretary of Education Terrell Bell in Washington, D.C. In that capacity, he led a study of private-sector executive attitudes toward involvement of business in education, which is the basis for his contribution to, and the impetus for, this book on the broader subject of business' role in social service delivery.

Ralph W. Conant obtained his doctorate in political science from the University of Chicago in 1959. He is presently president of Public Research Inc., a Maine consulting firm, chairman of the Shimer College Foundation, and a member of the Maine State Board of Education. He has been president of Shimer College in Illinois and of Unity College in Maine; the founding president of the Southwest Center for Urban Research in Houston, Texas; assistant director of the Joint Center for Urban Studies of MIT and Harvard University; and the associate director of the Lemberg Center for the Study of Violence at Brandeis University. His numerous books, papers, and lectures have dealt with social unrest, comprehensive health-care planning, education, urban and regional development, and other future-oriented issues. Most recently, he and Dr. Easton have collaborated to write books on consultants and entrepreneurs.

Robert P. Corman is a New Jersey native with a Juris Doctor from American University in Washington, D.C. In 1972 he joined the Appellate Section of the Office of the Public Defender. From 1974 to 1978 he served as a public interest lawyer, focusing particularly on the environment, with the Division of Public Interest Advocacy, Department of the Public Advocate, Trenton, NJ. In 1978 he became executive director of the Fund for New Jersey, a private foundation oriented to the state's critical issues. In addition to responding to hundreds of funding requests, he has created numerous organizations and projects, including the Center for Non-Profit Corporations and the Community Foundation of New Jersey. He has been particularly active in the grantmaking community and currently is the chair of the Council of New Jersey Grantmakers and a director of the New York Regional Association of Grantmakers. In addition, Mr. Corman serves as a trustee on many public and private boards, including those of the Center for Non-Profit Corporations, the Community Foundation of New Jersey, the Council of New Jersey Grantmakers, Ramapo College of New Jersey, the New York Regional Association of Grantmakers, the New Jersey Committee for the Humanities, the Institute for Not-for-Profit Entrepreneurship of New York University's Graduate School of Business Administration, and the Newark Local Initiative Support Corporation.

Harold W. Demone, Jr., is the Dean of the School of Social Work at Rutgers, State University of New Jersey. He is also a professor in the School, the Graduate Sociology Department, and the Center of Alcohol Studies. Formerly employed in two state health departments, Dean Demone has written more than 60 publications in the field of health. His chapter in this book evolved from a book he and Dr. Gibelman are writing on the purchase of human services, to be published by Rutgers University Press.

Thomas A. Easton obtained his doctorate in Theoretical Biology from the University of Chicago in 1971. Since then, he has written on scientific and futuristic issues for many magazines. His books include biology texts, two books on careers in science, and others, including those on consultants and entrepreneurs coauthored with Dr. Conant. He is also a contributing editor to *Biology Digest*, the book columnist for *Analog Science Fiction and Science Fact* magazine, and a Senior Associate in Public Research Inc. He is currently an adjunct assistant professor at Thomas College in Waterville, ME.

Norman Elkin has worked and written as an urban planner ever since obtaining his masters degree in social science from the University of Chicago in 1949. He has held posts with the city of Chicago, the state of Illinois, and consulting firms. He is now vice-president and manager of the Planning Department of Urban Investment and Development Co. He serves on the boards of directors of the Civic Federation of Chicago and the Greater State Street Council, among other civic activities.

Diane J. Garsombke is an assistant professor of business administration at the University of Maine, where she teaches in the MBA and undergraduate programs. Her research and publications deal with marketing issues facing U.S. businesses. She has worked in administrative positions with institutions of higher education, CARE, and the Peace Corps (Malaysia), and as a management consultant.

Thomas W. Garsombke is an associate professor of marketing and management at Thomas College, where he teaches marketing management, marketing research, and advertising in the MBA and undergraduate programs. Before completing his doctorate in administration at Northeastern University, he served as a Peace Corps volunteer in Malaysia. He has also worked as a marketing administrator in private business, as an administrator with the Social Security Administration, and as a marketing consultant. He is an active proponent of the "marketing concept" for non-profit organizations.

Gilbert Geis is a professor in the Program in Social Ecology at the University of California, Irvine. He has been a visiting professor at Sydney University Law School and a visiting fellow at Cambridge University and Harvard Law School. He is the former president of the American Society of Criminology. He has received the Edwin Sutherland Award for research from that group, as well as research awards from the National Organization for Victim Assistance and the Western Society of Criminology.

Margaret Gibelman is executive director of the Lupus Foundation of America, Inc., a national health organization devoted to research, government relations, public awareness, patient education, and services on behalf of those suffering from systemic lupus erythematosus. Previously, she was associate executive director of the Council of Social Work Education, a senior staff associate at the National Conference on Social Welfare, and director of the National Demonstration Project on Staff Development and Training at the American Public Welfare Association. She has also been on the faculty of Rutgers University School of Social Work. She holds a masters degree in social work and political science from Rutgers and a doctorate in social welfare from Adelphi University. She has published widely on the organization and delivery of human services, public–private sector relationships, purchase of services, child welfare services, and staff development and training. With Dr. Demone, she is coauthor of *Services for Sale: Purchasing Health and Human Services* (Rutgers University Press).

Justin F. Leiber is a professor of philosophy at the University of Houston. His work is primarily concerned with the interface between logic, linguistics, and theories of cognition and rationality. His degrees include a BA and a Ph.D. from the University of Chicago and a B.Phil. from Oxford. Among his books are *Noam Chomsky: A Philosophic Overview* (G. K. Hall), *Structuralism: Skepticism and Mind in the Psychological Sciences* (G. K. Hall), and *Can Animals and Machines Be Persons? A Dialogue* (Hackett Publishing Co.).

Frederick C. Thayer is professor of public and international affairs in the Graduate School of Public and International Affairs, University of Pittsburgh. He has long been immersed in the study of organization theory and behavior, dealing particularly with the question of why organizations, regardless of ideology, do what they do under conditions of regulated and unregulated competition. He is a continuing critic of policies that have recently deregulated such industries as airlines, trucking, buses, telecommunications, and banking. His most recent books are *An End to Hierarchy & Competition: Administration in the Post-Affluent World*, 2nd ed. (Franklin Watts), and *Rebuilding America: The Case for Economic Regulation* (Praeger).